FORCED MARRIAGE AND 'HONOUR' KILLINGS IN BRITAIN

Forced Marriage and 'Honour' Killings in Britain

Private Lives, Community Crimes and Public Policy Perspectives

CHRISTINA JULIOS

Birkbeck, University of London, UK and The Open University, UK

ASHGATE

Published by
Ashgate Publishing Limited
Wey Court East
Union Road
Farnham
Surrey, GU9 7PT
England

Ashgate Publishing Company
110 Cherry Street
Suite 3-1
Burlington, VT 05401-3818
USA

www.ashgate.com

British Library Cataloguing in Publication Data
A catalogue record for this book is available from the British Library.

The Library of Congress has cataloged the printed edition as follows:
Julios, Christina.
  Forced marriage and "honour" killings in Britain : private lives, community crimes and public policy perspectives / by Christina Julios.
     pages cm
  Includes bibliographical references and index.
  ISBN 978-1-4724-3249-0 (hardback) -- ISBN 978-1-4724-3250-6 (ebook) --
ISBN 978-1-4724-3251-3 (epub) 1. Forced marriage--Great Britain. 2. Honor killings--Great Britain. I. Title.

  HQ613.J86 2015
  306.840941--dc23

2015002210

ISBN 9781472432490 (hbk)
ISBN 9781472432506 (ebk – PDF)
ISBN 9781472432513 (ebk – ePUB)

Printed in the United Kingdom by Henry Ling Limited, at the Dorset Press, Dorchester, DT1 1HD

Contents

Preface and Acknowledgements

At the core of this book lie countless stories of young girls and women living in Britain who have experienced 'honour' violence. Within the confines of the family home, they have been coerced into unwanted marriages, subjected to physical and psychological abuse, abducted, imprisoned and in some cases killed by those closest to them. Whether teenage school girls, university students, working professionals, mothers or wives, their accounts expose the reality of everyday life for victims of 'honour' violence in Britain's minority ethnic communities; a reality that often involves the systematic violation of individual freedoms, civil liberties and human rights.

Against this background, the book explores the personal experiences of female survivors of forced marriage and victims of 'honour' killings as well as the prevailing public policy discourse underlying these phenomena. The volume features a wide range of often conflicting views from various stakeholders including policymakers, community leaders, grassroots service providers, scholars and those at the receiving end of 'honour' transgressions. Such an array of voices and narratives will contribute to further the ever fluid debate on the 'honour' question. The book not only unveils deep divisions between those at opposite ends of the 'honour' violence ideological spectrum; but raises wider questions about minority group entitlements, legal pluralism and women's rights. In doing so, it ultimately highlights the gender equality challenges facing Britain's particular brand of multiculturalism.

By shining a light on the private lives of victims and survivors of 'honour' violence, the book provides unique insights into a complex web of patriarchal, social, cultural and religious influences shaping the unequal status enjoyed by male and female migrants to the detriment of the latter. It is such imbalances in power relationships that continue to see ordinary law-abiding members of the Pakistani, Bangladeshi and Indian Diasporas, among others, turn filicide and fratricide in the name of 'honour'. Two 'honour' killings in particular provided the motivation for this book, namely the murders of a 16-year-old British Pakistani school girl from Cheshire in 2003, and of a 20-year-old Iraqi Kurdish woman from South London in 2006. The book is thus dedicated to the memory of Shafilea Ahmed and Banaz Mahmod.

I would like to thank colleagues at Birkbeck College Library, University of London, for their assistance in locating relevant materials; particularly Bob Burns for helping me to navigate through the Law archives. Thanks are also due to academic peers for their helpful suggestions during the course of this project. I should like especially to thank Dr Anne Kershen for her generosity, patience and insightful comments to the manuscript, which have greatly benefited the volume. Thanks are also due to Claire Jarvis at Ashgate whose enthusiasm, continuing support and guidance have steered the book in the right direction. Colleagues from Ashgate's editorial team have furthermore provided me with invaluable assistance during the production process. Lastly, I am indebted to my friends and family for their forbearance, especially my parents Adelaida and Rafael for their unconditional love and Nick for all the wonderful times through the years.

Sadly during the writing of the book, my beloved brother-in-law Juan Carlos passed away unexpectedly. He was an inspiration to us all, full of life and laughter. The eternal optimist, he made the most of what he had and triumphed over adversity time and again with a smile. He will be sorely missed and live on in all of us who knew him and loved him. I would therefore like to extend the dedication of the book both to Juan Carlos' memory and to my sister Adela, his widow, for her love and fortitude. Unlike the many unhappy unions depicted in the book, Adela and Juan Carlos truly loved each other and enjoyed a long and blissfully happy marriage.

List of Abbreviations

ACPO	Association of Chief Police Officers
BAMER	Black, Minority Ethnic and Refugee
BME	Black and Minority Ethnic
CAADA	Co-ordinated Action Against Domestic Abuse
CCRT	Community Cohesion Review Team
CEDAW	Convention on the Elimination of All Forms of Discrimination Against Women
CPS	Crown Prosecution Service
DCI	Detective Chief Inspector
DCSF	Department for Children, Schools and Families
DFID	Department for International Development
DV	Domestic Violence
DVAW	Domestic Violence Against Women
EHRC	Equality and Human Rights Commission
FCO	Foreign and Commonwealth Office
FGM	Female Genital Mutilation
FMPO	Forced Marriage Protection Order
FMU	Forced Marriage Unit
FMU DPF	FMU Domestic Programme Fund
FOI	Freedom of Information
GCSE	General Certificate of Secondary Education
GMP	Greater Manchester Police
IKWRO	Iranian and Kurdish Women's Rights Organisation
LGBT	Lesbian, Gay, Bisexual and Transgender
MCB	Muslim Council of Britain
MENA	Middle East and North Africa
MPS	Metropolitan Police Service
MWNUK	Muslim Women's Network UK
NGO	Non-Governmental Organisation
NSPCC	National Society for the Prevention of Cruelty to Children
OCD	Obsessive Compulsive Disorder
SBS	Southall Black Sisters
UNAMI	United Nations Assistance Mission for Iraq
UNESCO	United Nations Educational, Scientific and Cultural Organisation

| UNFPA | United Nations Population Fund |
| Unicef | United Nations Children's Fund |

PART I
Private Lives

Chapter 1
Introduction:
British Multiculturalism, 'Honour' Violence and Gender Inequality

Britain's 'Honour' Violence Landscape

On Easter Sunday 2012, national newspapers' headlines reported how a five-year-old girl had become 'Britain's youngest known victim of forced marriage' (Bingham, 2012; Lakhani, 2012; Doughty, 2012; Taneja, 2012). She was 'among 400 children dealt with by the Home Office's dedicated Forced Marriage Unit [FMU]' the previous year (Bingham, 2012). At the time, amid the press coverage of the child bride, an interview with a former five-year-old spouse called Samina (assumed name) also featured in the news (Baig, 2012: 2G). Given the timing of Samina's story, her experience serves to illustrate the plight of vulnerable young girls and women in Britain at risk of being forced into marriage.

At home, in the midst of an English northern town, Samina had been dressing up in a new outfit for what she thought was a birthday party; instead she was wedded off in an arranged marriage having barely turned five. Although decades have now passed since the ceremony took place, Baig notes how it 'effectively ended her childhood and paved the way for years of abuse' (Baig, 2012: 2G). As Samina explains:

> I was denied the right of childhood, play and innocence. When you are married at the age of five you no longer live like a normal child. I was deprived of my basic human rights. (Samina cited in Baig, 2012: 2G)

Discouraged from pursuing education, Samina was removed from school aged 13. On her fourteenth birthday, 'a formal wedding service was held, marking the bride's transition from her parents' home to the home of her husband' (Baig, 2012: 2G). The next two years would be spent in Pakistan, where 'the marriage was consummated against her will after she suffered a horrific beating' (Baig, 2012: 2G). Back in England, Samina gave birth to a daughter at the age of 20 and went on to develop Obsessive Compulsive Disorder (OCD). Defying the wishes of her husband, she subsequently managed to return to education and finally left him, aged 37. Nowadays a business entrepreneur in her early forties, Samina still ponders why she became a child bride:

 I don't know exactly why I was married off at such a young age, but it was all to do with maintaining traditions and making sure we didn't question anything. (Samina cited in Baig, 2012: 2G)

Samina's case is by no means an isolated incident or the first of its kind in the UK, but as the literature suggests (Hansard, 2011a; Brandon and Hafez, 2008; Khanum, 2008; CPS, 2008; Samad and Eade, 2002), it is the tip of a rather large and elusive iceberg, with thousands of young minority ethnic women and girls believed to be routinely promised in marriage from birth. 'People will be horrified' Jasvinder Sanghera remarks 'that a five-year-old girl in Britain could enter into a marriage' (Sanghera, 2012: 2G). Promised herself in matrimony whilst still a minor by her Indian-born Sikh parents, a teenaged Sanghera ran away from their Derby family home to escape the impending nuptials. She still recalls the moment her mother told the then school girl that she was to get married:

I came home from school, I was fourteen. My mother sat me down and she presented this photograph to me. And she said 'Jasvinder, this is the man you are going to marry'. And I said 'but mum, I want to finish school'. She said 'no; where you are going, you don't need an education. You are going to get married'. (Sanghera featured in BBC *Panorama*, 2012)

Sanghera's experience is a familiar one for many young girls and women who have found themselves at the receiving end of their parent's unilateral choice of prospective husbands. In an almost identical scene as the one Sanghera described earlier, Sarbjit Kaur Athwal (2013) recalls how her father told the then teenager about the man he had chosen to marry her:

it came as a shock when, one evening … Dad pushed an envelope to me across the dining table. Inside was a small photograph of a man I'd never seen before. 'Who's this?' I asked.
Dad smiled.
'That's the man you're going to marry'. (Athwal, 2013: 59)

Reflecting now on Samina's case, Sanghera notes 'Sadly, I am not at all surprised. Alongside many others, her [Samina's] life was mapped out before her. Her life was not her own to live but for others to take' (Sanghera, 2012: 2G). Karma Nirvana, the support group founded by the author of *Shame* and *Daughters of Shame* (Sanghera, 2007, 2009) in 1993, deals with similar cases of forced marriage on a daily basis including hundreds of 'honour' violence victims every year; with the 'Honour Network' Helpline having received 22,000 calls between April 2008 – when it was launched – and June 2012 (Karma Nirvana, 2012). The Association of Chief Police Officers' (ACPO) own reported estimates indicate that up to 17,000 females in Britain are exposed to 'honour' related abuse each year, including 'girls falling victims of forced marriage, kidnappings, sexual assaults, beatings and even murder by relatives intend on upholding the "honour" of their family' (Brady, 2008: 8). In 2008, ACPO's 'Honour Based Violence Strategy' stated:

> On average, to the best of our knowledge, 12 people are murdered every year for transgressing someone else's perverted notions of honour. We do not know how many commit suicide as an alternative or an escape. We know that around 500 men and women report to us every year their fear of being forced into marriage, or their experience of rape, assault, false imprisonment and much more as the consequence of being in a marriage without their consent. (ACPO, 2008: 4)

Although 'honour' violence is inflicted upon both male and females, young girls and women remain by and large the main targets. In 2012, for instance, out of the 1,485 cases where the government's Forced Marriage Unit (FMU) gave 'advice or support related to a possible forced marriage', '82% involved female victims and 18% involved male victims' (FMU, 2012). This book therefore focuses on the experiences and accounts of females at the receiving end of 'honour' transgressions. As for the narratives of male victims and perpetrators of 'honour' crimes, there is some literature that provides partial insights into these largely under-researched groups (Onal, 2008).

In line with mainstream violence against women, a combination of unavailable 'standardised data', 'significant under-reporting' and reluctance by victims to come forward for 'fears of retribution' is broadly understood to account for a continuing lack of 'honour' related evidence across the board (Hansard, 2008: 6; Brady, 2008: 8). While relevant government departments, criminal justice agencies and grassroots women's groups collect their own statistics, a clear national picture is yet to emerge. In 2008, Commander Steve Allen, lead officer of ACPO's 'Honour Based Violence Strategy', noted how the police and the Home Office's FMU may typically share about 500 cases between them during the course of a year, with the actual toll of 'honour'-based violence believed to be much higher than official figures suggests (Allen cited in Brady, 2008: 8). In his own estimation 'If the generally accepted statistic is that a victim will suffer 35 experiences of domestic violence before they report, then I suspect if you multiplied our reporting by 35 times you may be somewhere near where people's experience [of "honour" violence] is at' (Allen cited in Brady,

2008: 8). Six years earlier, Baroness Amos, Parliamentary Under-Secretary of State at the Foreign and Commonwealth Office (FCO), had highlighted this seemingly intractable problem: 'we are working with the cases that have come to our attention, but we believe that we only see a small proportion of the total number of cases' (Amos, 2002). At the time, the FCO acknowledged the challenges faced when seeking to obtain accurate figures on the real extent of 'honour' violence in Britain. In its Annual Report to the House of Commons Select Committee on Foreign Affairs, the FCO stated:

> We have dealt with approximately 250 cases in the past year ... But despite ... increased awareness, we are conscious that we deal with only a fraction of the total number of cases. As with domestic violence and child abuse, the nature of the problem of forced marriage makes it extremely difficult to quantify; in many cases victims will never speak out. We know that the police in West Yorkshire alone deal with around 200 cases per year, and that NGOs [Non-Governmental Organisations] working in this area deal with a similar number ... Some media reports have suggested that there are over 1000 cases per year in the UK. We fear that the true number may be even higher. (Hansard, 2002a: paras 11–12)

At the time of writing, we are not significantly closer to an overall figure; but a more comprehensive picture is gradually emerging as increased awareness, higher reporting rates and new evidence continue to fill the gaps in our existing knowledge. In 2010, data available from the House of Commons Home Affairs Committee on 'Forced Marriage' showed that the FMU dealt with 400 cases of forced marriage; while the figure of recorded instances in England reached between 5,000 and 8,000 during the previous year (Hansard, 2011a: 3–4).

It is partly this incomplete picture of the British 'honour' violence landscape that makes the UK an important context for the study of such phenomenon. Over the past two decades, furthermore, the issue of 'honour' violence has steadily made its way onto the British government's public policy agenda. A combination of prominent media reporting of forced marriage and 'honour' killing cases, increased levels of public awareness aided by high profile lobbying and campaigning have led to unprecedented government interventions, including the introduction of new legislation. All of which renders the UK an ever more relevant contemporary setting for the study of this now indigenous and self-perpetuating social problem. Against this background, the book aims to provide as full a picture as possible of the extent of 'honour' transgressions in Britain, in particular those situated at the most extreme end of the violence against women spectrum, that is, forced marriage and 'honour' killings. In doing so the volume unveils the many layers of this seemingly intractable issue, while mapping out the geography of 'honour' practices, recalling the experiences of 'honour' victims and survivors as well as following the development of policy initiatives aimed at tackling 'honour' crimes. Underlying them all, the book considers an array of contrasting views, perspectives and theoretical approaches that strive to make sense of multicultural Britain's very own 'honour' violence conundrum.

Defining 'Honour' Violence

So-called 'honour' transgressions are largely viewed as a form of 'gender-based violence' in terms of 'who commits it, who experiences it, and why' (Begikhani et al., 2010: 15). The Crown Prosecution Service (CPS) and ACPO share a generic definition of 'honour' violence that conceptualises such offences as fundamental violations of human rights. 'Honour' violence is accordingly understood as 'a crime or incident, which has or may have been committed to protect or defend the honour of the family and/or community' (CPS, 2013). 'Honour' offences therefore comprise a whole scale of behaviour designed to coerce individuals into submission, often ranging from abduction, captivity, physical harm and rape to emotional blackmail, verbal threats and psychological mistreatment.

The conceptualisation of this type of domestic abuse as a culturally based practice is disputed in the literature, with some observers viewing the 'honour' terminology as misguided (Gill and Anitha, 2011; Thiara and Gill, 2010). Welchman and Hossain, on the other hand, have described 'honour' transgressions as manifestations both of violence against women as well as patriarchal cultural practices; 'crimes of honour' consequently encompass:

> a variety of manifestations of violence against women, including 'honour killings', assault, confinement or imprisonment, and interference with choice in marriage, where the publicly articulated 'justification' is attributed to a social order claimed to require the preservation of a concept of 'honour' vested in male (family and/or conjugal) control over women and specially women's sexual conduct: actual, suspected or potential. (Welchman and Hossain, 2005: 4)

Four main categories of 'honour' infringements have been commonly identified, namely: forced marriage, 'honour' killings, domestic violence and female genital mutilation (Brandon and Hafez, 2008; Khanum, 2008; Welchman and Hossain, 2005). Given the scope of this book, only the first two types of 'honour' violence will be considered here, with domestic violence understood as an inherent part both of forced marriage and 'honour' killings.

Despite evidence of a significant 'honour' violence problem in Britain, the actual extent of the challenge remains unknown; partly due to the difficulties associated with the reporting and measuring of this phenomenon. What it is known however is that 'honour' crimes in the UK are on the increase. A Freedom of Information (FOI) request by the UK-based Iranian and Kurdish Women's Rights Organisation (IKWRO) revealed that in 2010 'more than 2800 incidents of "honour"-based violence were reported to police across the UK' (IKWRO, 2011). All 52 police forces across England, Wales, Scotland and Northern Ireland were asked to disclose recorded incidents of 'honour' violence during the course of a year. On the whole, '39 police forces responded with a total of 2823 incidents', but 'IKWRO estimates that a further 500 incidents may have been reported to the 13 forces who did not respond' (IKWRO, 2011). Of the 12 police forces that did provide additional figures for the year 2009, nine 'showed an increase in "honour" crime between 2009 and 2010'; here 'The overall increase across the twelve forces was 57%. In London "honour" crime has doubled to more than 5 times the national average, and in Northumberland it has tripled in a year' (IKWRO, 2011). The top five worst areas affected were listed as follows: London with 495 incidents, followed by the West Midlands (378 incidents), West Yorkshire (350 incidents), Lancashire (227 incidents) and Manchester (189 incidents) (IKWRO, 2011). These figures, IKWRO concludes, 'demonstrate that "honour"-based violence is not a minor problem but a very serious issue which affects thousands of people each year, many of whom will suffer high levels of abuse before they seek help' (IKWRO, 2011).

The unabated rate of 'honour' violence in Britain has drawn attention to the Diaspora communities where it is found to be most prevalent. Two minority groups above all have come to be widely identified with 'honour'-based cultural practices, namely: South Asians and Muslims.

An 'Asian' and/or a 'Muslim' Issue? The Contested Framing of 'Honour' Violence

By and large the literature recognises the far-reaching ambit of 'honour' violence affecting a wide range of communities and cultures, whilst cutting across age, gender, social strata and ethnic background. In 2007, Hester et al.'s (2007) Home Office-commissioned study into forced marriage in Tower Hamlets, Manchester and Birmingham identified a variety of population groups where forced marriage was seen as taking place, including South Asian (over 54 per cent), African (over 49 per cent), Middle Eastern (over 21 per cent), Latin American (over 8 per cent) and Muslim (43 per cent) (Hester et al., 2007: 24). To a lesser extent forced marriage was also identified among Eastern Europeans, Albanians, Chinese, Jewish, and some Christian denominations such as Mormon and Greek Orthodox (Hester et al., 2007: 24). The geography of forced marriage cases dealt by the FMU similarly spans 60 different nations including South Asian, Middle Eastern, African and Eastern European countries (FMU, 2012). Amy Cumming, Joint Head of the FMU, has accordingly indicated that forced marriage 'affects many communities and cultures' including both white and non-white ethnic groups (FCO, 2012a).

Notwithstanding the recognised breadth of the 'honour' violence phenomenon, evidence also suggest a prevalence of 'honour' crimes among South Asian and Muslim communities both in the UK and abroad. In Britain, figures from the FMU recording forced marriage cases by country of origin provide a case in point, with almost half of the cases (47.1 per cent) involving Pakistan followed by Bangladesh (11 per cent), India (8 per cent), Afghanistan (2.1 per cent), Somalia, Turkey and Iraq (over 1 per cent each) (FMU, 2012). In other words, over 66 per cent of forced marriage instances dealt with by the FMU pertain to individuals from Pakistani, Bangladeshi and Indian origin alone; whereas 'Asian or British Asian' communities account for less than 6 per cent of the total population in England and Wales (ONS, 2011: 6). In the same way, 'honour' killings in Britain over the past two decades, including the high profile cases featured in this book together with the many more instances reported in the press, as well as actual murder trials, have also disproportionally involved South Asian and Muslim perpetrators.

The UK 'honour' violence national picture is in turn replicated at international level. The United Nations Population Fund (UNFPA) estimates that 'Throughout the world, perhaps as many as 5,000 women and girls a year are murdered by members of their own families'; such occurrences have been reported in countries as far apart as 'Bangladesh, Brazil, Ecuador, Egypt, India, Israel, Italy, Jordan, Morocco, Pakistan, Sweden, Turkey, Uganda and the United Kingdom' (UNFPA, 2000). Gill likewise notes how 'patterns of family honour killings and violence are evident in Latin American and Mediterranean societies, various European cultures, communities in many countries of the Middle East and parts of South Asia, and in some migrant communities, including … several in the UK and other Western countries' (Gill 2010 cited in Begikhani et al., 2010: 16). Yet the same international indicators point markedly towards the South Asian (and neighbouring regions) as the global geographical epicentre of 'honour' transgressions, and members of the Muslim community as the main perpetrators. The UNFPA has accordingly singled out South and Western Asia together with North Africa as the world's territories where 'honour' killings predominantly take place; with 'At least 1,000 women' having been 'murdered in Pakistan in 1999' (UNFPA, 2000). In the same way, the Kurdish region of Iraq and Turkey has among the highest rates of 'honour'-based violence in the world and especially honour killings per capita recorded (Brandon and Hafez, 2008: 54). The UN estimates that as many as 1,000 women in Iraqi Kurdistan may be killed by their families every year (UN Security Council, 2006). In 2000, Asma Jahangir, UN Special Rapporteur on Extrajudicial, Summary or Arbitrary Executions, went as far as to say that:

important

The practice of 'honour killings' is more prevalent although not limited to countries where the majority of the population is Muslim. In this regard it should be noted that a number of renowned Islamic leaders and scholars have publicly condemned this practice and clarified that it has no religious basis. At the same time, it is reported that some Governments of countries where Muslims are in a minority do not take a firm position against such violations of human rights on the pretext of not wanting to hurt cultural sensitivities among the minority population. (UN Economic and Social Council, 2000: para. 78: 27)

Against this background, 'honour' violence has often come to be framed as a mainly 'South Asian' and/or a 'Muslim' specific issue. In the UK context, Gangoli et al. explain how 'currently available data from the Forced Marriage Unit indicates that forced marriage is prevalent in all South Asian communities … However, there is a general perception that this is an issue that is predominant among Muslim communities' (Gangoli et al., 2006: 4). Hester et al. have likened the construction of forced marriage in recent times to a 'pathology' within these groups 'steeped in cultural assumptions' (Hester et al., 2007). The framing of 'honour' violence as an 'Asian' and/or 'Muslim' issue is nonetheless contested in the literature and wider public debates, particularly in a post-9/11 and 7/7 setting (Shackles, 2012). Heightened attention on these specific ethno-religious Diasporas has seen some analysts raise concerns about 'generalised Islamophobia in the UK' where state intervention in 'honour' violence may be construed as a 'veiled threat' against minority cultural values and traditions such as arranged marriages (Gangoli et al., 2006: 4). Others point to what they perceive as the 'racialisation' of the 'honour' violence phenomenon, in a manner akin to ethnic profiling, through misguided depictions, problematising and stigmatising of marginalised groups. Gill, for instance, maintains that 'it is not possible to associate honour-based violence with one particular religion (for example, Islam), or culture', since 'The practice is spread across a variety of religious and cultural groups' (Gill cited in Begikhani et al., 2010: 17). Sen similarly argues that notions of 'honour' are 'neither new nor a purely Islamic feature' (Sen, 2005: 61). In line with Said's 'orientalist' analysis of socially engineered imageries of 'non-Western' cultures (Said, 2003), Sen points to international misrepresentations of Islamic cultures 'as deeply imbued with backward approaches to gender relations, associating Islam intrinsically with honour killings, and highlighting Islamic cultures as therefore inherently problematic' (Sen, 2005: 42). Varying representations of the 'honour' question in the British media can be seen in this light (see for instance Marsden, 2012; *Mirror*, 2012; Corbin, 2013). Phillips and Dustin furthermore suggest that the 'honour' issue has been more likely to 'get caught up in a potentially racist immigration debate' as a result of the government's primary focus on cases involving 'transcontinental marriage' and 'overseas spouses' (Phillips and Dustin, 2004: 543).

In contrast, some literature considers 'racialist' arguments as a form of veiled racialism itself, within a prevailing liberal discourse unwilling to confront its own failings. Ali, for instance, has drawn attention to the apparent duplicity of some 'Western intellectuals' who readily question 'native white' majority cultures in developed countries, but avoid challenging Islamic minority Diasporas, as doing so is generally regarded as 'Islamophobia and Xenophobia'; she argues that:

> Withholding criticism and ignoring differences are racisms in its purest form. Yet these cultural experts fail to notice that through their anxious avoidance of criticising non-Western countries, they trap the people who represent these cultures in a state of backwardness. The experts may have the best of intentions, but as we all know, the road to hell is paved with good intentions. (Ali, 2007: xviii)

Other commentators moreover regard unwarranted emphasis on 'cultural sensitivities' and differential treatment of minority groups, particularly in Britain, as mere expressions of political correctness. Diana Nammi, Director of IKWRO, for example, contends that:

> We have got a policy in the UK: it says 'politically correctness' [sic], which sometimes is 'politically wrong'. And it's happened [regarding] ... how to deal with issues that [are] happening within [the] Muslim community. A wrong is a wrong, crime is crime, within any religion or any communities; then we have to act equally for the same community, equal to a British community. I mean, it must be no [sic] any differences in terms of dealing with the crime. So it [political correctness] has been an element and ignorance, I believe. But I'm afraid, the majority of the ['honour' violence] victims are from [the] Muslim community and we need to believe that reality. (Nammi featured on BBC News, 2011)

Siddiqui equally recognises that 'Most of the reported cases of "honour killings" in Britain involve women from South Asian (Indian or Pakistani) or Middle Eastern, and mainly Muslim, backgrounds', with notions of 'honour' and 'shame' being 'propped up by orthodox and conservative cultural and religious values' (Siddiqui, 2005: 265). She has criticised the British government for prioritising engagement with minority 'community and religious leaders' over that of 'honour' violence survivors and women's groups (Siddiqui, 2005: 265). As for the Metropolitan Police Service's approach to dealing with 'honour' violence involving minority communities, Commander Allen has declared that:

> The police response to this issue ['honour'-based violence] has nothing to do with political correctness and nothing to do with inappropriate sensitivities. The police response is about saving life, protecting those at risk of harm and

bringing perpetrators to account. We have an absolute duty to uphold the law and to protect the Human Rights of our fellow human beings. (ACPO, 2008: 4)

Despite the disputed framing of the 'honour' violence phenomenon, the reality of forced marriage and 'honour' killings in Britain raises profound questions about the very nature of British society. In particular, the official protection of the rights of minority communities engaged in such practices at the expense of the rights of the victims. The scale of the 'honour' violence problem moreover calls into question successive governments' efforts to effectively address culturally led gender inequalities.

Multicultural Dilemmas: A Feminist Critique

Everyday 'honour' violence in Britain presents a direct challenge to the state's prevailing multicultural public discourse, which broadly views the British nation as 'a community of communities' (Runnymede cited in Julios, 2008: 147). 'Honour' crimes bring into question the consequences of the unbridled application of such an ideological approach to the lives of ordinary citizens; for nowhere the gulf separating liberal multicultural principles from their unintended effects appears more evident than in the private lives of victims of 'honour' violence. The picture that emerges from their domestic realm frequently reveals patriarchal control structures, sex discrimination and human rights abuses. There is little doubt – even among advocates of state multiculturalism (Kymlicka, 1995; Modood, 2005; Parekh, 2000) – that practices such as forced marriage and 'honour' killings are incompatible with the core tenets of a modern liberal democratic society. Kymlicka, for instance, admits that 'liberalism has been blind to grave injustices which limit the freedom and harm the self-respect of women' (Kymlicka, 1999: 33). Reflecting on the 'complacencies' of the liberal approach to multiculturalism and group rights, he argues that:

a liberal egalitarian … approach to multiculturalism must look carefully at intragroup inequalities, and specifically at gender inequalities, when examining the legitimacy of minority group rights. Justice within ethnocultural groups is as important as justice between ethnocultural groups. Group rights are permissible if they help promote justice between ethnocultural groups, but are impermissible if they create or exacerbate gender inequalities within the group. (Kymlicka, 1999: 31)

The patriarchal nature of mainstream contemporary societies has long been discussed in the feminist literature (Walby, 1993; Crompton, 1997; McDowell,

1997; Abbott et al., 2005), in particular, the dichotomy between what Walby (1993) describes as the 'private patriarchy' and the public domain of an individual's life. Here, the socially sanctioned position of a man at home – as father, brother or husband – sees him as 'the direct oppressor and beneficiary, individually and directly, of the subordination of women' (Walby, 1993: 178). This male-dominated social hierarchy, she argues, 'is importantly maintained by the active exclusion of women from the public arenas' (Walby, 1993: 178). Black feminists have in turn sought to address the marginalised status of Black, Minority Ethnic and Refugee (BAMER) women, believed to have been neglected by mainstream 'white' feminists (Crenshaw, 1991). Critics of the tensions between multiculturalism and gender have drawn attention to culturally based gender inequalities in minority communities that oppress women (Okin, 1999; Phillips and Dustin, 2004). Okin (1999), for instance, views gendered power differences most acutely manifesting themselves in the domestic sphere and criticises multiculturalists for failing to acknowledge such inequalities:

> Despite all this evidence of cultural practices that control and subordinate women, none of the prominent defenders of multicultural group rights has adequately or even directly addressed the troubling connections between gender and culture or the conflicts that arise so commonly between feminism and multiculturalism. (Okin, 1999: 20)

Siddiqui (2005) also refers to the shortcomings of multiculturalism, which 'at its best aims to promote racial tolerance, and at its worst fails to address power inequalities such as sexual oppression within communities or the structural basis for racism' (Siddiqui, 2005: 278). Such gender imbalances and the cultural values that sustain them have come to be viewed in the literature as symptomatic of the wider failings of multiculturalism (Vertovec, 2010; Vertovec and Wessendorf, 2010; Gozdecka et al., 2014).

The case of Fatima, featured in Sanghera's (2009) *Daughters of Shame*, vividly illustrates the gendered social conditioning of females within Britain's 'honour' cultures. An Asian mother of two, Fatima was sentenced to two years in jail for an arson attack that her brothers had coerced her into carrying out. Sanghera explains how Fatima 'had been a victim of emotional cruelty all her life. She had grown up believing that her brothers' controlling behaviour was reasonable and her fear of them was such that she had allowed herself to be bullied into her crime' (Sanghera, 2009: 244). Fatima's description of her newly found freedom behind bars can be seen in this light as an indictment of Britain's multicultural ideology:

> Prison is great ... I've been to the gym. I've been to the library – I can read what I like for the first time in my life. I've watched *EastEnders* – I've never been

13

allowed to do that before. I don't feel I'm being watched by my family all the time. I can make friends with whoever I like. I have company. I'm not treated like a slave … Prison is freedom for me … For the first time in my life I'm my own person, I'm in control. (Fatima cited in Sanghera, 2009: 245)

The literature is filled with similar personal stories 'told by women who have been drugged, beaten, imprisoned, raped and terrorised within the walls of the homes they grew up in' (Sanghera, 2009: 3). It is as much to protect the lives of these women 'whose families treat them like slaves' (Sanghera, 2009: 3) as to address 'conflicts between the recognition of cultural diversity and securing women's equality' (Phillips and Dustin, 2004: 531) that the book seeks to explore British society's response to 'honour' violence.

Theoretical Framework, Methodological Challenges and Structure of the Book

In line with the literature on 'honour' violence, a number of methodological challenges were encountered during the writing of this book. Two key issues in particular relating to the framing and measuring of forced marriage and 'honour' killings are worth mentioning here. Reflections on research methods are in turn followed by an outline of the structure of the book, including a breakdown of individual chapters.

Theoretical Framework

Given the multilayered nature of 'honour' violence encompassing various social, cultural, religious and health factors, explanations of this phenomenon are increasingly being developed through the theoretical lens of 'intersectionality' (Crenshaw, 1991). Thiara and Gill highlight the need to recognise that the different experiences of 'honour' violence victims are 'complicated by and mediated through the intersection of systems of domination based on "race", ethnicity, class, culture and nationality' (Thiara and Gill, 2010: 18). In order to fully comprehend the 'honour' violence phenomenon, they claim, it is imperative to move beyond mere – and occasionally simplistic – explanations of culture and faith; instead taking into account the structural foundations of abuse (Thiara and Gill, 2010). The CPS has also acknowledged the importance of using an intersectionality paradigm when dealing with 'honour' violence, particularly as 'victims may experience multiple disadvantages' that 'may have the effect of increasing vulnerability', for example:

Some Lesbian, Gay, Bisexual and Transgender (LGBT) people may face actual or threatened forced marriage and the potential for other forms of honour based violence as a result of how their sexuality or gender identity is perceived within their family or community. There is an increasing body of evidence to support the fact that LGBT people from within affected communities are being forced into marriage to cure their sexuality or address their gender issues. This may also include honour based practices such as corrective rape. (CPS, 2013)

This book takes accordingly a holistic approach to the multiple, interrelated dimensions of the 'honour' violence equation that shape the status and personal circumstances of those who experience it. Here the 'intersectionality' paradigm may not only serve to explain the multilayered nature of 'honour' offences, but inform the political discourse aimed at addressing this social problem.

Methodological Challenges

In the first instance, defining what 'honour' violence amounts to and who engages in this practice is not a straightforward task. On the contrary, as this chapter has already illustrated, the nature and scope of Britain's 'honour' violence problem is strongly contested in the literature. Whether viewed as a manifestation of violence against women, a patriarchal cultural practice, an 'Asian' and/or a 'Muslim' specific phenomenon or an illustration of the failings of state multiculturalism; the 'honour' question is, to quote Hester et al. (2007), a 'complex topic that can be difficult to define and involves popular understandings of communities that experience' it (Hester et al., 2007: 10). Whilst ascribing to the official CPS/ACPO definitional version here stated, the book encapsulates the many contrasting views, perspectives and theories on the subject by drawing from a wide range of documentary sources. These include official publications such as parliamentary debates, legislation and court reports, particularly of murder cases for 'honour' killings (Hansard, 2007 and 2008; Home Office, 2000 and 2012; R v. *Athwal and ors* [2009] EWCA Crim 789; R v. *Mahmod (Mahmod Babakir)* [2009] EWCA Crim 775; R v. *Nazir* [2009] EWCA Crim 213; R v. *Yones* [2007] EWHC 1306 (QB)). Scholarly books, journals and recent academic research (Pope, 2012; Gill and Anitha, 2011; Penn, 2011; Begikhani et al., 2010; Thiara and Gill, 2010) together with biographical accounts from survivors (Ahluwalia and Gupta, 2008; Athwal, 2013; Mushen and Croft, 2004; Sanghera, 2007 and 2009; Shah, 2010; Younis, 2012) are also drawn upon as well as grey literature mostly from think-tanks, interest groups and grassroots service providers dealing with 'honour' violence victims (Karma Nirvana, 2012; IKWRO, 2011; SBS, 2014b; Brandon and Hafez, 2008). In addition, media reporting, newspapers articles and audio materials featuring 'honour' violence related films/documentaries are furthermore examined (Bingham, 2012; Erdem, 2012; H.O.P.E., 2009; BBC *Panorama*, 2012).

With regard to quantifying the extent of 'honour' violence in Britain, the continuing lack of nationally standardised reliable data makes it virtually impossible to ascertain the actual scale of the problem. Figures from the FMU, the Home Office and ACPO, for instance, largely reflect underestimates (FMU, 2012; Home Office, 2000; ACPO, 2008); whereas data from women's groups such as Karma Nirvana, IKWRO and SBS are similarly limited in their reach (Karma Nirvana, 2012; IKWRO, 2011; SBS, 2013). Scholarly studies have also frequently provided snapshots of localised areas such as Khanum's (2008) Luton case-study or Hester et al.'s (2007) Tower Hamlets, Manchester and Birmingham-based research on forced marriage. International indicators placing the UK's 'honour' violence experience into a wider context, such as those from various United Nations (UN) agencies, present comparable limitations (UNFPA, 2000, 2012 and 2013; UN Security Council, 2006). The book nevertheless relies on the available – if flawed – evidence on forced marriage and 'honour' killings to produce as accurate a British national picture as possible. By unveiling a wealth of information, perspectives and data on the subject through the use of secondary sources, the volume's research process affords a level of triangulation conducive to realising this goal. Ultimately, the book's analytical methods and findings have been shaped by the methodological challenges encountered from the outset. Conversely, they have served to highlight the complex and often contentious nature of 'honour' violence and the difficulties associated with any government's efforts to deal with it.

Structure of the Book

The book is divided into three parts. Part I outlines the significance and focus of the book together with its methodology and theoretical framework. It then maps out the scope of forced marriage and 'honour' killings in Britain as well as exploring the experiences of victims. Part I comprises chapters 1, 2 and 3.

This opening chapter provides a contextual background to the phenomenon of 'honour' violence in Britain, and in particular two of its most significant and far-reaching manifestations: forced marriage and 'honour' killings. Generally understood as part of a wider spectrum of 'honour' related offences, including domestic abuse and female genital mutilation (FGM), increasing attention on forced marriage and 'honour' killings in recent times has seen such practices shaping the UK public policy discourse in unparalleled ways. It is against this background that the chapter maps out the nature and scope of these so-called 'honour' transgressions. The chapter situates the book's analysis within a mainstream feminist scholarly and political tradition driven by questions of gender inequality and patriarchal control (Walby, 1993; Crompton, 1997;

Abbott et al., 2005). In particular, it considers feminist critiques of state multiculturalism, which view women's rights as being superseded by the rights of minority ethnic patriarchies (Okin, 1999; Phillips and Dustin, 2004; Siddiqui, 2005; Ali, 2006a). As expressions of culturally based gender discrimination, the continuing presence of forced marriage and 'honour' killings in Britain presents a direct challenge to the country's liberal values that are inherently contrary to women's oppression. While recognising the presence of 'honour' violence across different communities and cultures, the chapter points to evidence suggesting a prevalence of such practices among South Asian and Muslim Diasporas. The broad conceptualisation of 'honour' violence as a 'South Asian' and/or a 'Muslim' specific problem however is contested in the literature and such debates are therefore explored here. On the one hand, there are the views from advocates of a 'racialist' approach to 'honour' crimes, which see distorted depictions of these marginalised communities as stigmatising and stereotyping (Gangoli et al., 2006; Begikhani et al., 2010; Sen, 2005); and on the other hand, counterviews from critics of such arguments that view them as either 'racialist' themselves, a by-product of misguided 'cultural sensitivities' or mere expressions of political correctness (Ali, 2007; Nammi featured on BBC News, 2011). The chapter finally reflects on how the unabated rate of 'honour' violence in Britain, by now spawning successive generations of UK-born migrants, conflicts with the UK state's ideologically liberal discourse.

Chapter 2 deconstructs the institution of marriage within the context of 'honour' cultures and explores its two main manifestations, namely 'arranged' and 'forced' marriage. Largely sanctioned as an acceptable cultural practice, arranged marriages require the full and free consent of both interested parties. The construction of the arranged marriage as a harmless tradition is nevertheless contested in the literature by some observers and survivors of arranged marriages who point to the potentially fluid boundaries between free and enforced consent, together with the impact that social expectations and cultural traditions may have on those entering into such unions as well as those wishing to exit them (Sanghera, 2007 and 2009). Research moreover points to the long-term health related implications associated with so-called 'cousin marriages' (Hope, 2013). The chapter then turns its attention to the practice of 'forced' marriage, where free consent is superseded by a plethora of coercive measures designed to obtain compliance from the victims, ranging from physical to psychological mistreatment, abduction and imprisonment (Brandon and Hafez, 2008; Khanum, 2008; Welchman and Hossain, 2005). Here, forced marriage is discussed within the context of feminist critiques conceptualising this phenomenon as a form of violence against women as opposed to a 'cultural' practice (Gill and Anitha, 2011; Thiara and Gill, 2010). Drawing from survivors' accounts, often reported in autobiographies, the media and grey literature, the chapter explores the nature of this variant of domestic violence and government initiatives aimed at tackling it. In line with the book's theoretical framework, the chapter investigates women's experiences of violence within marriage through the lens of 'intersectionality', which recognises the intersection of systems of male control based on gender, ethnicity and culture, among others (Crenshaw, 1991; Thiara and Gill, 2010). The 'intersectionality' paradigm thus recognises that the personal circumstances of potential and actual victims of marital abuse may be influenced by a multiplicity of interrelated dimensions pertaining to the 'honour' violence equation. These should not only inform any analysis of this social problem, but policy responses striving to eradicate it.

Chapter 3 examines the phenomenon of 'honour' killings in Britain over the past two decades. Unlike mainstream domestic violence and extemporary 'crimes of passion', the planned, premeditated and collaborative nature of what Brandon and Hafez have termed as 'community crimes' is explored at length (Brandon and Hafez, 2008). The chapter features five high profile case-studies of 'honour' killings that span nearly 10 years, as follows: first, Surjit Athwal, a 27-year-old Sikh customs officer at Heathrow Airport believed to have been killed in India on the orders of her mother-in-law and husband in 1998 (Siddique, 2007; Athwal, 2013). Second, Heshu Yones, a 16-year-old school girl from Acton who was stabbed by her Kurdish Muslim father in 2002 (Dodd, 2003). Third, Shafilea Ahmed, a 17-year-old girl from Cheshire murdered by her Pakistani parents in 2003 (Carter, 2012). Fourth, Samaira Nazir, a 25-year-old recruitment consultant stabbed by her brother and cousin in 2005 (Steele, 2006). Fifth, Banaz Mahmod, a 20-year-old woman from South London gang-raped, tortured and killed on the orders of her Kurdish Muslim father and uncle in 2006 (McVeigh, 2007a). These five case-studies were chosen as much for the extensive media coverage they received at the time as for their wider significance, within varying degrees, in public policy, social and legal terms. Featuring one Indian, two Pakistani and two Kurdish female victims as well as Sikh and Muslim perpetrators, these instances serve to illustrate the complex and diverse nature of such 'honour' related offences as well as the many social and cultural factors underlying them. By providing insights into the culturally based, gendered power relations governing 'honour' killings, the selected examples afford empirical evidence to substantiate the critical feminist analyses of multiculturalism framing this volume.

Part II of the book explores the evolution of Britain's public policy relating to 'honour' violence offences as well as the various political and legislative debates accompanying it. The section comprises chapters 4, 5 and 6.

Chapter 4 traces the development of government policy and legislative processes regarding 'honour' violence. In particular, it examines the introduction of the *Forced Marriage (Civil Protection) Act 2007* (Hansard, 2007), which saw the UK become the first country to use civil law to give protection and legal remedies to victims of a forced marriage. This has been largely achieved through the provision of Forced Marriage Protection Orders (FMPOs) under the Act. While the arrival of new legislation has been broadly welcomed as a step in the right direction, the drafting of the legislation was accompanied by complex and often difficult debates and ideological divisions among policymakers, stakeholders and community representatives. In trying to unravel the main strands of this rather entangled conceptual thread, the chapter draws from relevant legislative and parliamentary debates, public consultations and political statements as well as wider press and media reports (Hansard, 2011a; Home Office, 2000; Lord Lester, 2007; White, 2007). Such discussions are underlined by the equally conflicting views of feminist scholars, activists and politicians concerned with gender and diversity issues, particularly as they strive to square the UK's gender-equality-and-multiculturalism circle.

Chapter 5 examines the collaborative nature of forced marriage and 'honour' killings and the role played by families, community networks and individuals in position of authority both in eradicating as well as perpetuating such offences. Variously labelled as 'community' or 'cultural' crimes, 'honour' offences are often carried out with the acquiescence of members of the immediate family circle and the broader community, who either aid the perpetrators or are drawn into the ensuing conspiracy of silence (Brandon and Hafez, 2008). From relatives and friends to local representatives and community leaders; by and large 'honour' crimes are known to be collective endeavours as much in their planning and execution as in the disposal of incriminating evidence. Time and again family members have been unveiled as witnesses to 'honour' killings during the course of murder trials; others knew that these crimes were happening in their midst. Fathers, brothers and cousins will accordingly plan and carry out premeditated attacks on their own daughters, sisters and nieces. Media reports have specifically highlighted the issue of so-called 'bounty hunters', who have been charged by families of those fleeing forced marriages and 'honour' violence with tracking the runaways down (McVeigh, 2009). Understanding the nature and significance of these formal and informal networks within 'honour' cultures becomes therefore central to unravelling the gendered power structures that sustain them. The existence of socially sanctioned patriarchal hierarchies among minority ethnic communities further supports critical feminist analyses of multiculturalism. In particular, those who view gendered power differences most acutely manifesting themselves in the private sphere of an individual's life, and thus criticise multiculturalists for ignoring such differences (Ali, 2007). The presence of family networks in cases of forced marriage and 'honour' killings also serves to explain the home-grown intergenerational trend that now characterise these offences. The chapter therefore explores the extent to which the existence and use of networks is integral to the 'honour' violence equation. It also considers the role that those in positions of authority, community and religious leaders may play in either challenging or preserving the *status quo*.

Chapter 6 considers a number of key challenges identified by front-line practitioners regarding the provision of services and support to victims of 'honour' violence. Drawing from the wide-ranging expertise of these professionals, several issues are briefly examined including the government's multi-agency approach to tackling forced marriage and 'honour'-based violence, shortcomings in service delivery as well as best practice across the board, lack of adequate funding to grassroots groups together with the position of domestic violence victims of 'insecure immigration status' with no recourse to public funds (Amnesty International UK and SBS, 2008). The chapter also highlights the difficulties faced by 'honour' violence victims in accessing legal support and their experiences of dealing with the police. The education sector is furthermore scrutinised and in particular the reluctance of schools to engage in raising awareness of issues relating to 'honour' violence and forced marriage, for they are deemed to be culturally sensitive and problematic.

Finally, Part III sums up the main findings of the book and reflects on the future direction of 'honour' violence in multicultural Britain. It comprises the concluding chapter.

Chapter 7 draws from the key themes and findings of the book and reflects on the challenges facing British multiculturalism in the face of an unrelenting 'honour' violence problem. The chapter brings together debates relating to the evolving nature of the UK's approach to diversity running through the book; in particular, feminist critiques of a liberal discourse unable or unwilling to recognise culturally based gender discrimination, especially relating to 'honour' traditions that overtly oppress and control women. Within the context of the wider British nation, the accounts of 'honour' violence victims serve to illustrate the reality of everyday life for some female members of minority ethnic communities; a reality that often involves violations of civil liberties and human rights. While the book's feminist theoretical framework has helped to deconstruct such gendered power relationships; the chapter goes on to interrogate the critical feminist analyses here presented, reflecting on their advocates' contrasting views and considering the shortcomings of these approaches, especially as seen by long-term supporters of state multiculturalism (Kymlicka, 1995; Modood, 2005; Parekh, 2000). The chapter also considers the merits of using an 'intersectionality' paradigm to better understand the experiences of victims of 'honour' violence. In this way, the book not only contributes to further the debates on gender and diversity, but challenges the scholarly traditions underlying them. Lastly, the chapter brings into focus the enduring dilemmas facing contemporary British society: on the one hand, respect for minority rights and cultures while, at the same time, protecting gender equality, civil liberties and ultimately the rights of the majority. With state-sponsored multiculturalism largely viewed as unable to resolve these tensions, the chapter turns to the latest literature on 'post-multiculturalism' (Vertovec, 2010; Gozdecka et al., 2014).

Conclusion

Forced marriage and 'honour' killings have been part of the British social fabric for decades now. Within local communities across the country, inside family homes, girls and women continue to experience daily abuse by those closest to them. While the scale of this phenomenon is not fully known, available evidence seem to suggest that it is a widespread practice affecting many communities and particularly prevalent among South Asian and Muslim Diasporas. A combination of high profile cases, improved services provision for victims and successful prosecutions of offenders have placed the 'honour' violence phenomenon firmly on the UK government's political agenda. The resulting public and academic debates though have been characterised by profound disagreements as to how best define, frame and resolve this seemingly intractable problem. Within the disputed context of a British 'post-multicultural' nation, unresolved issues remain regarding minority and majority group rights, as well as the simultaneous safeguarding of cultural and religious traditions, gender equality and individual freedom. Such tensions not only present the UK government with a difficult political and ideological quandary, but give rise to equally profound questions. Should Britain tolerate oppressive traditions that disadvantage women and girls on gender grounds? Are minority cultures to be respected regardless of the values they espouse? How far should British society go in accommodating minority rights and how should those be balanced with the rights of the majority? Is it acceptable for the country's dominant culture to impose a moral universalism on ethnic communities? Or should the former be compelled into cultural relativism by the latter? By exploring female experiences of 'honour' violence through a myriad of personal and public narratives, the book makes a positive contribution to the growing debate on 'honour' violence, multiculturalism and gender in Britain. The volume's feminist theoretical underpinnings moreover shed light on the multiple intersections of gendered power structures that continue to disadvantage minority ethnic girls and women in contemporary British society. As for the many silent victims who have already paid the ultimate 'honour' penalty, it is hoped the individual narratives here depicted will afford them a voice.

Chapter 2
Till Death Do Us Part?
From Arranged to Forced Marriage

Marriage, 'Honour' and Culture

Sociologists have traditionally drawn a broad distinction between so-called 'individualist' and 'collectivist' cultures (Eysenck, 2013; Hofstede, 1980). Eysenck explains how individualist cultures, mainly associated with Western societies, are often seen to 'emphasise independence, personal responsibility and each person's uniqueness'; whereas collectivist systems 'such as many in the Far East' appear to 'emphasise interdependence, sharing of responsibility, and group membership' (Eysenck, 2013: 8). Sardar's (2008a) description of the 'archetypal Asian family' serves to illustrate this point:

> The Asian family is not a [mainstream British] nuclear unit of parents and 2.4 children. It is an extended social unit that includes grandparents, in-laws, aunts and uncles and a long list of relatives, each with a specific title in relation to everyone else in the family. And Asian family values are focused on keeping the unit together – in one physical place if possible – and providing support. The corollary is that you have to accept them on the same terms. It can be onerous, inconvenient, not to say downright demanding. (Sardar, 2008a: 3)

Sanghera (2007) similarly notes the communal nature of the Asian family and wider community which, unlike their Western counterparts, seem to emphasise the interests of the collective; as she puts it 'In the Asian community the will of the family still comes first' (Sanghera, 2007: 273).

The crude 'individualist vs. collectivist' characterisation can be seen as an oversimplification of a far more intricate reality and is therefore disputed in the literature (Triandis et al., 1993). Nonetheless, the principle of 'cultural differences' has come to underline wider debates regarding multiculturalism and 'honour' violence against women. Brandon and Hafez (2008), for instance, point to the paternalistic social attitudes prevalent in many minority ethnic communities and religious cultures including South Asian, Middle Eastern and ultra-orthodox Jewish groups. Here, every male member of the family is usually assigned the role of 'guardian of cultural norms and values', while their female counterparts are expected to abide by such established principles or else risk repercussions, including violence (Brandon and Hafez, 2008: 29); hence:

> Patterns of violence in the Jewish community can be similar to those of more recent immigrants – even though many Jewish families have lived in the UK for centuries. As in South Asian and Middle Eastern cultures, many Jews from conservative backgrounds can may [*sic*] see women as the upholders of family and community values and put a high premium on traditional family values. In addition, Jewish women are often seen as being the carriers of their community's religious identity. As in other communities, however, this can become a pretext for violence and abuse. (Brandon and Hafez, 2008: 30)

Women and young girls growing up in Britain's 'honour' cultures may accordingly be afforded a different social status to that of their male peers; one which is heavily laden with patriarchal, cultural and religious symbolism. Innumerable personal accounts in the literature attest to the culturally construed gendered experiences of 'honour' violence victims (Ahluwalia and Gupta, 2008; Sanghera, 2007 and 2009; Athwal, 2013; Younis, 2013; Shah, 2010; Muhsen and Croft, 2004).

The many stories of victims and casualties of 'honour' violence portrayed in this book further illustrate that reality. Kiranjit Ahluwalia, for instance, whose decade-long abusive 'arranged marriage' is further recounted in this chapter, depicts her Indian 'honour' culture and religious traditions as permeating every aspect of her life in a way that privileges men, but is fundamentally oppressive to women:

> My culture is like my blood – coursing through every vein of my body. It is the culture into which I was born and where I grew up which sees the woman as the honour of the house. In order to uphold this false 'honour' and glory, she is taught to endure many kinds of oppression and pain, in silence. In addition, religion also teaches her that her husband is her God and fulfilling his every desire is her religious duty. A woman who does not follow this path in our society has no respect or place in it. She suffers from all sorts of attacks and much hurt entirely alone. She is responsible not only for her husband but also his entire family's happiness. (Ahluwalia and Gupta, 2008: 243)

Sarbjit Kaur Athwal likewise warns that 'Being [born] a girl in an Indian family is not the best way to start life. In many people's eyes, that was the first time I brought shame on my family' (Athwal, 2013: 16). Originally from Hounslow, West London, Athwal recalls how having been brought up by her Indian parents 'to be a respectful Sikh, to honour and obey my family and community', her life became marked by gender discrimination from the outset:

Sikhism is about equality, about all castes of men being the same and about the similarities, not the differences, between men and women. So, looking back, why was I the one not allowed to go out unaccompanied? Why was I forced to cover up if I set foot outside the house? Why did I have to cover my head with a scarf if a male so much as entered the same building, even if it was one of my own uncles? If it had to do with my religion I would have not minded. But this appeared to be only about my gender.

I really should have been a boy …

My male cousins were excused everything I had to endure … It really was one rule for them and another rule for me. (Athwal, 2013: 44–5)

In Athwal's case, two significant 'honour' related events were to shape her adult life in fundamental and unanticipated ways: first, her 'arranged marriage' as a teenager to Hardave Athwal; and second, the subsequent 'honour' killing of her sister-in-law Surjit Athwal at the hands of her husband, Sukhdave Athwal, and mother-in-law, Bachan Kaur Athwal. In her biographical account *Shamed*, Athwal (2013) narrates her everyday life in the midst of a patriarchal 'honour' culture as well as the events leading to the conviction of Sukhdave and Bachan Kaur for the murder of Surjit (Athwal, 2013). Surjit's own story is in turn reported in the following chapter.

In line with Athwal's experience, British-born Samina Younis describes how her strict Pakistani Muslim parents saw her and her twin sister as 'a burden due to the fact that we were not born as males' (Younis, 2013: 5). Having had her life mapped out from a young age by her family, Younis reflects on a violent upbringing in which:

I was constantly reminded by my parents that a woman's place is in the home and women do not have a voice in society and to only speak when I am spoken to. From childhood to a teenager I became emotionally and mentally scarred with the violence and abuse I experienced from my parents. I grew to learn the honour of my family was more important to my parents than the lives of my sisters and I. (Younis, 2013: 5–6)

Such culturally based gender differentials are by no means limited to minority ethnic communities and/or religious cultures. On the contrary, there is ample evidence of a continuing global gender gap in mainstream societies across the world (WEF, 2013; OECD, 2012; EC, 2005). But there is equally compelling evidence of 'honour' related paternalistic traditions that are intrinsically prejudiced against women (UNFPA, 2000, 2012 and 2013; UNFPA-UNICEF, 2012). These include, Okin explains, 'elaborate patterns of socialization, rituals, matrimonial customs, and other cultural practices (including systems of property ownership and control of resources) aimed at bringing women's sexuality and reproductive capabilities under men's control' (Okin, 1999: 14). Okin furthermore argues that these practices prevent women from making informed choices about how to live autonomous lives independent from men; choices that may include not getting married, not having children and not being in a relationship either with a man or a woman. As she puts it:

> While virtually all of the world's cultures have distinctly patriarchal pasts, some – mostly, though by no means exclusively, Western liberal cultures – have departed far further from them than others. Western cultures, of course still practice many forms of sex discrimination ... But women in more liberal cultures are, at the same time, legally guaranteed many of the same freedoms and opportunities as men. In addition, most families in such cultures, with the exception of some religious fundamentalists, do not communicate to their daughters that they are of less value than boys, that their lives are to be confined to domesticity and service to men and children, and that their sexuality is of value only in marriage, in service to men and for reproductive ends. This situation ... is quite different from that of women in many of the world's other cultures, including many of those from which immigrants to Europe and North America come. (Okin, 1999: 16–17)

Okin's earlier assertions have been validated by later literature (Abbott et al., 2005). Satz, for instance, has argued that:

> In every country of the world, women fare far worse than men on a number of important indices: income and wealth, political participation, vulnerability to sexual assault, and degree of access to the most prestigious social positions. In many developing countries the inequalities based on gender are especially stark: girls are less likely to be educated, receive health care, or even be fed than their male siblings. In India, for instance, girls are 40 per cent more likely to die before the age of five than boys. (Satz cited in Okin, 2013: ix)

It is against this background that Penn's (2011) characterisation of marriage in contemporary society must be understood. Two types of marriage can accordingly be identified worldwide today: on the one hand, there are 'love marriages' which 'dominate Western nations such as the United States and those in Europe'; and on the other hand, 'arranged marriages' prevalent 'in many parts of Asia and Africa' (Penn, 2011: 637). Penn argues that both types of marriage 'co-exist in countries such as Britain, France and Germany' as a consequence of international migration from developing to developed nations particularly in Western Europe (Penn, 2011: 637). Drawing from empirical research with 'young Asians and non-Asians in the North West of England' (Penn and Lambert, 2009), he elucidates how 'both arranged marriages and love marriages share *similar* structural properties as value systems. Both strongly advocate the *superiority* of their own system of marriage and, as a corollary, *derogate* the other' (Penn, 2011: 638). Consistent with Penn's findings, Samad and Eade (2002) point to the continuation of 'endogamous marriages' within Britain's Pakistani and Bangladeshi communities based on 'caste and status' (Samad and Eade, 2002: 108). The practice of transcontinental marriages is understood to persist largely 'due to difficulties in finding appropriate partners; from the same caste group, educational background and class background' (Samad and Eade, 2002: 108). Encouraging the preservation of in-group unions therefore not only serves to strengthen social capital and kinship; but is seen as a significant 'cultural asset' that can ultimately be transformed into 'economic advantage' (Samad and Eade, 2002: 119).

An Arranged Marriage: A Matter of Consent?

The public debate on the nature and types of conjugal unions among Britain's 'honour' cultures has by and large been characterised by a simplified depiction of two seemingly clear-cut practices. On the one hand, the socially sanctioned 'arranged' wedding is broadly construed as a legitimate tradition involving consenting adults. On the other hand, the objectionable 'forced' marriage is invariably seen as involving coercion and violence. Government publications, political commentary and official pronouncements have time and again reiterated this unambiguous version of such marital traditions. The views expressed in *A Choice by Right*, the report of the Home Office Working Group on Forced Marriage (2000) provide a case in point:

> A clear distinction must be made between forced and arranged marriages … The Working Group is clear that the distinction lies in the right to choose. In the tradition of arranged marriages, the families of both spouses take a leading role in arranging the marriage, but the choice whether to solemnise the arrangement remains with the spouses and can be exercised at any time. The spouses have the right to choose – to say no – at any time. In forced marriage, there is no choice … The tradition of arranged marriage has operated successfully within many communities and many countries for a very long time and remains the preferred choice of many young people who spoke to the Working Group. (Home Office, 2000: 10)

In a recent speech on immigration, Prime Minister David Cameron reinstated this prevailing narrative:

the most grotesque example of a relationship that isn't genuine is a forced marriage, which is of course completely different from an arranged marriage where both partners consent, or a sham marriage where the aim is to circumvent immigration control or make a financial gain. (Cameron, 2011)

Advocates of arranged marriages often point to the socialising aspects of this long-held custom, which not only involves the bride and groom, but their close families and extended circle of relatives. An arranged marriage, Sardar stresses, 'is not just a marriage between two individuals, but two families' (Sardar, 2008a: 3). Having entered into an arranged marriage as a young man, the author of *Balti Britain: A Journey through the British Asian Experience* maintains that 'marriage is too important to be left to so precarious and potentially perverse and headstrong a basis as the dreams and delusions of a would-be bride and groom' (Sardar, 2008a: 3). An integral part of his British-Asian identity, the practice of arranged marriage, Sardar maintains, is 'the heartbeat of Asian tradition' (Sardar, 2008a: 3); a tradition that inextricably bound him to his future spouse well before any of them had been born:

I have always been married. My mother harboured a specific plan for my marriage before I was born. I was married generations before my birth, just as my wife Saliha was destined to be my companion before we ever met. We met but briefly and never alone before we were married. As it was, so it is and ever will be, because it works. (Sardar, 2008a: 3)

In spite of the generally recognised socio-cultural role and status of arranged marriages, their conceptualisation as a harmless tradition is increasingly being interrogated in the literature. Questions have been raised about the nature of 'free' consent when agreeing to enter into an arranged marriage, the circumstances under which approval may be granted, the social pressures and expectations that may lead to an arranged marriage as well as the consequences of choosing to opt out or exit such a union. Hester et al. (2007) argue that the boundaries between an arranged and a forced marriage are far from unambiguous:

Normally a forced marriage is taken to mean a lack of consent at the point of entry into a marriage, but if the marriage arrangements are very rushed and the young person does not really understand what is happening, or does not have time to respond, or has been given inadequate information, then the notion of consent is questionable. In particular, there can be a 'slippage' or blurring between arranged and forced marriage. (Hester et al., 2007: 10)

Phillips and Dustin (2004) furthermore point to the evolving and fluid nature of the notion of 'consent' upon which the arranged marriage is ostensibly based. Reflecting on recent forced marriage related case law, they reveal how 'the dichotomy between coercion and consent has been approached in a more nuanced way' in the '(relatively few) cases of forced marriage to come before the English and Scottish courts' (Phillips and Dustin, 2004: 537). The legal definition of 'duress' has accordingly evolved from an earlier 'very restrictive' version to 'one that recognizes the force of moral and emotional blackmail' (Phillips and Dustin, 2004: 537). As a result, 'many marriages currently regarded as arranged would more accurately be described as forced' or 'non-consensual' (Phillips and Dustin, 2004: 537–40). Citing empirical studies of potential brides in arranged marriages (Bhopal, 1999; Bradby, 1999), Phillips and Dustin conclude that 'the pressures to agree [to an arranged] marriage are clearly enormous' with the women involved seeing themselves as 'having minimal power to refuse' (Phillips and Dustin, 2004: 540). Would-be brides in arranged marriages thus 'felt that it was harder for a young woman than a young man to resist parental pressure, and that a daughter who refused too many prospective partners would seriously undermine her parents' standing in the local community' (Phillips and Dustin, 2004: 540). Athwal's (2013) description of the centrality of the 'arranged marriage' tradition to her family's history and identity further corroborates the literature's empirical findings on the nature of consent. Aged 17, Athwal was shown a picture of a man her parents intended her to marry:

> As they pointed to the low-resolution, grainy image, my parents explained that this was how marriages worked. Parents of a boy contacted parents of a girl and arranged a match. That was it, simple. The children had no say. They certainly didn't seek out their own husband or wife. That's how my grandparents in India had married, that's how my grandparents in the UK had married, and that's how my aunts and uncles had found each other as well. (Athwal, 2013: 61)

Despite the weight of expectation, Athwal refused to marry the man depicted in the photograph on that occasion; but the teenager was in no doubt that she 'was running out of chances' and could not continue to reject prospective husbands indefinitely:

> Dad had honoured my view, and taken into account my younger years. He'd listened to my opinion, but we both knew that only went so far. Yes, I could veto this man. What I couldn't do was say I would not get married. My marriage was already a foregone conclusion. That was the Sikh way. That was our family way. And that was the way it would be for me. *Next* time ... (Athwal, 2013: 63)

Two years later, and a further potential spouse rejected, Athwal finally relented and went ahead with an arranged marriage. Having begged her father not to marry her off, she admits to family and 'community' pressures playing a crucial part in the final outcome. As an older sibling to her young sister, she was 'the example' to follow, she had 'the family's honour to think of' and 'many lives' may be affected by her decision; there was, Athwal concedes, 'a lot of weight on my young shoulders and I thought I might collapse under the pressure' (Athwal, 2013: 66). The reasons behind her decision to go ahead with the arranged marriage clearly illustrate the problematic nature of 'consent' within the socially sanctioned arranged marriage. As Athwal explains:

> I was no more interested in marrying this stranger from Hayes than I had been the day before. But I'd said I would and, in all honesty, acquiescing was a tremendous weight off my shoulders. There were no more arguments to be had, no more emotional blackmail or plaintive looks, no more pressure from the community. All I had to do now was see it through. (Athwal, 2013: 73)

It is precisely the backdrop against which decisions about 'arranged marriages' are made and the many environmental factors underlying 'consent' that have come under closest scrutiny. Anitha and Gill (2009) argue that the established 'binary' distinction between arranged and forced marriage fails to acknowledge 'the context in which consent is constructed' (Anitha and Gill, 2009: 165). They contend that:

> consent and coercion in relation to marriage can be better understood as two ends of a continuum, between which lie degrees of socio-cultural expectation, control, persuasion, pressure, threat and force. Women who face these constraints exercise their agency in complex and contradictory ways that are not always recognised by the existing exit-centred state initiatives designed to tackle this problem. (Anitha and Gill, 2009: 165)

In keeping with Athwal's experience, survivors of arranged marriages invariably point to the impact that parental, family and community's expectations have on individuals, particularly young people, when considering whether to enter an arranged union (Sanghera, 2007 and 2009; Ahluwalia and Gupta, 2008; Athwal, 2013). They also emphasise the social implications and cultural penalties awaiting those who either refuse to enter into arranged marriages or choose to exit them afterwards, including domestic violence, social exclusion and isolation. Sanghera (2009) recalls her life-changing decision to flee home as an adolescent after refusing to marry the prospective husband her Indian parents had designated for her:

> I run away rather than go through with that marriage and my family disowned me: 'You have shamed us. You are dead in our eyes', my mum said … As I

struggled to make my way in life I kept my head down and my eyes averted: I
didn't want people knowing how worthless I was. (Sanghera, 2009: 1)

Ahluwalia, in turn, describes how notwithstanding years of domestic violence
following her arranged marriage, she would face grave social consequences as a
member of Britain's Indian Diaspora, if she chose to leave her abusive husband:

> I had no way out. Divorce carried such stigma. If I lived on my own, I would
> be condemned by [UK's Indian] society. If I lived with my family, I would be a
> burden to them. (Ahluwalia and Gupta, 2008: 109)

Ahluwalia's case is particularly relevant in understanding the complex and often
overlapping socio-cultural layers integral to the 'arranged marriage' scenario;
for unlike most women in her position, she went on to kill her husband.

The Story of Kiranjit Ahluwalia

In 1989, after a decade of domestic abuse ensuing from an arranged marriage,
Kiranjit Ahluwalia, a UK-based Indian immigrant, killed her husband by
setting his bedroom alight and was convicted of his murder and sentenced
to life imprisonment. 'For ten whole years', she recalls, 'I lived with fear, fear,
fear. It was only when I went to prison that I got my confidence … that I
got to know what it was like to be free of fear' (Ahluwalia and Gupta, 2008:
78). In 1992, with the assistance of Southall Black Sisters (SBS), the Asian
women's grassroots organisation, Ahluwalia won an appeal 'on the grounds
of diminished responsibility based on new psychiatric evidence of her long
standing depression due to her experiences of violence and abuse' (SBS, 2013).
Here, Ahluwalia describes the extent to which her husband sought to control
every aspect of her life during their marriage:

> He wanted complete control – to hit me, to have sex, to take me out, to keep me
> in, to take me upstairs. I couldn't watch TV, I couldn't eat or drink – not a thing
> could I do without his approval. (Ahluwalia and Gupta, 2008: 85)

At the subsequent retrial, she was found guilty of manslaughter 'on the basis
of diminished responsibility' and 'sentenced to three years and four months
imprisonment, exactly the time she had already served'; she was therefore
released immediately (SBS, 2013). Her high profile case contributed to changes
in the law regarding the partial defence to murder for abused women who go
on to kill. In her autobiographical book *Provoked*, Ahluwalia openly criticises the
prevailing patriarchal customs and 'cultural restrains' of her Sikh community
that overtly discriminate against women:

> Ours is a culture that imprisons women, while allowing men the freedom to do what they like. They have neither the barrier of religion nor that of *izzat* ['honour'] standing in their way. Only women are made to suffer like this. There are hundreds of thousands of women who are tied down by these restrictions … When a daughter is born in our society; it is a matter of grief. She is a drain, she will have to be fed and educated and clothed, and then a dowry will have to be found for her so that she can become an asset in someone else's home. And she is the vehicle for the *izzat* of the whole family, whether the one into which she was born or the one into which she marries. This *izzat* is a noose around her neck. It curtails her freedom to study, to work, to do what she wants, because family honour is always at stake. This *izzat* kills her off, bit by bit. (Ahluwalia and Gupta, 2008: 112)

Such paternalistic attitudes are often internalised both by male and female members of 'honour' cultures, with men typically seeking to regulate the lives of their female peers as keepers of the family 'honour', and women aiming to fulfil their designated roles by avoiding bringing shame upon themselves and their families at any cost. The many instances of 'honour'-based violence, and in particular 'honour' killings, depicted in this book show the collaborative nature of such offences frequently involving male and female relatives of the victims. Unsurprisingly, Ahluwalia recalls how not only her husband, but also her own brothers actively strived to exercise control over her life:

> When I told my brothers I wanted to work, their response was, 'You want money, don't you? Tell us how much. We'll give it to you. You can't do a job'. For the first time I realised that they were letting me study only to help me pass the time. There was no question of a career. All my dreams lay in pieces. I wasn't ready to be a housewife. (Ahluwalia and Gupta, 2008: 53)

Sanghera's own account of her upbringing within a similar patriarchal tradition, which saw the all-encompassing codes of 'honour' permeate every aspect of her parents' existence, closely resonates with Ahuwalia's narrative:

> I was brought up to keep secrets, ugly secrets about bullying, coercion and fear which were all part of everyday life in our family. I believed it was shameful to discuss things with outsiders and that if I did I would compromise our honour – izzat – the most important thing in my mum's life. That's why I didn't tell anybody when she showed me a photograph of the man she said I had to marry. I knew it wasn't right; I knew I was too young to leave school or get married, and it felt all wrong being forced to marry a man I didn't know, but I didn't tell. I kept the secret and it festered inside me, feeding on my feelings of shame, resentment, fear and guilt. (Sanghera, 2009: 1)

In her autobiographical book *Shame*, Sanghera laments the extent to which the culture of 'honour' presiding over her parents' lives was more important to them than the wellbeing of their own daughter. 'My parents', she says, 'care more about honour than they do about me' (Sanghera, 2007: 261). After running away from home and being 'disowned' by them, Sanghera could not understand 'How could anyone turn their back on their own child for the sake of a concept? How could that be considered honourable? To me it seemed a cause of shame' (Sanghera, 2007: 261).

Just as 'shame and dishonour' were what Sanghera's mother, in particular, 'dreaded more than anything' (Sanghera, 2007: 3), so it seems was the case with the mother-in-law of another young Asian bride who had entered into an arranged marriage: Gina Satvir Singh. Like Sanghera's parents, Ahluwalia's husband and brothers before her, Singh's mother-in-law, Dalbir Kaur Bhakar, sought to exert complete control over her daughter-in-law's behaviour.

The Story of Gina Satvir Singh

In 2006, Singh made news headlines when she successfully brought a landmark legal case against her mother-in-law and was awarded £35,000 in damages (*Singh v. Bhakar*, 2007; Brady, 2008; Jones, 2006; Sears, 2006). Singh used the *Protection from Harassment Act 1997*, which covers actions such as 'religious or racially motivated harassment' and stalking, to take Dalbir Kaur to court. It is believed to be the 'first time the act has been used in such a way' (*Singh v. Bhakar*, 2007; Jones, 2006).

Four years earlier, following Singh's arranged marriage aged 26 to fellow Sikh Hardeep Sing Bhakar; she moved to her husband's extended family home in Ilford, Essex. By the time of her marriage, which she consented to freely, Singh had risen to a managerial position in her family's clothing business. She would be later described in Nottingham County Court as having 'considerable experience of the wider world' (Jones, 2006). Once in her new home though, Singh's mother-in-law subjected her to daily and sustained abuse, humiliation and social isolation aimed at controlling her behaviour. The Court heard how Singh was not allowed to leave the house and 'forced to work 17 hours a day', often doing menial and demeaning domestic chores (Brady, 2008: 9). Dalbir Kaur refused to give Singh a house key, 'made her wash the lavatory with her hands', forced her to have her long hair cut to shoulder-length in contravention of Singh's religious beliefs and referred to her as a 'poodle'. Singh was also banned from watching TV, had her mobile phone confiscated and was 'only allowed to make and receive one call a week from her family', while being 'refused permission to wear her own clothes but forced to wear those chosen by her mother-in-law' (Sears, 2006). Singh was not permitted to register with her local GP either, and 'a hand infection, the result of the excessive cleaning she was forced to do, went untreated' (Jones, 2006). After four months into the marriage, Singh returned to her parental home and sought medical attention for depression. Divorce from her husband ensued soon after.

During the court proceedings against Dalbir Kaur, Judge Scott QC described Singh and Bhakar's marriage as 'four months of hell' (*Singh* v. *Bhakar*, 2007; Sears, 2006). At that time, Singh 'was utterly miserable and wretched' and 'suffering from what was for her an incomprehensible personal attack'; as for her mother-in-law's behaviour, he stated that: 'The course of conduct which I have found on the part of Mrs Bhakar is very serious, far more than enough to amount to harassment for the purpose of the Act' (*Singh* v. *Bhakar*, 2007; Sears, 2006). He concluded that Dalbir Kaur's actions were designed to show Singh that the older woman was in charge. Originally from India, Dalbir Kaur had lived in England for three decades, but as the judge explained 'until recently she spoke no English. She has no daughters. I think she was anxious at the prospect of having a daughter in law who had been born and brought up in England and who had spent several years in the workplace' (*Singh* v. *Bhakar*, 2007; Sears, 2006). Rosley, Singh's solicitor, in turn indicated that Singh's ordeal was neither uncommon nor at the life-threatening end of the domestic violence spectrum, when taking into consideration the extent of abuse that women in comparable situations are known to be subjected to (Rosley, 2006).

The legal implications of the *Singh* v. *Bhakar* (2007) ruling for victims and perpetrators of 'honour' violence could potentially see anyone being held to financial account for the 'ill-treatment of their relatives or visitors to their homes, even if it is not serious enough to be a crime' (Sears, 2006). Whereas Singh was able to leave her marriage swiftly, young girls and women in a similar position are frequently not able to do so as the literature and the many instances depicted in this volume illustrate. Such outcomes may be partly attributed to a continuum of socio-economic and cultural expectations and pressures that are present at every stage of an arranged union, from inception through to exit. Athwal's parents, for example, who by her own account enjoyed a successful arranged marriage, originally pressurised the then young woman into marrying against her will, and subsequently persuaded Athwal not to leave her husband and bring 'shame' on the family when she attempted to do so, as she recalls:

> However pious they'd been during our childhood, my parents had not enjoyed watching me flounder in my arranged marriage. It had worked for them, the same as it had worked for millions of others around the world. But although they never mentioned it, I think they felt guilty having pushed me, with the encouragement of their family, into marriage with an unsuitable match. As a result, I was the last one to endure an arranged union. (Athwal, 2013: 214)

A final aspect of the arranged marriage practice that periodically comes under examination in the literature relates to the long-term health risks associated with unions between close blood relatives or so-called 'first cousin marriages' (Hope, 2013). While 'consanguinity' has long been acknowledged as a 'major risk factor for congenital abnormality', recent research has identified it as accounting for almost a third of anomalies in newborns of Pakistani origin in Bradford (Sheridan et al., 2013). Anne Cryer, Labour MP for Keighley who has long campaigned for women's rights within 'honour'-based communities, has openly criticised the practice of first cousin marriages as harmful to children and costly to the NHS; while Phil Woolas, Environment Minister, has viewed the issue as a 'matter of public health' (Hope, 2013; Boseley, 2013). The health implications and potential consequences of first cousin marriages are frequently considered at best as highly sensitive and at worst as intrinsically laden with 'racialist' undertones. Consequently this aspect of the arranged marriage tradition remains both under-researched and inadequately discussed in the literature. Thus it has only been briefly raised here.

Forced Marriage: A Human Rights Approach

While recognising that 'issues of culture form a backdrop to the experiences of minority women' (Kelly, 2010: 12), feminist scholars, practitioners and policymakers have by and large moved away from 'cultural' explanations that problematise 'honour'-based communities. Kelly (2010) has accordingly warned of the dangers of 'culturalising' gender-based abuse, whilst challenging 'simplistic notions of culture' that seek to explain violence against women (Kelly, 2010: 12). Instead, the literature tends to view forced marriage as a variant of domestic violence and a transgression of individual human rights (Gill and Anitha, 2011; Thiara and Gill, 2010). Thomas (2009) has thus characterised forced and early marriages as 'serious human rights violations' (Thomas, 2009). Gill and Anitha (2011), in turn, point that 'Forced marriage, which is generally viewed as encompassing child marriage because minors are deemed incapable of giving informed consent, is specifically recognised as an abuse of human rights in a number of UN treaties and other international instruments' (Gill and Anitha, 2011: 5). This prevailing approach is indeed consistent with current international legal conventions and protocols, including the UN's *Convention on Consent to Marriage, Minimum Age for Marriage and Registration of Marriages 1962* and the *Convention on the Elimination of All Forms of Discrimination against Women (CEDAW) 1979*, that have long positioned forced and child marriages within the realm of human rights infringements (UN, 1962 and 1979).

Against this background, Brandon and Hafez (2008) examine the underlying reasons behind young women and men being coerced by their families into conjugal unions against their wishes:

> Often parents force their children to marry in order to control their sexual behaviour and to pre-empt any actions that could shame the family. In other cases however, families use forced marriage to strengthen family, community and caste ties and preserve and maintain the family's material wealth. In many cases, forced marriages are carried out to prevent or limit the influence of 'western' ideas on children from traditional backgrounds who are brought up in the UK. (Brandon and Hafez, 2008: 12)

By its very nature, the process of forcing somebody to marry typically involves varying degrees of physical and emotional abuse being exerted on the victims, including imprisonment, social isolation, withdrawal from education – in the case of school children – and abduction both at home and abroad. Many individuals at risk of a forced marriage will run away from home rather than going ahead with the wedding; as a result, they may face additional problems such as homelessness and violence from strangers (Brandon and Hafez, 2008: 16). Those unable to avoid being coerced into an unwanted marriage will invariably experience domestic violence once the wedding ceremony has taken place; as Nazir Afzal, Director of the CPS London West, explains:

> Forced marriage is the earthquake and what's followed is a tsunami of domestic abuse, sexual abuse, child protection issues, suicide and murder … If we can tackle forced marriage then we can prevent all these other things from happening. (Nazir Afzal cited in *Independent*, 2012)

In her capacity as Joint Head of the Forced Marriage Unit (FMU), Amy Cumming observes how 'Every day in the unit we see the devastating impact forced marriage has on individuals. Many of the victims who contact us have experienced horrendous sexual and physical violence. They endure intense pressure in many forms – whether emotional, financial or otherwise' (FCO, 2012a). During 2012, the FMU recorded 1,485 instances in which forced marriage related advice and support had been provided; of those, 82 per cent involved female victims and 18 per cent males, 114 cases featured individuals with disabilities and 22 victims who identified themselves as Lesbian, Gay, Bisexual and/or Transgender (LGBT) (FMU, 2012).

Young people and children are particularly vulnerable to being forced into marriages and unsurprisingly comprise the bulk of the FMU's casework. During 2012, 30 per cent of the victims dealt by the Unit were aged 18–21, 22 per cent aged 16–17 and 13 per cent aged under 15; only 8 per cent of the cases related to victims aged 31 and over (FMU, 2012). Before the end of that year, the FMU had identified a two-year-old girl as the youngest victim of a 'possible' forced marriage in Britain to date, with the oldest being a 71-year-old woman (FMU, 2012). In line with the FMU's data, Cumming highlights the existence of a significant proportion of 'children involved in the practice [of forced marriage] across the school age range' (Cumming cited in Taneja, 2012). By March 2012, the FMU had dealt with 400 cases alone involving children, nearly a third of which were minors (Taneja, 2012). The Iranian and Kurdish Women's Rights Organisation (IKWRO), which typically handles over 100 forced marriage related cases in the course of a year, similarly counts children and teenagers among their constituents. Fionnuala Murphy, IKWRO's campaigns officer, describes how 'We have had clients who are in their very early teens, 11-year-olds, 12-year-olds, the youngest case we had was nine years old' (Murphy cited in Taneja, 2012). Such prospective young victims of 'honour' violence are often taken overseas in the course of school holidays to be married off without their consent. In 2008, during her evidence to the *House of Commons Home Affairs Committee on 'Domestic Violence, Forced Marriage and "Honour"-Based Violence'*, District Judge Marilyn Mornington noted that 'We are bringing three girls a week back from Islamabad as victims of forced marriage. We know that it is the tip of the iceberg, but that is the failure end' (Hansard, 2008: Q65, Ev 11–12). During the first half of 2012, assistance from the Foreign and Commonwealth Office (FCO) was sought in 46 cases involving forced marriage overseas, over half of the cases featured 19–25-year-olds and over a third under 18-year-olds; the overwhelming majority of the victims were females, with only 15 per cent males (FCO, 2012a). At the time, the FCO issued an official 'Forced Marriage warning' in the run-up to the annual school holiday, including three films as part of their 'Right to Choose' campaign (FCO, 2012a). Spelling out the heighten risk of forced marriage during the summer vacation for would-be victims, the FCO's notice stated:

> Summer holidays are the peak time for young people to be taken overseas and forced into a marriage against their will. In some cases they are taken on what they have been told is a holiday to visit family abroad, but in fact a marriage has been planned. Once abroad, victims are often even more isolated than they might have been in the UK and getting help is more difficult. (FCO, 2012a)

The transition between GCSE and Sixth Form College, Tickle explains, is customarily the time when 'young girls, and sometimes boys, can simply disappear off school rolls' (Tickle, 2012). Landau Forte College in Derby provides a case in point. With about one-third of the school intake comprising students from minority ethnic backgrounds, including Pakistani and Indian, this otherwise ordinary college has dealt with at least six cases of pupils reporting being at risk of a forced marriage in recent years. Liz Coffey, Landau Forte's principal, recounts one such case: a 15-year-old boy who disappeared from the school as he was about to take his GCSE exams, only to return later in the year having been married off. Coffey says 'He never really opened up about it … He did talk about the fact that he had to go and get married. And then he just didn't turn up for his exams. We took that to social services, but of course he was 16 by then' (Coffey cited in Tickle, 2012). Similar accounts of pupils being withdrawn from school, teenage girls taken abroad to be wedded off and young runaways fleeing forced marriages have steadily made national headlines over the past two decades. The following four cases exemplify this trend.

In 1983, teenage sisters Zana and Nadia Mushen, from Birmingham, were supposedly taken on a family holiday to Yemen, but once there, they discovered their father had actually 'sold them for a few thousand dollars' into a life of slavery (Brady, 2008: 9). Both girls were taken to a remote rural village, held prisoner, forced into marriages and endured daily abuse, including rape and enforced pregnancy. In her autobiographical account, *Sold*, Zana recalls how:

> When a girl marries into a Yemeni family, she is expected to share the burden of the work with the other women in the family, relieving the older ones of some of the worst chores … Neither of the families we had been forced into were unrealistic enough to expect Nadia and me to take on the work from the first day. They were breaking us in gradually, curtailing our freedoms bit by bit, and building up our workloads. We were like animals who needed to have their spirits broken before they could be properly trained. (Muhsen and Crofts, 2004: 66)

Zana and Nadia's case was one of the earliest instances of UK related forced marriages to enjoy a high profile media campaign that culminated with the involvement of British and Yemeni authorities (McGirk, 2003; Frean, 2000). Zana eventually was allowed to return back to Britain after eight years in Yemen, but was forced to leave her baby son, Marcus, behind. Her sister Nadia remained there (Finn, 2002).

In 1996, the *Independent* featured a different story relating to school girls at risk of forced marriages entitled 'The Mystery of the Missing Muslim Girls' (Abrams, 1996). The broadsheet pondered the whereabouts of 'hundreds, possibly thousands' of female Muslim pupils, as Bradford Local Education Authority reported up to 700 children absent from the school rolls (Abrams, 1996). Many of them, Abrams, the article's author, explains were assumed to have been 'sent to Pakistan or Bangladesh to sit out the remaining years until they are 16. But large numbers simply drop out, spending their days at home with parents who believe daily contact with boys and with Western attitudes could place them in moral [*sic*] danger' (Abrams, 1996).

In 2001, the *Daily Telegraph*'s article, 'My Escape from a Forced Marriage', related another case similar to that of the Mushen sisters involving a 22-year-old British student, Marina Anwar, and her two younger sisters, who were held captive in Pakistan for six months while their relatives attempted to coerce them into prearranged marriages. The siblings had travelled from their Bolton home to Pakistan on an apparent visit to their dying grandmother, only to be presented with their prospective husbands on arrival: three boys from their parents' village in the Gujarat province. Marina recalls having become 'virtual prisoners' in their grandparents' home as pressure was exerted on the three sisters to go along with the arranged marriages:

> They wanted me to marry my first cousin. He was 26 and I had not seen him since I was 11. He was uneducated and could not speak English or even write Urdu ... There were also husbands found for my sisters aged 21 and 15. Part of the arrangement was that when we were married I would apply for permission to bring him to Britain. (Marina cited in Johnston, 2001: 15)

Marina and her sisters eventually managed to escape to Lahore, where the British High Commission arranged for their safe passage back to the UK.

In 2010, a further case of two attempted forced marriages hit the news headlines. Under the caption 'Court Stops Girls Being Sent Abroad for Marriage', the *Belfast Telegraph* reported how a court ruling had prevented two British Pakistani Muslim sisters aged 12 and 14 from travelling overseas for suspected forced marriages. In this instance, thought to be the first of its kind, High Court Judge Mr Justice Stephens, sitting in Belfast, granted a Forced Marriage Protection Order (FMPO)[1] on behalf of the minors, directly contravening their parents' wishes (*Belfast Telegraph*, 2010: 12). The youngsters were originally expected to travel to Pakistan, Justice Stephens suggested, 'so that they could learn "respect" as an overarching filial duty which I hold in the context of this family means obedience overriding their full and free choice' (*Belfast Telegraph*, 2010: 12). With a precedent in the family pertaining to the enforced nuptials of the sisters' own two brothers and claims by the authorities that 'false documents were produced as part of a planned deception by their parents', Justice Stephens ruled against the couple. He stated 'I find as a fact that there is a present real and substantial risk that G and D [the sisters] will be forced by their parents to marry against their wishes' (*Belfast Telegraph*, 2010: 12).

---

1   Created by the *Forced Marriage (Civil Protection) Act 2007*, such legal instrument is designed to protect 'a person from being forced into a marriage or from any attempt to be forced into a marriage' or 'a person who has been forced into a marriage' (Hansard, 2007: c.20, 1).

Despite the hundreds of cases featured in the media over the years, reports from grassroots organisations, figures from law enforcement agencies and the government's own estimates, no one knows precisely how many minors at risk of forced marriage are taken out of British schools every year. 'Where they go and whether they come back is not known' Taylor and Hughes remark, but it 'is feared that many are forced to marry abroad' (Taylor and Hughes, 2008). The lack of certainty here seems hardly surprising given that systematic data collection is still not carried out at national level, with questions regarding the amount, location and welfare of these children therefore remaining largely unanswered. Only under parliamentary scrutiny, the government has protractedly acknowledged the persistent absence of robust evidence regarding youngsters who are regularly removed from schools across the country. As early as 2008, Kevin Brennan, Parliamentary Under-Secretary of State for Children, Schools and Families, admitted this much. During his evidence to the Home Affairs Committee investigating 'honour' violence, Brennan stated that 205 children under the age of 16 had disappeared from Bradford schools, '172 of these children were tracked to an alternative destination or known to be on roll at a school. That does still leave a number of young people unaccounted for' (Hansard, 2008: Ev 64, Q374). Further cross-examination from David Davies MP and the Committee's Chair, Keith Vaz MP, saw the minister concede his government's inability to provide accurate national figures:

Q381 David Davies: Do you know how many other cities [in addition to Bradford] have up to 20 girls who have disappeared under the age of 16 across the UK?

Kevin Brennan: It is fair to say that the issue of forced marriage is particularly prevalent in certain areas. I understand that the areas which government offices have been asking questions about are the areas which are particularly of concern. I should imagine it is those areas where we would have a similar problem. Government offices inquired of, I think, 14 different areas in the country, Chairman.

Q382 Chairman: … What is the global figure of the missing children?

Kevin Brennan: That figure, as I explained earlier on, Chairman, is not available at national level, but we are looking with the Forced Marriage Unit … to find a way to be able to collect that statistic at national level. (Hansard, 2008: Ev 64, Q381–382)

The BBC's coverage of the Bradford story at the time summed up the reality of 'More than 30 girls' still 'missing from schools in Bradford' despite the government's 'efforts to track them down'; these were, the BBC concluded, 'Lost girls in "forced marriages"' (BBC, 2008).

Conclusion

Notwithstanding the prevailing official rhetoric conceptualising the arranged marriage as an unproblematic cultural practice based on the free consent of the parties involved, the evidence here presented suggests a need for a less one-dimensional and more nuanced approach to understanding this phenomenon. Rather than a clear-cut distinction between the arranged and forced marriage, attention must be paid to the complex and fluid nature of the notion of 'consent' and the manner and circumstances in which it is procured. The autobiographical accounts and empirical studies depicted in this chapter clearly illustrate how individuals, particularly young people, who enter into arranged marriages may face a heavy burden of family expectations, social, economic and cultural pressures to acquiesce that would effectively render their consent void. Given the vulnerable position of young women and school girls, often dependent on their parents, they are at the greatest risk of becoming susceptible to such pressures.

While the arranged marriage tradition may result in successful marriages for many individuals, it certainly does not for all. Here, the typically patriarchal outlook of 'honour'-based communities and cultures, with gendered notions of *izzat*, places additional caveats on those wishing to exit an arranged marriage, as Ahluwalia, Sanghera and Athwal, among others, discovered. Social isolation, ostracism and stigma may await spouses intent on leaving an arranged marriage, even if they are experiencing domestic violence.

Whereas the issue of free consent is, in principle, assumed in an arranged marriage, it is universally understood to have been irretrievably denied in a forced union. At this point in the marital spectrum, any semblance of individual choice is altogether abandoned in favour of coercion and abuse. Codes of 'honour' become thereby internalised both by men and women; as parents, husbands and siblings will seek to exercise control over their daughters, wives and sisters' behaviour at any cost. The outcome consistently results in domestic abuse and human rights transgressions, of which females continue by far to be the main targets. Unsurprisingly, the feminist literature has come to conceptualise forced marriage as a variant of domestic violence against women and therefore it frames this practice within a human rights perspective. When considering the unabated scale of the forced marriage problem in Britain, especially among the school population, serious questions remain about the effectiveness of government interventions, community leadership and grassroots provision, which will be discussed in detail during the course of the book. The next chapter, however, will specifically focus on the most extreme expression of 'honour' violence, which perpetrators will only resort to when all other avenues to exert control over their victims have failed, namely: the 'honour' killing.

Chapter 3
Two Decades of 'Honour' Killings: Five Key Case-Studies

'Control' Crimes

Over the past two decades, many lives have been lost to 'honour' killings in Britain. Other victims have met their end abroad through 'organised overseas killings of UK citizens' (Hansard, 2008: Ev312). As the most extreme manifestation of 'honour'-based violence, these deadly crimes represent a final act of control over a person's behaviour after all attempts at eliciting compliance have failed. Since the mid-1990s, the British media have chronicled a seemingly endless catalogue of 'honour' related deaths, largely featuring young minority ethnic women murdered by their families either at home or away. Among the most documented examples are the untimely deaths of Tasleem Begum (killed in 1995), Rukhsana Naz († 1998), Surjit Athwal († 1998), Tulay Goren († 1999), Nuziat Khan († 2001), Heshu Yones († 2002), Shafilea Ahmed († 2003), Samaira Nazir († 2005), Banaz Mahmod († 2006) and Geeta Aulack († 2009) (Saner, 2007; *Telegraph*, 2004). In order to understand the nature of such crimes, the following sections will specifically examine five case-studies, namely, the 'honour' killings of Surjit Athwal († 1998), Heshu Yones († 2002), Shafilea Ahmed († 2003), Samaira Nazir († 2005) and Banaz Mahmod († 2006).

While every year new instances of 'honour' related deaths come to light, there are still no official figures as to the exact numbers of casualties or the extent of this phenomenon, specifically 'honour' crimes committed on British soil. A picture is slowly emerging through a combination of casework by governmental and criminal justice bureaux including the Forced Marriage Unit (FMU), the Metropolitan Police Service (MPS) and the Crown Prosecution Service (CPS), together with grassroots providers' own estimates, academic studies and news reporting. Of the lack of reliable data, Nazir Afzal, Director of the CPS London West, says:

> We don't know the true figure of honour killings. It's anything between ten and twelve a year in this country [UK]. I don't know how many other unmarked graves there are in our green and pleasant land. I don't know; and that suggests to me that we are underestimating this issue. (Afzal featured in BBC *Panorama*, 2012)

Although 'honour' killings cut across different demographics and social strata, their prominence among some minority communities, specifically South Asian groups, has frequently seen these offences labelled as 'community' or 'cultural' crimes (Brandon and Hafez, 2008). A categorisation that, as already indicated in this volume, is contested in the literature (Gill, 2006). Nevertheless, when in 2012, Laura Wilson, a white teenage mother, was fatally stabbed by her Asian boyfriend, Ashtiaq Ashgar, she was unsurprisingly described at the time as 'Britain's first known white honour killing victim' (Marsden, 2012). Regardless of the ethnic background of victims and perpetrators of 'honour' related deaths, the underlying reasons behind these offences remain closely linked to those present in other forms of 'honour'-based violence such as forced marriages. They comprise a variety of socio-cultural factors together with patriarchal attitudes to masculinity, female sexuality and the role of women (Samad and Eade, 2002). Brandon and Hafez have specifically highlighted the paternalistic cultural attitudes and anti-Western sentiment present in 'honour' related South Asian communities:

> Such ['honour'] killings are … often more indicative of the extent to which a family will go to defend its own traditions against ideas of female independence and freedom of thought and action which they regard as 'western' and therefore as morally and ethnically inferior to their own South Asian value system. A woman's own willingness to break traditional cultural, social and religious taboos is also an important factor. (Brandon and Hafez, 2008: 39)

'Honour' killings may accordingly be 'justified through an appeal to traditional values – the authority and wisdom of parents, children's duty of obedience, customary patterns of marriage within specific ethnic, religious, clan, caste or class groupings, the honour of the family, etc.' (Khanum, 2008: 8). The 'honour' killing of Tulay Goren in 1999 provides a case in point. A 15-year-old girl from Woodford Green in North London, Tulay was murdered by her Turkish Kurd Muslim father Mehmet Goren after he kidnapped, drugged and tied her up. Tulay had run away from home to live with her boyfriend, 'a fellow Turkish Kurd twice her age whom the family disapproved of because he was from a different branch of Islam' (Coleman, 2011). The school girl's remains, believed to have been temporarily buried in the family garden, have never been recovered. In contrast with other types of crimes, 'honour' killings are characterised by their controlling and collaborative nature. They typically involve a number of close family relatives working together in the planning and execution of the victim's murder. Such joint undertakings are primarily aimed to protect the offenders from a perceived loss of family 'honour' and the public consequences of such loss. Victims of 'honour' killings will therefore witness their parents and adult relatives turn perpetrators of such transgressions, as usually male elders seek to exert control over the behaviour of their young female charges. Afzal of the CPS London West, with national responsibility for forced marriage and 'honour'-based violence, has referred to 'honour' crimes as 'control crimes':

> Thousands of women, usually women, are suffering every year in this country [UK] harm by those who claim to love them the most: their families. The reality is it's simply about men controlling women. It's a power and control issue. These are control crimes where women are told that there're certain things they can do and there're certain things they can't. And if they overstep the line, or they threaten to do so, or somebody gossips about them having done so; then they are entitled to suffer some kind of threat or violence. And ... people ... try and paint it into some kind of theological or ideological issue; but it's not. It's about men saying to women: you can't do that; if you do that, you will pay the penalty. (Afzal featured in H.O.P.E., 2009)

Detective Chief Inspector (DCI) Caroline Goode of the MPS, who led the landmark investigation into the 'honour' killing of 20-year-old Banaz Mahmod in 2006, also recognises the collective and premeditated nature of 'honour' crimes:

> every single one of these ['honour' killing] cases ... involved extreme violence; because the murders are committed to send a message to the wider community. But quite often there are multiple perpetrators; there's a degree of high organisation, quite often precipitated by a family meeting. (DCI Goode featured in BBC *Panorama*, 2012)

Besides the inherently controlling character of 'honour' killings, the involvement of successive generations of relatives within the same family in the execution of a murder is seen as a significant development. It is indeed worth considering that despite a minority ethnic presence on British soil often spanning decades, 'honour' violence is no longer the preserve of first-generation migrants. On the contrary, such practices are being handed down through successive cohorts of UK-born nationals. Brandon and Hafez argue that '"honour" violence is now, to all intents and purposes, an indigenous and self-perpetuating phenomenon carried out by third and fourth generation immigrants who have been born, raised and educated in the UK' (Brandon and Hafez, 2008: 1). This intergenerational trend is well documented in numerous British murder trials and press reports of 'honour' related offences, including the five case-studies of 'honour' killings examined in this chapter. Here, fathers, brothers and uncles will typically take a leading role in the planning and execution of premeditated attacks on their own daughters, sisters or nieces.

While the majority of 'honour' killings involve male perpetrators and female victims, many instances of such crimes feature the active participation of

45

female family members, frequently the victim's mother or mother-in-law, with the remaining siblings either witnessing the assault, joining in or being drawn into the ensuing conspiracy of silence. The 'honour' killing of Rukhsana Naz, a 19-year-old Pakistani girl from Derby, by her mother Shakeela and elder brother Shazad, serves to illustrate this point. In 1998, Rukhsana's mother 'helped her eldest son strangle her daughter using a plastic flex ... They then placed her body in a homemade sack and dumped her in a farmer's field 100 miles away' (Watson-Smyth, 1999). Mother and son believed Rukhsana 'had bought shame on their family by refusing to have an abortion after becoming pregnant by her lover while her husband [from an arranged marriage when she was 15 years old] was in Pakistan' (Watson-Smyth, 1999). On the day of the murder, Shakeela held Rukhsana's legs down while Shazard 'tightened a plastic flex around her neck for three to four minutes. Her younger brother Iftikhar watched helplessly. He told the court his brother had threatened him with a knife and forced him to help with the disposal of the body' (Watson-Smyth, 1999). Both Shakeela and Shazad were jailed for life.

Five Stories of Family Crimes

The five case-studies of 'honour' killings examined in the following sections further illustrate the deliberate and cooperative nature of 'honour' crimes. The murders of Surjit Athwal († 1998), Heshu Yones († 2002), Shafilea Ahmed († 2003), Samaira Nazir († 2005) and Banaz Mahmod († 2006) often required a multiparty effort involving several relatives of the victims, in some instances extending to members of the larger community. All the casualties in these accounts were young women living in Britain either born and raised here or belonging to migrant families long settled within their local community. With the exception of Surjit, who was killed abroad, the rest met their deaths on British soil. In the midst of our liberal UK society, these sisters, wives and mothers were murdered after efforts to exert control over their seemingly 'Westernised' lives proved futile. Like many 'honour' killing victims before then, they suffered domestic abuse prior to their deaths.

The five 'honour' killings here depicted have been well documented in the media and have therefore been selected as much for their prominent role in bringing the issue of 'honour' violence into the British national consciousness as their impact in shaping the country's public policy agenda. A number of cases made legal history and their courtroom outcomes have seen incremental improvements to service provision for victims and survivors of 'honour' violence. Some of the relatives of the victims behind the headlines have subsequently spoken publicly about their experiences, published biographical accounts as well as leading public awareness campaigns. Overall, these troubling stories of family life – and hundreds more like them – have raised serious questions about the status of women from minority cultures within the UK and the protection afforded to them by the state.

Case-Study 1: The Story of Surjit Athwal

On 4 December 1998, Surjit Athwal, a 27-year-old mother and HM Customs & Excise officer at Heathrow Airport, flew to Delhi on a hastily arranged family trip with her mother-in-law, Bachan Kaur Athwal. A fortnight later, Bachan returned home as planned, but Surjit never did and 'has not been seen or heard of since then' (R v. *Athwal and ors*, 2009). Bachan had in fact plotted with her relatives to have Surjit killed in India after discovering that she was having an affair with a work colleague and planned to divorce her husband, Sukhdave Athwal (McVeigh, 2007c). Bachan lured Surjit to the overseas journey under the pretext of two family weddings. Of Surjit's disappearance, her brother, Jagdeesh Singh, would say years later: 'Surjit was taken away mysteriously and suspiciously from London by her in-laws and she disappeared in Punjab. Clearly she hadn't disappeared. She'd been murdered and her body had been very secretly and very conveniently disposed of' (Singh featured in H.O.P.E., 2009).

Surjit's sister-in-law, Sarbjit Athwal, witnessed first-hand the murder plot and subsequently played a crucial role in securing the criminal convictions of Bachan and Sukhdave for Surjit's death. In her autobiographical book, *Shame*, she describes the events leading to her sister-in-law's demise (Athwal, 2013). Sarbjit depicts how the arranged marriage of Surjit and Sukhdave, which Surjit entered into aged 17, spiralled into a vicious circle of domestic violence and abuse. In 1988, Surjit had first moved out of the family home at the behest of her husband and mother-in-law who accused her of 'murdering her own unborn baby' following a miscarriage (Athwal, 2013: 126). Surjit nevertheless returned to her husband. 'As much as she wanted to say "no"', Athwal speculates, 'a Sikh woman who'd left a marriage was not looked on too well in the community. Whether it was pressure from her parents or brainwashing from her in-laws or simple faith, what the community might think played on Surjit's mind' (Athwal, 2013: 118). By 1994, Surjit had left the family home again, this time of her own accord, only to later return to her husband once more. But the relationship continued to deteriorate and events took a turn for the worse when Surjit embarked on an extramarital affair with an older married colleague, which produced a baby boy. 'I couldn't blame my sister-in-law', Sarbjit says of her sister's infidelity, 'How unhappy she must have been. Sukhdave had bullied her, belittled her, driven her from her house, abused her and hit her. Much of that had been at his mother's behest. Of course Surjit had wanted to escape from that. And by finding a new man to love, she figured that was the best way' (Athwal, 2013: 140).

As for the newborn son, Surjit let her husband 'believe the baby was his. But he knew. He always knew' (Athwal, 2013: 141). Further violence ensued when Surjit attempted again to leave her husband. Living next door to her sister-in-law, Sarbjit recalls how 'I could make out every smack that Sukhdave landed on his wife as she tried to leave. I felt sick as I heard my sister-in-law hit the floor. Then I gasped as I made out a different voice. It was Bachan Kaur. And she was attacking Surjit as well' (Athwal, 2013: 145). By 1998, Surjit had sought legal advice on divorce proceedings.

In late November 1998, Sarbjit describes how Bachan summoned her, together with her husband Hardave and brother-in-law Sukhdave, to the family living room in their Hayes, West London, home to make a momentous announcement concerning Surjit:

> 'I've spoken to a contact in India', she [Bachan] began. 'It's all going to be taken care of'.
> Sukhdave nodded. I didn't have a clue what she was talking about, and from the mood in the room I didn't dare interrupt.
> 'It's her own fault. She's out of control', Bachan Kaur continued. 'She's bringing shame on the family'. She looked sad. 'We're the laughing-stock of the community'.
> So now I knew who she was talking about – but what did it have to do with India? I didn't get the chance to ask.
> 'So, it's decided then', Bachan Kaur concluded, without any discussion having taken place. 'We have to get rid of her'. (Athwal, 2013: 147–8)

After Surjit's murder had been carried out, Bachan boasted that her daughter-in-law's body had been disposed of in the River Ravi (R v. *Athwal and ors*, 2009; *Daily Mail*, 2007). But with only circumstantial evidence to go on, it would take years for Surjit's blood family to find out what they believe really happened to her. Surjit's brother, Jagdeesh, who set up a campaign, Justice for Surjit, explains what is likely to have transpired during the last minutes of her sister's life:

> She was driven off in a car and taken to the banks of a nearby river. She was pulled out of the car, strangled, suffocated to death and then her body was thrown into the river with a view to it being lost for ever [*sic*]. (Jagdeesh Singh cited in John, 2003)

At the criminal trial for Surjit's death in 2007, it would be Sarbjit's witness account that proved 'central to the prosecution case' and was ultimately deemed by the presiding judges to have 'led to Bachan and Sukhdave being charged with conspiracy to murder' (R v. *Athwal and ors*, 2009). In their ruling, Lord Justice Maurice Kay and Justices Mackay and Stadlen noted that 'Bachan and Sukhdave were not charged until the police had obtained this [Sarbjit's] evidence and we are content to assume that neither would have been convicted without it' (R v. *Athwal and ors*, 2009). The CPS similarly acknowledged the significance of Sarbjit's evidence together with that of Bhajan Kaur Binder, another relative who also provided a witness statement to the police. After the verdict, Jaswant Narwal, Head of the Crown Prosecution Service Central Criminal Court Trials Unit, said:

> Nearly nine years after Surjit went missing and following long and protracted investigations and numerous international enquiries the prosecution have achieved a conviction for her so-called honour killing … This was a particularly difficult and complex case given that Surjit's body has never been found.
>
> The prosecution case rested largely on circumstantial evidence, and in particular crucial witness accounts from two members of the defendants' family, as there was virtually no forensic evidence. I applaud the bravery of these two individuals in coming forward and telling the court what they knew in extremely difficult circumstances.
>
> Bachan Kaur Athwal, mother-in-law, grandmother and matriarch of the Athwal family together with her son enlisted the support of their relatives in India to carry out this appalling murder, simply because they felt Surjit's behaviour was damaging their family honour. They wanted to 'get rid' of Surjit and thought it would be easier to do this in India and even thought they had got away with it. (CPS, 2007a)

At the time of Surjit's disappearance, her blood relatives sought to register her with two local police stations in Hayes and Coventry (her family home) as 'a missing person, with a strong risk of having been murdered' (Hansard, 2008). But their attempts were rejected and as a result of 'the disinterested and unresponsive response of the two local police stations, Surjit's family were left isolated and unclear as to what to do next' (Hansard, 2008). With the support of Southall Black Sisters (SBS), they embarked on a lengthy public campaign for an enquiry into Surjit's disappearance, which saw them engaging with 'police, MPs, the Foreign Office, the Foreign Secretary Jack Straw, the Punjab Police, the national media; all in a bid to secure a comprehensive process of investigation in the UK and robust UK government representations for an equally comprehensive investigation to be conducted in India by the Indian authorities' (Hansard, 2008). Surjit's case was eventually reopened in 2004, with a new investigative team led by DCI Clive Driscoll. Earlier police investigations into Surjit's disappearance had been characterised by 'slowness; failure to extract key evidence; a disproportionate reliance on the suspects' version of events;

and a failure to even treat the case as a murder and only a "disappearance"' (Hansard, 2008). In stark contrast, renewed efforts and a robust approach by the new team of officers lead 'to a criminal prosecution eight years after Surjit's disappearance and a conviction following a 13-week trial' (Hansard, 2008). In 2007, the landmark trial at the Old Bailey saw Sarbjit waive her anonymity as a witness in court and resulted in Bachan and Sukhdave becoming 'the first in UK legal history to be convicted of an outsourced honour killing where the murder was plotted in the UK but carried out abroad' (Gilbert, 2013). Despite their efforts to disrupt police inquiries by writing 'forged letters to the Indian police in order to deter them from investigating Surjit's disappearance' (R v. *Athwal and ors*, 2009; Ward, 2007), mother and son were sentenced to life imprisonment. Bachan was 71 years old at the time (R v. *Athwal and ors*, 2009).

In 2008, the memorandum submitted by the Justice for Surjit campaign to the *House of Commons Home Affairs Committee's Sixth Report on 'Domestic Violence, Forced Marriage and "Honour"-Based Violence'* reflected on what had proved to be a long and difficult journey. It read: 'The nine year experience of this ordeal, has elicited many issues, lessons and questions about the adequacy and efficiency of current procedures and practises, from UK government, Foreign Office, Home Office, UK Police to the Indian Government and its associated departments and its police authorities' (Hansard, 2008). The protracted campaign and its eventual outcome had thus not only drawn attention to the 'honour' killing of Surjit, but to the wider challenges that so-called 'remote control killings' (Hansard, 2008) present both to Britain, where such murders of UK citizens are organised, as well as the overseas countries where they are ultimately carried out.

Case-Study 2: The Story of Heshu Yones

On 12 October 2002, Heshu Yones, a 16-year-old school girl from West London was knifed to death by her Kurdish Muslim father, Abdalla Yones,[1] in a frenzied attack at their family home. Heshu was involved in 'a relationship with a young Lebanese Christian', which Abdalla disapproved of (R v. *Yones*, 2007). During the fatal stabbing, she 'suffered 11 wounds to her face, neck and body' (R v. *Yones*, 2007), and as she struggled to fend off the sharp blows, her body was left covered in defensive wounds (Husseini, 2009: 159; Pope, 2012: 134). Describing the violent nature of Abdalla's actions, Sanghera explains how he stabbed Heshu frantically 'before slitting her throat and leaving her to bleed to death in the bathroom of their council flat in Acton. The knife he used was twisted, bent, and the tip of it was broken off with the ferocity of his attack'

---

1 The literature on Heshu Yones' 'honour' killing features different spellings for Abdalla Yones' first name including Abdalla and Abdullah. For consistency purposes, it will spelt here as Abdalla as shown in official court records (R v. *Yones*, 2007).

(Sanghera, 2009: 24). The forensic 'scene-of-crime photographs' were 'almost unbearable', Sanghera adds, in them:

> Heshu's mutilated body, slumped on the bath, looks like a human sacrifice, which in a way I supposed it was. Heshu was sacrificed in the name of honour; killed by her Kurdish Muslim father because – as he saw it – she had shamed him by having the temerity to choose a Christian boyfriend. (Sanghera, 2009: 24)

In the aftermath of the murder, Abdalla 'tried to cut his own throat before jumping from a third floor balcony. He made a further attempt to take his own life whilst in custody awaiting trial' (*R v. Yones*, 2007). A Kurdish refugee 'who had spent most of his life involved in the Kurdish struggle for independence', Abdalla fled 'Saddam Hussein's Iraq at the time of the first Gulf War' and 'brought his family to the UK when Heshu was five' (Pope, 2012: 133; *R v. Yones*, 2007). But as the years went by and an adolescent Heshu asserted her independence, Abdalla 'found his daughter too "Western" and could not accept that she had a boyfriend' (Pope, 2012: 133). Diana Nammi, Director of IKWRO, explains how Heshu's family reacted on discovering her relationship:

> [They] took her back to Iraq and wanted to force her into a marriage. But because she was not virgin [*sic*] anyway, her family decided to not put her in a marriage because by not being a virgin … she will bring shame to the community. They brought her back to the UK with a condition to stop her relationship with boyfriend. But later on anyway she was killed by her father. (Nammi featured in H.O.P.E., 2009)

As tensions increased at home, Heshu's life began to unravel. In the months preceding her death, she suffered 'very significant physical abuse' at the hands of her father; although 'it was never reported to the police' (Allison, 2003). Fearing for her life, she had 'told her teachers at school that she thought she was in danger; three times she sought help from them and three times she somehow got ignored' (Sanghera, 2009: 24). Nobody at school, Husseini notes, took Heshu's warnings seriously and 'no one (except for her close friends who saw the bruising) knew that by 2002 she was regularly beaten by her father' (Husseini, 2009: 158). On one occasion, Heshu wrote a farewell letter to her family – later read out in court – as she was poised to run away from home; in a passage, she says:

> Goodbye mum, I will see you again one day. Thank you a thousand times for trying so hard for me. I'm sorry I was such a bad friend. Some day I will try and make it up to you. Keep letting off that gas in your fat stomach. Enjoy life – now that I'm gone, there's no more trouble. I promise you I will be good.

Bye dad, sorry I was so much trouble. Me and you will probably never understand each other. I'm sorry I wasn't what you wanted, but there's [*sic*] some things you can't change. Hey, for an older man you have a good strong punch and kick. I hope you enjoyed testing your strength on me; it was fun being on the receiving end. WELL DONE. (Heshu cited in Husseini, 2009: 159–60)

Events meanwhile continued to accelerate on a downward spiral. Heshu's 'progress at college deteriorated' to the point where she 'failed her examinations'; the teenager also 'incurred substantial bills with use of her mobile phone' (R v. *Yones*, 2007). On 10 October 2002, Abdalla 'received an anonymous letter in which the author described Heshu as a prostitute and slut who regularly slept with her boyfriend' (R v. *Yones*, 2007). Two days later, Abdalla 'was left alone with Heshu in the flat' and heard his daughter talking on her mobile telephone; he later claimed to have 'no recollection of how he acquired the knife nor of the actual attack on Heshu' (R v. *Yones*, 2007).

Initially, Abdalla denied any involvement in Heshu's killing; but subsequently admitted culpability and was convicted of her murder in 2003. The trial over Heshu's death 'resulted in the first ever life sentence for an honour killing in Britain' (Pope, 2012: 133). Legal history was therefore made as the term 'honour killing' had now entered the British legal system. The investigation into Heshu's murder moreover marked a decisive moment in the police force's strategy towards 'honour' crimes. Following Abdalla's conviction, Scotland Yard announced a major national drive to examine historic suspected killings by reviewing 'nearly 120 murders' (Bennetto and Judd, 2004: 20). The operation included examination of 'murder files going back 10 years – 52 in the London area and 65 in other parts of England and Wales' (Bennetto and Judd, 2004: 20). Commander Andy Baker, Head of the Metropolitan Police's Serious Crime Directorate, stated that 'We are not reopening these cases – many of them have been through the courts with convictions. It is a matter of looking at these cases and learning how we can prevent killings in the future' (Bennetto and Judd, 2004: 20). By June 2004, '13 suspected "honour killings" between 1993 and 2003 had been identified'; among the cases scrutinised were 'deaths involving women who have been burnt to death or run over by cars. In some instances, they were previously thought to have been accidents. Many of the female victims were from South Asian communities' (Bennetto and Judd, 2004: 20). Reflecting on the impact of Heshu's case, Pope argues that while 'Previous cases had already lifted the veil on honour killings ... Heshu Yones' case marked a turning point not only because it triggered a review of investigation methods for this type of crime, but also because this time, the justice system made no allowance for Yones's cultural background and locked him up for life' (Pope, 2012: 134–35). Cultural issues, however, remain central to Heshu's murder and the wider 'honour' violence phenomenon; as Sanghera notes 'Heshu's father was sentenced to life with a minimum tariff of just eight years before he was considered for release. Apparently the judge said it was "a tragic story arising out of irreconcilable cultural differences between traditional Kurdish values and the values of Western society'" (Sanghera, 2009: 25).

At the time, the role of community networks in particular was identified as a main obstacle in bringing the perpetrators of 'honour' killings to justice. Commander Baker refers to 'the problem of the silence within communities about what is going on' (Commander Baker cited in Allison, 2003). A recurring theme in 'honour' related offences, the conspiratorial muteness that often surrounds 'honour' crimes saw members of the Kurdish community being complicit in concealing Heshu's murder. Commander Baker says:

> We are completely satisfied that some members of the community, or his friends, tried to assist him [Abdalla] in that cover-up. It's not about one person committing the murder, it's about the few that acknowledge it and support it and are involved in it. (Commander Baker cited in Allison, 2003)

Such assessment was further corroborated by Detective Inspector (DI) Brent Hyatt of the Metropolitan Police Directorate and a member of its Honour Killings Working Group as he recalled the reactions from some quarters of the Kurdish community to Abdalla's crime:

> I thought Heshu's dad might need protection when people found out what he'd done. I thought he'd be attacked by the other blokes in prison but I was wrong on both accounts. He was congratulated on redeeming the family's honour and the other Kurds in Belmarsh [prison] gave him a hero's welcome. (DI Brent Hyatt cited in Sanghera, 2009: 24)

Husseini similarly reported on efforts made by the local Kurdish community to help Abdalla 'raise £125,000 bail while threats were made against those who planned to give evidence against him'; the police moreover uncovered plans to help Abdalla 'flee the country' (Husseini, 2009: 159).

Barely a year after Heshu's tragic death, cultural issues relevant to 'honour' crimes including paternalistic attitudes, anti-Western sentiment and the influence of community networks were at play again in another 'honour' killing; that of Shafilea Ahmed.

Case-Study 3: The Story of Shafilea Ahmed

The eldest daughter of a family of five, Shafilea Ahmed was an ordinary teenage school girl of Pakistani descent living in Warrington, in the early 2000s (*Ahmed* v. *HM South and East Cumbria*, 2009). She was described by one of her school teachers, Mrs Joanne Code, as 'a very good student who was keen on her work … and had an ambition to be a lawyer' (*Ahmed* v. *HM South and East Cumbria*, 2009).

Shafilea's family life, however, had long been marred by a history of domestic violence and parental abuse: the Ahmeds were known to social services. In mid-2002, aged 16, Shafilea was first broached by her taxi-driver father, Iftikhar Ahmed, on the subject of having an arranged marriage, after a relative in Pakistan had made enquiries about her prospects. From that moment onwards, Shafilea consistently said 'she did not want such a marriage' (*Ahmed* v. *HM South and East Cumbria*, 2009). In the autumn, Shafilea left home for a day or two over a family disagreement regarding money being withdrawn from her bank account. After she returned home, her teacher Mrs Code would later give evidence that Iftikhar had spoken with her over the telephone and 'told her Shafilea had decided not to persist with her schooling, that she would burn or destroy her books' (*Ahmed* v. *HM South and East Cumbria*, 2009). Mrs Code had also a telephone conversation with Shafilea who in turn explained 'she was being held against her will' (*Ahmed* v. *HM South and East Cumbria*, 2009). As a result, social services were called to the school to meet with Shafilea, 'but after a discussion with them she felt that she could be confident in dealing with her difficulties at home herself' and decided to remain with her parents (*Ahmed* v. *HM South and East Cumbria*, 2009). On 31 January 2003, however, Shafilea left home again for a few days and travelled to Blackburn with a male companion, Mushtag Bagas. After returning from Blackburn, Shafilea spoke with Mrs Code and told her 'They are going to get me married off, I am frightened and I don't want to go back home' (*Ahmed* v. *HM South and East Cumbria*, 2009).

Over two weeks later, Shafilea flew to Pakistan with her father on a family visit, and during the course of their stay the issue of an arranged marriage was raised with her once more. On this occasion, a 'discussion took place between Mr Ahmed and his uncle resident in Pakistan, whose son was at least a possibility as a prospective bridegroom for Shafilea' (*Ahmed* v. *HM South and East Cumbria*, 2009). Asked what she thought about the idea of the potential union, Shafilea answered 'no way' (*Ahmed* v. *HM South and East Cumbria*, 2009). While still in Pakistan, an incident happened in which Shafilea swallowed some sort of bleach or similar caustic liquid. Her mother, Farzana, explained the episode away as an accident in which 'Shafilea mistook a bottle of bleach for mouthwash' during a power cut (*Ahmed* v. *HM South and East Cumbria*, 2009). Years later, during the trial for Shafilea's murder, her sister Alesha would give a very different account of events in court. She described how Shafilea 'had been drugged and sedated' for the family trip to Pakistan, where her parents had tried to coerce her into an arranged marriage (Smith, 2012: 7). Fearing she would be left stranded there, Shafilea drunk the corrosive fluid to ensure she was taken back to the UK. 'What else could I do', she had told Alesha (Smith, 2012: 7).

By 18 March 2003, Iftikhar had arrived back to the UK without Shafilea and the following day 'cashed in' her return ticket (*Ahmed* v. *HM South and East Cumbria*, 2009). On 27 May 2003, when Shafilea finally flew back home to the UK with her sister Mevish, she was admitted to hospital in Warrington with breathing difficulties. Shahin Munir, a close friend of Mevish, who would later provide the police with letters and diary entries describing her friend's account of Shafilea's killing, recalls the youngster's stay in hospital:

> Oh my god. Today I met with Mev[vish] ... Shafilea was very ill. She lost a lot of weight, but her mum told Mev to stop caring for her, like stop trying to feed her etc. They came home and she went to the hospital but her mum looked as though she didn't want her to survive and the doctors didn't think she would either. But she did. (Shahin Munir cited in Smith, 2012: 7)

Despite extensive damage to her oesophagus, Shafilea was eventually discharged from hospital and seemed to have made a good recovery; so much so that by early September 2003, she had resumed her education in the sixth form at Priestly College. On 11 September 2003, however, Shafilea vanished without a trace. Her family did not report her disappearance to the police, and only when her college teacher Mrs Code raised the alarm with the Cheshire Constabulary did an official investigation into Shafilea's case begin, about two months after she went missing (*Ahmed* v. *HM South and East Cumbria*, 2009). From the outset, the police 'took the view that this was a homicide inquiry' and Shafilea's parents and some relatives were interviewed as suspects (*Ahmed* v. *HM South and East Cumbria*, 2009).

On 4 February 2004, Shafilea's body was found 'in a site in what is usually dense undergrowth by the River Kent, at Sedgwick in Cumbria ... The body had been concealed' (*Ahmed* v. *HM South and East Cumbria*, 2009). It was ascertained that Shafilea had died 'early, at or after the time of her disappearance' (*Ahmed* v. *HM South and East Cumbria*, 2009). During the subsequent inquest into Shafilea's death four years later, the Coroner for South and East Cumbria, Mr Ian Smith, delivered his assessment:

> How did she die? Well, quite simply she was murdered. I am convinced of that by a number of facts: Firstly, the way that her body was disposed of; it was hidden, it was taken many miles from where she lived. I am satisfied beyond all reasonable doubt ... I think everyone accepts that she was murdered. She was unlawfully killed I agree.

> So what remains? A great deal of speculation, a fair amount of non-information, but nonetheless, what certainly remains is that Shafilea was the victim of a very vile murder. There is no two ways about that. I believe that she was taken from

> her home on 11 September or the early hours of 12 September 2003, she was
> removed, she was murdered somewhere else, either in a vehicle or at some other
> premises, and she was quickly disposed of. I do not believe she ran away … I do
> not know who did it, there is no evidence whatever before the court as to who
> did it. (*Ahmed* v. *HM South and East Cumbria*, 2009)

In early January 2008, the inquest led accordingly to a verdict of 'unlawful killing'
(*Ahmed* v. *HM South and East Cumbria*, 2009). But it would take a further four
years for the many questions left unanswered by Shafilea's death to be finally
addressed in a court of law and her killers brought to justice. On 3 August 2012,
Iftikhar Ahmed and his wife Farzana were jailed for life for the murder of their
daughter Shafilea at Chester Crown Court (Brown, 2012: 9). Echoing the earlier
imprisonment of Surjit Athwal's relatives, Shafilea's parents were convicted
after an eyewitness came forward to testify against them in court. On this
occasion, it was Shafilea's sister Alesha who provided the crucial evidence. She
described how Shafilea had been suffocated at the family home in Warrington
after her parents pinned her down on a sofa and 'stuffed a plastic bag into her
mouth' (Brown, 2012: 9; Smith, 2012: 7). Both 'Farzana and Iftikhar held their
hands over their teenage daughter's nose and mouth. Shafilea gasped for air, wet
herself and then was still. Her eyes remained open. Her father dragged her on
to the floor and punched her once in the chest' (Smith, 2012: 7). Alesha testified
that 'the whole family had witnessed the killing', but her brother Junyad and
sister Mevish denied any foul play (Smith, 2012: 7). Alesha, who was involved
in a mysterious armed raid at the family home prior to giving her eyewitness
account of Shafilea's murder to the police, entered witness protection (Evans,
2012). Of her decision to speak up at the trial, she said:

> When you get used to something, it becomes normal and that's when I saw it
> wasn't normal, really. I think what happened to my sister was wrong, but because
> it's your parents you think it's normal because you still love them. I think at
> uni[versity] I did feel the way my sister had – you want to fit in with everyone
> else but you are still being forced to live in a different way. I think that's what
> made me crack. (Smith, 2012)

The court proceedings, which saw family members pitted against each other,
took on a dramatic turn when Farzana unexpectedly disowned her husband.
After years of colluding with him to conceal the truth, she now accused Iftikhar
of violent and controlling behaviour. The prosecutor, Andrew Edis, dismissed
her actions as a mere attempt 'to save herself'; Farzana was now 'Telling new
lies' in the hope they 'were better than the old lies' (Smith, 2012: 7). In his ruling,
Mr Justice Roderick Evans condemned the couple's 'unrealistic, destructive
and cruel' expectations that their daughter should live in a 'sealed cultural

environment separate from the culture of the country in which she lived'; 'You wanted your family' he said 'to live in Pakistan in Warrington' (Brown, 2012: 9). Following the verdict, Paul Whittake, Chief Crown Prosecutor for CPS Mersey-Cheshire, said:

> Despite the best efforts of the defendants to derail the investigation into her death by subverting witnesses, including their own children, the Crown Prosecution and Cheshire Police have worked tirelessly to gather the evidence and present it to a jury. The statement of Alesha Ahmed, Shafilea's younger sister, was crucial to our case and today's result is a testament to her courage over the last two years.

> There are many ways to describe what happened to Shafilea: child abuse, domestic violence and honour-based violence being just three … The word 'shame' has been heard many times during the course of this trial, but the shame is not on Shafilea, it is on her parents.

> Why did they abuse her? Why did they kill her? Put it simply, it was because she challenged their regime and refused to conform to their expectations. She wanted to choose how she lived her life and who she married, choices that are fundamental freedoms for any citizen of the United Kingdom. (CPS, 2012)

While the murder convictions of Shafilea's parents brought closure to the case, questions remained about the amount of time elapsed between her death and the successful prosecutions. As in previous instances, the inherent difficulties of investigating domestic abuse were compounded by procedural errors and a wider reluctance by police, educators and social services alike to intervene within a minority ethnic family setting. Despite Iftikhar's know violent character, the *Guardian* notes:

> interviews were conducted while he remained in the same room [with Shafilea]. To avoid answering difficult questions the Ahmed parents claimed they were victims of racism. The authority of the father over his family repeatedly interrupted attempts to support Shafilea and, after her disappearance, thwarted the police investigation. It was only when one sister was persuaded to break with her family and give evidence against them that a prosecution became possible. (*Guardian*, 2012: 42)

Questions also remain regarding the conspiracy of silence that once more shielded perpetrators of an 'honour' crime for so long. As Brown points out, it had taken almost a decade 'to bring the Ahmeds to justice after police faced a wall of silence both within the family and the community' (Brown, 2012: 9).

Such conspiracy of silence would again make its presence felt in the 'honour' killing of another young woman two years after Shafilea's disappearance; that of Samaira Nazir.

Case-Study 4: The Story of Samaira Nazir

On 23 April 2005, Samaira Nazir, a 26-year-old recruitment consultant of Pakistani origin living in Southall, was killed in a frantic and sustained knife attack at her parental family home. Witnessed by several relatives, the murder was jointly perpetrated by Samaira's brother Azhar Nazir, aged 30, and Imran Mohammed, a 17-year-old distant cousin 'who was seeking asylum under a false name' (Steele, 2006). Both would be later convicted of her murder. Afzal of CPS London West has described how Samaira 'was slaughtered … in the presence of two infant nieces who were splattered with her blood' (Afzal featured in H.O.P.E., 2009). The girls, aged two and four, saw Samaira trying to 'flee the knife blows from her cousin', but 'her brother dragged her back from the door by her hair' (Steele, 2006). While Samaira's screams for help could be heard by the family's neighbours, her own mother 'stood and watched as she was murdered' (Sieghart, 2006). Four knives were used in the fatal stabbing (Butt, 2006). Samaira's death was described in court as 'terrifying and painful':

> She was stabbed ten times, twice in her side, twice in the legs, once in the back, twice in the abdomen and once in the neck. When police arrived at the scene, a scarf had been tied so tightly around her neck that an officer had to cut it to remove it. She had bled profusely. It was obvious that a very violent and prolonged struggle had taken place. The cause of her death was haemorrhaging compounded by the compression of her neck. (R v. *Nazir*, 2009)

Samaira had apparently been killed in an attempt to stop her from marrying Salman Mohammed, her Afghan boyfriend who was deemed unsuitable by her family. Described as 'the cleverest in the family', Samaira graduated from university after studying Travel and Tourism and was made a director at a recruitment company owned by her brother, who also ran a grocery store (Steele, 2006). Samaira and Salman had met in 2000, 'following his illegal entry into the UK, after he found his way to Nazir's greengrocer's shop looking for advice on employment and accommodation' (Butt, 2006). Nazir helped Salman procure both work and lodgings, and the newcomer and Samaira's relationship slowly developed. Salman would later rely in court how they were 'boyfriend and girlfriend for about five or six years. But we couldn't tell her family because Samaira said her father was a very strict man who would not allow any female in his family to marry outside of his caste or tribe' (Butt, 2006). So when the couple announced their engagement, death threats were made against them.

Salman recalls how in a telephone conversation about two weeks before the murder, Azhar had 'threatened to kill him and Samaira' if they went ahead with the marriage (R v. *Nazir*, 2009). Having already turned down prospective suitors in Pakistan, Samaira was summoned to the family home in Southall, where angry relatives lay in wait. Both of her parents, her brother and his two young daughters as well as Samaira's cousin were there.

At the time of Samaira's death, Imran maintained 'he was alone responsible' for her murder and declared that 'he had not intended to kill her, but only to scare her' (R v. *Nazir*, 2009). Azhar admitted he objected to the marriage because Salman was 'dishonest and carrying on illegal activities' (R v. *Nazir*, 2009); but denied any involvement in his sister's murder. During Azhar's evidence at the trial, he accepted he was present at the crime scene, but was 'horrified by what he saw happen' and 'could not imagine doing anything like that' (R v. *Nazir*, 2009). Azhar described how there was an argument 'over Samaira's plan to marry Salman. She was shouting and swearing', he went upstairs where more yelling could be heard and then down into the front room, only to find his mother crying. A next-door neighbour, who heard the commotion, knocked on the front door to enquire about the disturbance. Azhar's explanation was that his sister 'was losing it' [having fits] (R v. *Nazir*, 2009). Next, he heard 'someone running through the hallway and the door opening and his sister shouting for help'; Azhar said he 'came out of the front door' and saw his cousin 'holding his sister from the shoulders. There was a struggle going on' and he saw 'all the blood' (R v. *Nazir*, 2009). Azhar 'could not think what to do except call the police as soon as possible' (R v. *Nazir*, 2009).

Despite Azhar's claims, witness statements and forensic evidence presented in court cast serious doubts over his version of events. On returning home after knocking at the Nazirs' front door, the next-door neighbour recalled the ensuing sequence of events:

> I came back into my house and closed my front door. The screaming continued. I went back to the sitting room and was looking after the baby, then I went to my front room for a while. Somebody tried to get out. Someone opened the front door at 36 [Abbott's Road]. I saw a bloody arm. I couldn't make out whose. Then I heard a voice, 'Help, help'. It was Samaira's voice. Somebody pulled her back. I couldn't see which part of her was being pulled and then the front door closed. (R v. *Nazir*, 2009)

An anonymous witness separately testified to have seen Azhar pulling Samaira, 'who was already injured, back into the house when she was trying to escape' (R v. *Nazir*, 2009). Forensic evidence furthermore showed that 'the blood staining' found on Azhar's clothes was 'inconsistent with his account of what he had done and where he had been during the murder' (R v. *Nazir*, 2009). On

14 July 2006, Azhar was sentenced at the Central Criminal Court together with his cousin for the murder of Samaira. On sentencing them, Judge Christopher Moss declared that Samaira had 'suffered a brutal, gruesome and prolonged death in her own home' (Judd, 2006). Turning to Azhar, he added 'You were Samaira's judge and jury. You may not have been alone in that respect. You claimed you loved your sister dearly when you orchestrated her murder' (Judd, 2006). Speaking on behalf of the CPS, Afzal said after the verdict:

> Samaira was murdered because she loved the wrong person in her family's eyes. In that sense it was an 'honour killing' to protect the perceived status of the family, to mark their disapproval of Samaira's intention to marry someone her family considered 'an unsuitable boy' … We hope that Samaira's death and the investigation and prosecution that followed will deter others who may wish to harm their own family members because of practices that are as tragic as they are outdated. (CPS, 2006)

In line with other 'honour' killings, the death of Samaira at the hands of her brother and cousin saw family members colluding and actively taking part in her murder. Afzal has described her murder as being both 'organised' and 'premeditated' (Afzal featured in H.O.P.E., 2009). Patriarchal and cultural attitudes to women also played a central role in precipitating her untimely death. Her family, Afzal adds, 'you would have thought were upstanding, modern, part of the society that we all belong to. However, she decided that she wanted to marry somebody of her own choice' and was killed as a result; 'Now what that tells me', Afzal goes on, 'is that … people who claim to be modern are not immune from this kind of behaviour, and that ultimately she paid the price for what you and I might think was the most pathetic and petty of reasons' (Afzal featured in H.O.P.E., 2009). Following the sentencing of Samaira's killers, District Judge Marilyn Mornington, who specialises in 'honour' violence cases, reiterated the need for members of the communities where 'honour' crimes are prevalent to break their conspiracy of silence:

> We need people from the communities themselves to come forward and speak. This is not easy for people to do because of the whole issue of honour. They could be putting themselves at risk.
> But the most important part of this is to change hearts and minds in the community.
> For every killing there are 1,000 women living in fear for their lives, living lives totally constrained by this distorted view of honour. (District Judge Mornington cited in *The Star*, 2006)

Ann Cryer, the Labour MP and veteran campaigner against forced marriage and 'honour'-based violence, has gone further in criticising the government's approach to multiculturalism as detrimental to women's rights:

> it's time the authorities stopped pussyfooting around cultural sensitivities and took a stronger stand on women's rights and the broader notion of multiculturalism. If not, they'll soon have the blood of another young woman on their hands. (Ann Cryer MP cited in Dhaliwal, 2006)

Dhaliwal moreover has argued that the boldness of Samaira's crime, committed 'in broad daylight in a residential suburb of London' shows how 'indifferent her killers were to the society around them and how confident they were that no one would hold them to account' (Dhaliwal, 2006). Such 'honour' related crimes, Dhaliwal contends, 'are the inevitable result of a liberal multiculturalism that encourages religious and ethnic minorities to regard themselves as separate entities within Britain. Some people are so removed from mainstream life, and accustomed to authorities turning a blind eye, they think they can behave with impunity' (Dhaliwal, 2006).

A year after Samaira's passing, another 'honour' killing would again draw attention to these seemingly intractable social issues. On this occasion, the death of Banaz Mahmod in 2006 saw members of her close family and the wider Kurdish community in London colluding in the planning, execution and concealing of her murder. An 'honour' related death in which the level of premeditation and organisation beforehand as well as the degree of violence and punitive measures inflicted on the victim reached new heights.

Case-Study 5: The Story of Banaz Mahmod

On 11 June 2007, Mahmod Babakir Mahmod, his brother Ari Mahmod Babakir Aga and a third man, Mohammed Marid Hama, were convicted of the murder of Mahmod's 20-year-old daughter Banaz in London and sentenced to life imprisonment (R v. *Mahmod*, 2009). The three men, together with two others, Mohammed Ali and Omar Hussain, who fled to Iraq after the crime, had plotted to kill Banaz. She was raped and strangled, her body stuffed in a suitcase and buried underground.

At the time of her death, Banaz had been living at her parents' home in the midst of a seemingly ordinary migrant Kurdish family in Mitcham, South London. But all was not well at home. Her father's patriarchal and anti-Western attitudes had seen Banaz's older sister, Bekhal, become a victim of domestic abuse early on. Bekhal's own experience provides the backdrop against which Banaz's murder took place and sheds some light on the mindset of her killers. Having been 'taken into care as a teenager' (Brandon and Hafez, 2008: 56),

Bekhal's everyday life during her time in the Mahmods' household was at the mercy of her father's wrath; she recalls how:

> One day I was walking home through the park and I'd taken my scarf off and my father saw me. He screamed at me: 'Who do you think you are? You are acting like a bitch'. He pulled me inside the house, spat in my face and then picked up his slippers to beat me around the head as he shouted: 'Don't you ever disobey me'. In the two years before I run away, I think he beat me more than 20 times. It would be over silly things like undoing the top button of my school shirt, or using hair gel. Once, he picked up a metal soup ladle and hit me round the head repeatedly with it. I didn't want to have boyfriends or go out at night or anything like that. I was respectful to my parents. I just wanted to be able to have friends, to give my opinion, very small things that British girls take for granted. (Bekhal Mahmod cited in Weathers, 2007)

By 2002, there had been an attempt on Bekhal's life. At the time, she was living with a 'black' boyfriend, which her family 'viewed with disfavour' (R v. *Mahmod*, 2009). On a particular occasion, Bekhal's boyfriend drove her to a park where she had arranged to meet her brother, Bahman. Court records would later describe what happened next:

> Bahman jumped out of the bushes and said: 'What are you doing with my sister?' She said that they were just friends although she believed he knew about their relationship. Her boyfriend then drove off. She walked in front of Bahman ... On a grassy area he ran up to her and hit her behind the ear with a barbell. He took hold of her around the neck and she bit his arm and she shouted for help. Bahman said: 'Don't make this harder than it is already, I have to do it. I am the son of the house. You have brought shame on the family, it is my duty to finish you off'. He then said it had been his father who had told him to do it. As she sat crying on a bench Bahman asked Bekhal to come home. He said he had been paid by his father and showed her £200 or £300 in £50 notes. (R v. *Mahmod*, 2009)

During the trial of Banaz's murder, Bekhal gave evidence under police protection that she had left home because 'she did not want to engage in an arranged marriage' and went to live with foster parents instead (R v. *Mahmod*, 2009). Her mother said Bekhal had 'brought shame on the family' and if she did not return home 'her father had threatened that he would kill her sister and their mother and it would be her fault' (R v. *Mahmod*, 2009). In the event, Bekhal's mother inauspicious prediction was to become a reality for Banaz.

Unlike her older sister, a teenage Banaz had entered into an arranged marriage to a Kurdish man. Her husband proved to be violent and abusive and she sought to divorce him. Banaz had subsequently fallen in love with Rahmat Suleimani, an Iranian from a different Kurdish clan, which her family disapproved of. Like her sister before her, Banaz went on to experience parental abuse, including threats against both herself and Rahmat as well as a failed attempt on Banaz's life by her father. Fearing for her safety, Banaz visited Mitcham Police Station in early December 2005, but her repeated efforts to alert the authorities of the danger she felt she was in were largely overlooked. On 12 December, a handwritten letter by Banaz was handed to the police with the names of the people she believed were intent on murdering her. DCI Goode of the MPS recalls how Banaz 'had been told who the people were who were going to be responsible for killing her. And the people that she named in there are the people who have been convicted for her murder' (DCI Goode featured in BBC *Panorama*, 2012). Banaz had ominously forewarned the police that 'In the future at any time if anything happens to me, it's them' (Banaz cited in Peachey, 2012).

Events escalated when, on New Year's Eve, Banaz was admitted to St George's Hospital in Tooting 'distressed and bleeding' (R v. *Mahmod*, 2009). Rahmat met her at the hospital, where he recorded on his mobile telephone's camera Banaz's account of the events that had led her there. The grainy footage 'shows Banaz still trembling, stammering out her story from a hospital bed in which she begged nurses to hide her from her father' (Sanghera, 2009: 133–4). In the recording, Banaz explained how:

> her father had asked her to go to her grandmother's house to sort out her divorce. Once there, her mobile phone had been taken away from her by her father and he had made her drink half a bottle of brandy. The curtains were closed and she was told to sit on the floor with her back towards him. When he went to another room, she ran out of the back door. She smashed a neighbour's window in her desperation. That was the cause of the bleeding. She made her way to a local cafe and the police were contacted. (R v. *Mahmod*, 2009)

Staff at the hospital recalled Banaz being 'too frightened to leave the ambulance on arrival' as she kept saying that 'her father and uncle were trying to kill her' (R v. *Mahmod*, 2009). But despite Banaz's pleas, the police 'refused to believe her story' and she was 'dismissed as a melodramatic and attention-seeking drunk' (Sanghera, 2009: 133–4). Of the police's response, DCI Goode said:

> What happened on that night was that the police were called, but the officer that turned up simply didn't understand what it was that she was being told. She had no prior knowledge of honour-based violence and simply didn't believe, in all fairness, what it was that she was being told. The police clearly did fail Banaz on that occasion. (DCI Goode featured in BBC *Panorama*, 2012)

In the aftermath of the hospital incident, Banaz and Rahmat pretended to have broken off the relationship, but continued to see each other in secret. On 22 January 2006, there was an attempt to kidnap Rahmat: while in the company of some friends, Omar, Hama and Ali tried to force him into a car. When Rahmat refused to go with them, Hama made a threat to the effect of 'Okay, Rahmat, it may not be tonight because of these people but we will kill you and Banaz' (R v. *Mahmod*, 2009). The following day Rahmat reported the incident at Kennington Police Station and Banaz did likewise at Mitcham Police Station. Court records show that Banaz 'said she was willing to give a statement but she also said that she was happy to continue living in the family home in Morden Road. She asserted that it was her uncle Ari who was controlling the situation' (R v. *Mahmod*, 2009). Banaz arranged to return to the police station again on that day, but never did. She was last seen alive on 24 January 2006. Two days later a missing person's report was filed.

On 28 April 2006, her body was found 'in a suitcase buried in a back garden in Birmingham' (R v. *Mahmod*, 2009). Banaz's corpse had been driven there by her killers. DCI Goode recalls the moment the young woman's remains were unearthed:

> After digging for the whole day, we finally discovered Banaz's body buried six feet deep … under the footings of the house. They'd gone to extraordinary lengths to ensure that we didn't find her. (DCI Goode featured in BBC *Panorama*, 2012)

As the details of Banaz's final moments were eventually pieced together, Afzal of the CPS London West recounts the sequence of events leading up to her death:

> In Banaz's Mahmod's case … what was her crime? Well, her crime was that she was seen kissing her boyfriend outside of the tube station [in London]. For that reason alone, her father, her uncle and six other men from the [Kurdish] community sat around a table, not unlike the one in this room, and said: she must die. The next day, she was abducted off the streets of London, she was raped – we talk about 'honour' issues here, you know – raped, and then she was strangled and buried in a suitcase in Birmingham. Now again, why did eight people feel including her father … that she'd done such … horrible thing … that she had to pay the ultimate penalty? (Afzal featured in H.O.P.E., 2009)

The level of violence and the ritualistic nature of the punishment inflicted on Banaz set her murder apart from other types of domestic crimes. Prior to her death by strangulation, Banaz had been beaten up and sexually abused. Under her father's instructions, she had been 'stripped by her killers and gang raped for two hours in the family home before being garrotted' (Brandon and Hafez,

2008: 59). One of her killers, Mohammad Hama, would later be recorded in prison under surveillance boasting about having 'slapped' and 'fucked' Banaz as her father watched (Brandon and Hafez, 2008: 59). She was strangulated for five minutes, but it took her 'half an hour to die' as one of her killers 'stamped repeatedly on her neck to "let her soul out"' (Brown, 2007). The 'ritualised' nature of such crimes, Brandon and Hafez argue, turns these murders into 'quasi-judicial punishments with a strong moral dimension ... intended as a warning to other women not to transgress the community moral "red lines"' (Brandon and Hafez, 2008: 59). Afzal of the CPS London West concurs:

> We don't see this as domestic violence – it's beyond that. The murder of Banaz was so brutal that it was a clear warning to others; it was a way of saying don't step out of line or this could be you. (Afzal cited in Brandon and Hafez, 2008: 59)

Afzal furthermore points to the collective character of the 'honour' killing phenomenon, which extends beyond the immediate family circle. In the case of Banaz's murder, he says, 'substantial numbers of the community actually did not assist and support prosecutors; instead they supported the family members who were responsible for the killing. They really didn't care, and it showed' (Afzal cited in Brandon and Hafez, 2008: 58).

During Banaz's murder trial, her father denied any wrongdoing. He said that 'he did not distinguish between his sons and daughters. He believed in human rights and women's rights. There were no restrictions on his children's friendships. Bekhal had left home of her free will and he denied ever hitting her' or that his son Bahman 'ever hit Bekhal'; he also said 'It is 100% untrue that Rahmat was unacceptable to us' (R v. *Mahmod*, 2009). Of Banaz's statements to the police, Mahmod claimed to be aware of his daughter's visit to the police station, but this was 'something to do with matters between Banaz and her husband'; Mahmod 'knew nothing of any threat by Ari towards Banaz' and challenged the prosecution's description of the events that took place on New Year's Eve (R v. *Mahmod*, 2009). On the contrary, 'he had seen Banaz in hospital and she had been pleased to see him' (R v. *Mahmod*, 2009).

Banaz's father, uncle and their accomplice Hama were eventually convicted of her murder in 2007. Reflecting on the challenges to bring them to justice, Paul Goddard, CPS London Senior Prosecutor said:

> The murder of Banaz Mahmod Aga by her father, uncle and their associates not only took away the life of a young woman, it left her boyfriend in fear of his life and also left members of the family and community in fear ...

The discovery of Banaz's body on 28 April 2006 was not the end of the case but the beginning of an even more challenging phase. Witnesses required assurance and measures to assist them; telephone and technological evidence of considerable volume and complexity required detailed analysis and re-analysis in order to reveal the truth of what happened to Banaz and avoid the false trails that had been laid down. (Goddard cited in CPS, 2007b)

It would take several more years and a determined joint effort by the UK and Iraqi authorities to bring the remaining two absconded accomplices Mohammed Ali and Omar Hussain before a British court. By 2010, the two men wanted over Banaz's death had been finally extradited from Iraq and jailed for her murder. Unlike the case of Surjit Athwal over a decade earlier, whose killers remain at large, this was the first time that perpetrators of an 'honour' killing in Britain were successfully extradited from abroad to face justice. The landmark investigation paved the way for changes in the police's handling of 'honour' killings and their wider understanding of 'honour' related crimes, as the successful convictions of Banaz's murders had also unveiled serious procedural shortcomings. One area however that has remained intractable thus far is the deep-seated cultural attitudes and collective muteness within communities that time and again has hindered police efforts to bring perpetrators of 'honour' crimes to justice. As DCI Goode put it at the time of Banaz's murder, 'If Rahmat hadn't reported her missing, we wouldn't have known ... You have to ask how many of those are going on in this country. It could well be that we're only seeing the tip of the iceberg' (DCI Goode cited in Peachey, 2012).

Conclusion

Each of the 'honour' killings depicted in this chapter chronicles a unique personal tragedy of unnecessary suffering and loss of life. The stories of Surjit, Heshu, Shafilea, Samaira and Banaz speak of domestic violence, human rights abuses and obsolete cultural attitudes at the heart of Britain's 'honour'-based communities. The combined narratives of these young women, and many others over the past two decades, serve to illustrate the behavioural patterns common to such 'control crimes': their conspiratorial and collaborative nature, the patriarchal and anti-Western outlook of the perpetrators, the involvement of family and community members and the ensuing conspiracy of silence that encircles them all. From Surjit's 'remote control killing', whose executioners are still at large, to the complicity of parents and relatives in the murders of Heshu, Shafilea and Samaira, to the family plot to kill Banaz hatched in collusion with the wider Kurdish community; they all share similar traits. Such 'honour' killings exemplify the extraordinary lengths individuals and groups bound by 'honour' codes will go in order to ensure compliance from their victims. Paternalistic cultural mindsets together with distorted notions of family 'honour' and 'shame' will translate into extreme levels of domestic and sexual violence against women who defy such norms. In a testimony to the power of the collective over individual agency in 'honour' cultures; those who fail to acquiesce will pay with their lives. Parents will murder their children, brothers kill their sisters and husbands slay their wives in order to exert the ultimate 'honour' penalty.

Just as potential victims of 'honour' killings risk losing their lives, the eyewitnesses who step forward to help them do so at a great personal cost. Intimidation, threats and fear of harm have accompanied bystanders in 'honour' crimes who dared to take a stand. From Surjit's sister-in-law Sarbjit testifying against her extended family, to Shafilea's sister Alesha entering witness protection to speak up for her dead sibling, to Banaz's sister Bekhal giving evidence incriminating her parents; they too have paid a heavy price. Despite the remarkable courage these individuals showed under extreme circumstances, many of their lives have been blighted as a result. Their plight continues to raise questions about the role communities play in perpetuating 'honour' crimes and the inability of their leaders to tackle it. Such questions will be examined in detail in the second part of this volume.

The stories described in this chapter have also drawn attention to the official investigative strategies deployed to deal with 'honour' crimes. The past two decades have proved a steep learning curve for the police, the CPS and related government agencies. But as knowledge of 'honour' crimes has developed, so have the approaches aimed to address them. The investigations into the murders of Surjit, Heshu, Shafilea, Samaira and Banaz have seen significant procedural failures as well as ground-breaking successes in resolving 'honour' killing cases and prosecuting the perpetrators. Some of the highs and lows in this ongoing journey saw Surjit's family embark in a protracted public campaign to bring her killers to justice; the introduction of the term 'honour killing' into the British legal system following Heshu's murder together with the ensuing national review of historic suspected killings; and Banaz's futile attempts to warn the police of her impending death, the successful prosecution of her killers and the unprecedented extradition of their accomplices from abroad.

Underlying them all there has been reluctance by the authorities, schools and social services to interfere in the domestic setting of minority ethnic families and communities. Such a pervasive, politically correct undercurrent has led critics to question the status of minority ethnic women within multicultural British society and the protection that is afforded to them. For the stories of Surjit, Heshu, Shafilea, Samaira and Banaz are indicative of the myriad of similar instances of 'honour' killings taking place in family homes across the country. To the outside world, there is nothing intrinsically unusual about victims of 'honour' crimes and their families, merely ordinary people inhabiting ordinary lives. A closer look, however, reveals a far more unsettling private realm; one that is largely at odds with the liberal values of the wider multicultural UK society they belong to. In order to understand how the British state attempts to square this particular circle, the second part of the book will put the 'honour' question to the political establishment, community leaders, service providers and survivors of 'honour' violence themselves.

PART II
Public Policy Perspectives

Chapter 4
Government, Westminster Parties and the 'Honour' Question

Constructing 'Honour' Violence as a Policy Issue: A Sociological Approach

In trying to understand how the phenomenon of 'honour' violence has come to be at the centre of the UK government's policy agenda, attention must be turned again to Sociology, which provides a suitable empirical framework for the study of social problems within a public policy setting. On this occasion, Fuller and Myers' (1941) classic proposition on 'The Natural History of a Social Problem' serves to explain 'honour' violence's transition from the margins of the public policy spectrum to the epicentre of the British government's legislative and political programme (Fuller and Myers, 1941: 320). Their model will therefore be explored here in some detail.

As a starting point, Fuller and Myers describe a 'social problem' as 'a condition which is defined by a considerable number of persons as a deviation from some social norm which they cherish' (Fuller and Myers, 1941: 320). Having traced the rise of trailer campsites in Detroit, between 1920 and 1937, they postulated that social problems have a 'natural history' consisting of a series of stages through which they inevitably evolve, namely those of 'awareness', 'policy determination' and 'reform' (Fuller and Myers, 1941: 320). From the outset, the 'awareness' or 'genesis of every social problem lies in the awakening of people of a given locality to a realization that certain cherished values are threatened by conditions which have become acute' (Fuller and Myers, 1941: 322). At this early stage in the development of the 'problem consciousness', stakeholders have not yet crystallised their definition sufficiently to suggest or debate exact measures for amelioration or eradication of the undesirable condition. Instead, there is unsynchronised random behaviour, with protest expressed in general terms. Analysis of newspaper coverage during the decade of 1925 to 1935, for instance, revealed editorials moving progressively from expressing 'curiosity and amusement' regarding the campsites to increasingly voicing 'concern and alarm' at the scale of the growing problem (Fuller and Myers, 1941: 322). Simultaneously complaints from neighbours, parent–teacher associations, women and men's clubs as well as government officials 'were articulated on the grounds of the unsightliness of the camps, noises, odours, immorality, crime, and property depreciation in the surrounding districts' (Fuller and Myers, 1941: 323). Conflict of interests over proposed solutions arose among groups who had different and incompatible interests. On the one hand, neighbourhood and real estate groups wanted the trailer campsites eliminated; whereas labour unions and civil rights groups championed 'the survival of trailer communities' (Fuller and Myers, 1941: 325).

The stage of 'policy determination' follows swiftly from the initial public awareness period, with 'debate over policies involved in alternative solutions' (Fuller and Myers, 1941: 324). Interest groups are now mainly preoccupied with 'what ought to be done', as a result, specific programmes and debates among participants occupy the focus of attention. On the 'resident trailer problem in Detroit', discussions among stakeholders involved questions such as 'should the trailer camps be prohibited entirely and expelled from the community, should they only be licensed, taxed, or otherwise restricted in growth, or should they be let alone in the hope that the situation would right itself?' (Fuller and Myers, 1941: 325).

The final stage of 'reform' in the natural history of a social problem witnesses 'administrative units engaged in putting formulated policy into action' (Fuller and Myers, 1941: 326). This is the 'institutionalised' phase of a social problem where action takes place and the outcomes of policy decision-making are actually implemented. In Detroit, legislation was enacted which 'placed the trailer camps within the city under certain prohibitions and restrictions', furthermore 'special requirements as to licensing, inspection, and supervision of the camps were enforced' and 'special rules of public health for the trailer communities' established (Fuller and Myers, 1941: 326).

Social problems such as the Detroit trailer campsites in the first half of the twentieth century or 'honour' violence in Britain decades later do not come into being 'full-blown, commanding community attention and evoking adequate policies and machinery for their solution' (Fuller and Myers, 1941: 321). Far from it, as Fuller and Myers argued:

> social problems exhibit a temporal course of development in which different phases or stages may be distinguished. Each stage anticipates its successor in time and each succeeding stage contains new elements which mark it off from its predecessor. A social problem thus conceived as always being in a dynamic state of 'becoming' passes through the natural history stages of awareness, policy determination, and reform. (Fuller and Myers, 1941: 321)

Fuller and Myers' original model has subsequently been challenged in the literature for its narrow understanding of the nature of a social problem and limited success in discovering a sequence of stages common to all social problems (Lemert, 1951; Becker, 1966; Spector and Kitsuse, 1977;

Best, 2002). Lemert, who sought to replicate Fuller and Myers' findings a decade after they postulated their 'natural history' thesis, viewed their generalising of the trailer camp problem to a much wider set of phenomena as premature and their model as too rigid (Lemert, 1951). Spector and Kitsuse similarly deemed Fuller and Myers' empirical findings as insufficient to support their oversimplified assertion regarding all social problems progressing through the stages of 'awareness', 'policy determination' and 'reform' (Spector and Kitsuse, 1977). They nevertheless recognised the intrinsic value of the 'natural history' approach to the study of social and human phenomena by identifying sequences of events that take place as these occurrences unfold over time (Spector and Kitsuse, 1977).

It is within this context that the 'natural history' model is understood as providing a valid conceptual tool for analysing the development of 'honour' violence in Britain as a social problem. We need not accept the specific stages Fuller and Myers posited or the inferences they made in order to share their core thesis: to fully understand a social problem, we must appreciate how it came to be constructed as such. The emergence of 'honour' violence in the UK over the past two decades can therefore be said to have undergone a 'natural history' featuring different and often overlapping stages of development. These junctures, which are broadly consistent with Fuller and Myers' original phases of 'awareness', 'policy determination' and 'reform' will each be explored in turn.

Awareness: From the Grassroots to the Mainstream

At the inception of any social problem, Fuller and Myers argue, there needs to be an 'awareness' or 'problem consciousness' among stakeholders without which 'no identifiable problem can be said to exist' (Fuller and Myers, 1941: 322). In the case of 'honour' violence, attention to this issue originally came as a by-product of grassroots service provision targeted towards domestic violence against women. The UK's mainstream charity sector has a long and well documented history of dealing with victims and perpetrators of domestic abuse across the board (Refuge, 2013; Women's Aid, 2014; CAADA, 2012; Respect, 2014). However, concern with the 'honour' violence variant, including forced marriage, female genital mutilation (FGM) and 'honour' killings, appeared originally limited to the communities mostly affected by these transgressions. It has accordingly been mainly minority ethnic and South Asian women's groups in particular that have spearheaded targeted initiatives to identify and meet the needs of those affected by 'honour' violence. Yet, despite decades of localised service provision by organisations such as the Southall Black Sisters (SBS), Karma Nirvana and Ashiana Network, among others, no meaningful nationwide engagement with the 'honour' question was to take place until the late 1990s (SBS, 2014a; Karma Nirvana, 2013a; Ashiana Network, 2012a). Before that period, a mixture of lack of reliable data, understanding and visibility of the 'honour' violence issue together with a prevailing multiculturalist political discourse rendered successive governments unwilling to actively intervene in an area of social life deemed both 'culturally sensitive' and confined to an individual's private realm (Julios, 2008; Okin, 1999; Ali, 2006a and 2007; Walby, 1993). The closing years of the twentieth century however witnessed a paradigm shift regarding British society's approach to harmful 'honour' practices. The literature has identified several contributing factors to changes in hitherto prevalent attitudes including 'increased representation of women after the 1997 election (which generated a larger cohort of MPs prepared to speak out against abuses of women)' together with a rise in parliamentary time devoted to debates on 'honour'-based violence and women's rights, specifically forced marriage and FGM (Phillips and Dustin, 2004: 534). This upsurge in political capital devoted to 'honour' related abuse was accompanied by growing media output from journalists and social commentators such as Yasmin Alibhai-Brown, who became a member of the Home Office Working Group on Forced Marriage in 1999 (Phillips and Dustin, 2004: 534). The convergence during that time of three high profile cases involving 'honour' offences has furthermore been credited with drawing public attention to the plight of victims of 'honour'-based violence and in turn prompting the government into action. The three instances refer first to the 'honour' killing of Rukhsana Naz in 1998 – featured in Chapter 3 – 'after she left an arranged marriage and became pregnant by another man'; second the plight of 'Jack' and 'Zena' Briggs, who spent years in hiding from bounty hunters employed by Zena's family after she refused to marry a cousin in Pakistan; and third the successful return to England of a young Sikh girl, 'KR', whose parents forcibly took her to India in an attempt to coerce her into marriage (Phillips and Dustin, 2004: 534). Nationwide media coverage of these 'honour' violence related cases elicited plentiful headlines and social commentary such as Hall's (1999) 'Life for "Honour" Killing of Pregnant Teenager by Mother and Brother', Johnstone's (1999) '"Shame" Murder Mother gets Life' or Hill's (2004) 'Runaways Stalked by Bounty Thugs', and many more (Sewell, 1999; Watson-Smyth, 1999; Rawstorne, 2006). All of which contributed to propel the issue of 'honour' crimes firmly into the public consciousness, thus signalling a transition from the initial 'awareness' phase of its 'natural history' towards the deliberation driven 'policy determination' stage.

Before exploring the latter, however, it is worth considering how the aftermath of the initial period of 'awareness' has seen public visibility of the 'honour' violence question rising exponentially. The early 2000s especially witnessed the unprecedented growth of an emerging body of knowledge relating to 'honour' violence. In addition to frequent media reporting, increasing numbers of personal narratives of survivors of 'honour' offences both at home and abroad have steadily come to light (Ali, 2006a and 2007; Sanghera, 2007 and

2009; Ahluwalia and Gupta, 2008; Athwal, 2013; Younis, 2013), together with new scholarly research, grey literature, including reports as well as evidence-based policy work (Home Office, 2000; Samad and Eade, 2002; Welchman and Hossain, 2005; Siddiqui, 2005; Gill, 2006; Khanum, 2008; Thiara and Gill, 2010; Gill and Anitha, 2011; Rehman et al., 2013). Over the past two decades, 'honour' violence can thus be said to have effectively transitioned from a marginal community concern to a mainstream social policy issue.

Policy Determination: Debating the 'Honour' Violence Problem

In 1999, with the issue of 'honour' violence commanding the attention of the New Labour government, Home Office Minister for Community Relations, Mike O'Brien MP, established the Working Group on Forced Marriage (Home Office, 2000). This was to signal the beginning of a period of 'policy determination' in the evolution of the 'honour' violence question. As Fuller and Myers note, this stage is characterised by 'debate over policies involved in alternative solutions' (Fuller and Myers, 1941: 324). The ground-breaking public consultation exercise carried out by the Working Group, including a broad range of interested parties, their deliberations and the eventual outcome, clearly illustrate this process.

From the outset, the stated aim of the Working Group was 'to investigate the problem of forced marriage in England and Wales and to make proposals for tackling it effectively' (Home Office, 2000: 6). Co-chaired by peers Baroness Uddin and Lord Ahmed, the Working Group featured a significant South Asian presence among its nine core members including the two co-chairs together with Lord Dholakia OBE, Yasmin Alibhai-Brown and Hannana Siddiqui from SBS. Their terms of reference comprised four main areas, namely to 'probe the extent of the [forced marriage] problem'; 'engage all of the relevant service delivery agencies, affected communities and relevant non-governmental organisations on this issue'; 'stimulate a public debate to raise awareness of … forced marriage'; and 'develop a comprehensive strategy … including preventive measures' to deal with it (Home Office, 2000: 28). In order to fulfil the brief, the Working Group carried out a public consultation running from August 1999 to April 2000 and involving stakeholders across the board. The consultative exercise featured 'written submissions and evidence, seminars, visits to women's organisations and meeting with victims of forced marriage and their families' (Home Office, 2000: 29). Participants included government departments and local authorities, police forces, social, education and health services, universities, charities, women's groups and victims of forced marriage, youth, advice and immigration services as well as lawyers and members of the judiciary (Home Office, 2000: 29).

The consultation laid bare the complexity of the issues under discussion and the many contrasting and often conflicting views held by the participants regarding how to best understand and deal with the 'honour' question. It is precisely, Fuller and Myers remind us, this 'interinfluence and cross-fertilization of debate among and between … participating discussants' that effectively 'represent the dynamics of policy determination' (Fuller and Myers, 1941: 324). The diversity of perspectives and the underlying tensions engendered were apparent when the Working Group published its findings in a report titled *A Choice by Right*, in June 2000 (Home Office, 2000). The Group's co-chairs claimed at the time that the consultative process had enabled 'dialogue and collaboration within and between the service providers, as well as with communities', with 'a broad consensus on important practical actions' having been reached; but they also acknowledged the challenges faced and the many unresolved issues that remained (Baroness Uddin and Lord Ahmed cited in Home Office, 2000: 1). In particular, there was a recognition that fundamental unanswered questions lingered such as how to empower communities so that forced marriage can be effectively addressed from within or how to achieve 'a commitment to tackle the lack of representation of women, particularly Asian women, in prominent public positions' (Baroness Uddin and Lord Ahmed cited in Home Office, 2000: 1).

A Choice by Right ultimately evidenced the seriousness with which the government had now come to view the issue of 'honour' violence and specifically forced marriage; as the Group's co-chairs put it, there was now a 'commitment at the highest levels of Government to tackle this ["honour"-related] violence and abuse' (Baroness Uddin and Lord Ahmed cited in Home Office, 2000: 1). A Labour administration-led initiative, the Working Group's report furthermore served to establish a politically sanctioned public narrative to define and frame 'honour' violence. The document accordingly provided a blueprint for future interventions including areas such as 'meeting the needs of victims', 'preventing forced marriage', 'international dimensions', 'guiding principles for effective action' and 'monitoring' (Home Office, 2000: 3). Some aspects of this 'official' discourse have subsequently come under scrutiny in the literature such as the 'clear-cut distinction' it postulates between a 'forced' and an 'arranged' marriage, particularly by reference to the nature of consent, as illustrated in Chapter 2 of this volume. Other areas however have kept broadly in line with prevailing thinking on the 'honour' phenomenon such as situating the issue of forced marriage within a 'human rights' perspective and the assertion that 'Forced marriage is not just an "Asian" issue'; although the Working Group's report also admits that 'British Asian communities … have been at the forefront of much of the existing action aimed at tackling forced marriage and domestic violence' (Home Office, 2000: 12). In contrast, its treatment of the cultural aspects of forced marriage and the role of community and religious leaders remains ambivalent, once more reflecting the multifarious nature of the matters under consideration. Similarly, *A Choice by Right* makes it 'clear that the issue of forced marriage should not be used to stigmatise any community'; but at the same time it recognises that 'one of the many motivations for parents forcing their children into marriages is the desire to … protect their cultures' (Home Office, 2000: 12 and 20). The Working Group furthermore declared 'disappointment' with the lack of engagement by community leaders in the subject and suggested that 'challenging and changing people's attitudes is the key to preventing forced marriage' (Home Office, 2000: 12 and 20).

One key area which proved especially contentious at the time was the debate over whether forced marriage should become a criminal offence. As it will be discussed in detail later in this chapter, the Working Group rejected the idea of criminalising forced marriage on the basis of already existing provision for related offences under the law. It argued that:

> Although there is no specific criminal offence of 'forcing someone to marry' within England and Wales, the law does provide protection from the crimes that can be committed when forcing someone into a marriage. Perpetrators – usually parents or family members – have been prosecuted for offences including threatening behaviour, assault, kidnap and murder. Sexual intercourse without consent is rape. (Home Office, 2000: 9)

Despite their stated joint position, strong disagreements on the matter of criminalisation persisted among stakeholders who continue to engage in protracted discussions over important topics such as the status of forced marriage and 'honour' violence before the law, protection afforded to victims and treatment of perpetrators as well as the various courses of action that should be followed. As Fuller and Myers discovered in the trailer campsites case in Detroit, during the 'policy determination' phase 'Ends and means are discussed and the conflict of social interests becomes intense. People who propose solutions soon find that these solutions are not acceptable to others. Even when they can get others to agree on solutions, they find agreement as to means a further difficulty' (Fuller and Myers, 1941: 324). This has certainly proven to be the case with the problem of forced marriage and 'honour' violence in the UK. Conflicting approaches to the 'honour' question have persisted all the way through to the final stage of 'reform' when the apparatus of government with its administrative and legislative bureaux is engaged in translating policy decision-making into practice.

Reform: Institutionalising 'Honour' Violence: From New Labour to the Conservative–Liberal Democrat Coalition Government

The publication of *A Choice by Right* in 2000 signalled the beginning of a lengthy period of governmental action in which a plethora of official policy initiatives and programmes together with new 'honour' specific legislation were to be implemented. At the time of Fuller and Myers' writing, the 'residence-trailer problem in Detroit' was 'just beginning to enter the reform stage in its natural history' (Fuller and Myers, 1941: 326). Similarly, the phenomenon of 'honour' violence in Britain is currently undergoing a period of 'reform'. In line with Fuller and Myers' findings, the focus now 'is no longer on the idea that "something ought to be done" or that "this or that should be done" but on the fact that "this and that are being done"' (Fuller and Myers, 1941: 326). As the following sections will illustrate, a range of public policy interventions and legislative measures relating to 'honour' violence and specifically forced marriage are being effected at the present time. This action-led process typically involves long-standing official bodies working in the execution of government policy, but it also may lead to the formation of new agencies dealing with particular aspects of the 'honour' problem. As Fuller and Myers noted, while the 'established public agencies may prove sufficient for the administration of reform ... it may be necessary to establish new agencies of administration' (Fuller and Myers, 1941: 326). The creation of the Forced Marriage Unit (FMU) in January 2005 provides a case in point.

Addressing Forced Marriage and 'Honour'-Based Violence: The Forced Marriage Unit (FMU)

A joint effort by the Home Office (HO) and the Foreign and Commonwealth Office (FCO), the FMU was set up to 'lead on the Government's forced marriage policy, outreach and casework' both in the UK and abroad, where 'consular assistance' would be provided to British nationals (FMU, 2014). Since its inception in 2005, the Unit has operated a 'public helpline to provide advice and support to victims of forced marriage as well as professionals dealing with cases', in addition to undertaking 'an extensive outreach and training programme of around 100 events a year' while carrying out media campaigns, such as the 'right to choose' in 2012 (FMU, 2014). Through its FMU Domestic Programme Fund (DPF), the FMU furthermore provides funding to grassroots charities and organisations engaged in delivering targeted 'honour' related activities and services (FMU, 2014). Successful tenders in the 2013–14 bidding round, for instance, featured among others Ashiana Sheffield's 'Bridge the Gap' project aimed at creating a forced marriage-based film as an interactive educational tool; Karma Nirvana's 'Practitioner Roadshows' designed to publicise information on current forced marriage legislation, particularly 'the practicalities of the criminalisation' and SBS's 'Consolidating support for repatriated victims of forced marriage' programme providing information and advocacy to this particular demographic cohort (Gov.uk, 2014b).

In addition to the setting up of official bodies such as the FMU, the Third Sector has witnessed in recent times the emergence of new 'honour' related grassroots organisations such as Freedom Charity, which reaches out to school children and young people at risk of forced marriage through its helpline as well as the use of social media and mobile technology (Freedom Charity, 2012). Even umbrella groups traditionally dealing with gendered domestic violence such as Refuge and those involved with children's welfare like the National Society for the Prevention of Cruelty to Children (NSPCC) now find themselves supporting victims of 'honour' related offences. Under the headline 'Forced Marriage Feared by Schoolchildren', the NSPCC, for example, recently reported how its ChildLine is receiving growing numbers of calls from children as young as 12 years of age 'becoming worried they will be forced to marry against their will' (NSPCC, 2014). NSPCC figures from 2014 show 'the number of contacts – online and phone – about the [forced marriage] issue has shot up by two-thirds in the last year, to 141, with some victims saying they are suicidal' (NSPCC, 2014).

Providing Civil Remedies: The Forced Marriage (Civil Protection) Act 2007

Two years after the establishment of the FMU, another significant development in the 'reform' stage of the 'honour' violence social problem took place. On 26 July 2007, the UK ratified the *Forced Marriage (Civil Protection) Act 2007* (Hansard, 2007), which came into force on 25 November 2008. In doing so, the UK became the first country to use 'civil rather than criminal law' in this manner (Lord Lester, 2007). As Lord Lester, the Liberal Democrat Peer who introduced the original Private Members' Bill, put it, 'no other country has used civil law to give protection and legal remedies to victims [of forced marriage]. There are criminal laws in India and Pakistan but they are of little practical use' (Lord Lester, 2007). The new Act of Parliament was therefore designed to protect 'individuals against being forced to enter into marriage without their free and full consent' as well as those already coerced 'into marriage without such consent' (Hansard, 2007: c.20, 1). As has already been indicated in this volume, the Act provided for the use of Forced Marriage Protection Orders (FMPOs) to do so. When deciding whether to issue a FMPO, the courts would have to take into account 'all the circumstances' surrounding each case 'including the need to secure the health, safety and well-being of the person to be protected' (Hansard, 2007: c.20, 1). Vulnerable individuals at risk of a forced marriage

79

would therefore be afforded a civil recourse under the law. Shortly after the introduction of the Act, the first FMPO was issued over the high-profile case of Dr Humayra Adedin, a 32-year-old NHS trainee doctor from East London who was held hostage for four months in Bangladesh and forced into a marriage by her parents (Bingham, 2008; Lakhani, 2009). During her captivity 'the High Court in London had issued a landmark order under the new Forced Marriage Act calling for her release'; she was eventually freed and returned to the UK after a court in the Bangladeshi capital Dhaka 'ordered her parents to hand her over to the British High Commission' (Bingham, 2008).

While the introduction of the landmark *Forced Marriage (Civil Protection) Act 2007* was widely welcomed, the many debates that attended its birth unveiled fundamental ideological differences regarding how to deal with this variant of 'honour' violence. The issue of whether to criminalise forced marriage, which the Act had failed to do, proved a particular bone of contention. Advocates of criminalising forced marriage pointed to recent developments in Denmark where 'three members of the same family have been arrested for forcing a young female relative to marry – the first since forced marriage became a crime in 2008' (Lakhani, 2012). Critics, on the other hand, questioned the effectiveness of such a move into criminal law and warned of the dangers of driving the problem of forced marriage underground and stigmatising minority groups. Community leaders, in particular, largely rejected the introduction of new legislation. As previously noted, the Home Office Working Group on Forced Marriage did 'not support the creation of a specific offence on forcing a person to marry' (Home Office, 2000: 9). Sadiq Khan, a Muslim Labour MP, similarly opposed the establishment of new legal remedies that may reinforce 'stereotyping and "ghetto" legislation' (White, 2007), as did the Muslim Council of Britain (MCB, 2005). Meanwhile, SBS – whose representative resigned from the Working Group over its refusal to abandon the use of 'mediation' involving victims and their families – also rejected the introduction of new legislation. Lord Lester recalls how:

> The Southall Black Sisters were among many well-informed organisations opposing such an extension of the criminal law. They argued that a new criminal offence would add little to the existing body of law on murder, kidnapping and offences against the person; that police intervention would be counter-productive; and that it would be difficult to obtain sufficient evidence to satisfy the criminal burden of proof. (Lord Lester, 2007: 25)

In 2008, during a national conference on Forced Marriage and 'Honour' Based Violence, Bridget Prentice MP, Parliamentary Under-Secretary to the Ministry of Justice, explained the government's decision not to criminalise forced marriage as closely reflecting the opinions of the majority of interested parties at the time:

> We consulted with the people that work with young people, who work with the most vulnerable and with young people who've been forced into marriage or were potentially being forced into a marriage, and they told us quite clearly that overwhelmingly they felt that if we criminalised it, it would go underground. Because a young person really doesn't want to make a member of their family into a criminal. What they want is protection. What they want is the opportunity to make their own choices about who they marry … and that was the reason why we decided we would make it a civil protection order and not a criminal one. (Prentice featured in H.O.P.E., 2009)

The following year, she would report on the rates of prosecutions for forced marriages since the *Forced Marriage (Civil Protection) Act 2007* had been enacted:

> The Forced Marriage (Civil Protection) Act 2007 was implemented in November 2008 providing greater protection for those at risk, preventing forced marriage and enabling courts to make Forced Marriage Protection Orders (FMPOs). These are civil provisions. We continue to work with agencies including the police and local authorities to ensure they are aware of the Act's provisions.
>
> Since implementation of the Act on 25 November 2008 up to 31 October 2009 a total of 79 FMPOs have been made. (Prentice cited in Hansard, 2009)

Nonetheless, the debate over the merits and pitfalls of criminalising forced marriage continued unabated; and by 2011, a cross-party Parliamentary Committee reporting on Forced Marriage urged the government to introduce new legislation. The *House of Commons Home Affairs Committee – Forced Marriage, Eighth Report 2011* stated:

> It is not at all clear that the [Forced Marriage] Act is wholly effective as a tool in protecting individuals from forced marriage and from repercussions from family members. While the measures in the Act should continue to be used, we believe that it would send out a very clear and positive message to communities within the UK and internationally if it becomes a criminal act to force – or to participate in forcing – an individual to enter into marriage against their will. The lack of a criminal sanction also sends a message, and currently that is a weaker message than we believe is needed. We urge the Government to take an early opportunity to legislate on this matter. (Hansard, 2011a: 7)

Five months later, the newly elected Prime Minister, David Cameron, gave a speech on immigration in which he announced the government's plans to criminalise the breach of FMPOs:

> Forced marriage is little more than slavery. To force someone into marriage is completely wrong and I strongly believe this is a problem we should not shy away from addressing because of some cultural concerns. I know there's a worry that criminalisation could make it less likely that those at risk will come forward, but as a first step I'm announcing today that we will criminalise the breach of forced marriage prevention orders. It is ridiculous that an order made to stop a forced marriage isn't enforced with the full rigour of the criminal law. (Cameron, 2011)

On December 2011, a further public consultation was launched to seek wide ranging views on how 'to implement the criminalisation of a breach of a FMPO and whether forced marriage should be criminalised' (Home Office, 2012: 3). Contrary to the outcome of the original consultation exercise, the majority of respondents on this occasion supported the creation of a new criminal offence: of a total number of 297 responses, 54 per cent were in favour and 37 per cent against; an additional 9 per cent were undecided and 80 per cent 'felt that current civil remedies and criminal sanctions are not being used effectively' (Home Office, 2012: 5). Karma Nirvana, the 'honour'-based violence charity, conducted a separate postcard poll among members of the public that yielded over 2,500 responses, 98 per cent of which supported the government's proposals (Karma Nirvana, 2013b; Home Office, 2012: 4). Although the pendulum of public opinion had now decisively swung in the direction of regulation, the main arguments put forward by and large remained unchanged. The Home Office thus summarised the by now familiar views:

> Many of those in support [of criminalisation] felt that it would act as a deterrent and deliver a strong message that we would not tolerate this abhorrent practice and would prosecute perpetrators. It was also suggested that this approach would empower victims to come forward and report incidents of forced marriage because the issue of victims actually agreeing to marry under duress should not be under-estimated.

> Those against criminalisation felt that it could drive the issue further underground, as victims would be less inclined to want to come forward if it would ultimately lead to members of their family being imprisoned. There were concerns regarding the issues of intent and the 'burden of proof' and that it could result in victims being taken overseas for the purpose of marriage at a much earlier age. (Home Office, 2012: 5)

On 8 June 2012, the Prime Minister finally announced that forced marriage would become a criminal offence in England, Wales and Northern Ireland as it had already done so in Scotland under the *Forced Marriage etc. (Protection and Jurisdiction) (Scotland) Act 2011* (BBC, 2011; Hansard, 2011b). He declared 'forced marriage is wrong, is illegal and will not be tolerated' (Gov.uk, 2012). In welcoming the official announcement, Karma Nirvana's founder, Jasvinder Sanghera, said: 'The Prime Minister is right to send out a signal that such appalling acts of exploitation are simply unacceptable in 21st-century Britain … it will change a mind set for this [forced marriage] to no longer be dealt with as cultural but a crime' (Karma Nirvana, 2013b). Diana Nammi, Director of the Iranian and Kurdish Women's Rights Organisation (IKWRO), similarly hailed the impending criminalisation of forced marriage as 'a historical achievement in the fight for women's human rights and against cultural relativism and racism' (IKWRO, 2012a). Such views and others to the contrary would surface again two years later when forced marriage became a *de facto* criminal offence in England and Wales.

The Criminalisation of Forced Marriage: The Anti-Social Behaviour, Crime and Policing Act 2014

On 16 June 2014, the *Anti-Social Behaviour, Crime and Policing Act 2014* came into force (Hansard, 2014). Under provisions included in Part 10 of the Act, forced marriage became a criminal act in England and Wales; anyone knowingly in breach of a FMPO would therefore be 'guilty of an offence' (Hansard, 2014: 84). The Act states:

> **121 Offence of forced marriage: England and Wales**
> (1) A person commits an offence under the law of England and Wales if he or she –
> (a) uses violence, threats or any other form of coercion for the purpose of causing another person to enter into a marriage, and
> (b) believes, or ought reasonably to believe, that the conduct may cause the other person to enter into the marriage without free and full consent. (Hansard, 2014: 86)

The Act allows for law enforcement agencies to pursue perpetrators overseas, for it makes 'forcing a UK national into marriage outside the UK an offence under domestic law for the first time. The offence is triable in courts in England and Wales' (Gov.uk, 2014b). Victims of forced marriage will be able 'to pursue a civil or criminal option' as 'the new criminal offences will work alongside existing civil legislation [that is FMPOs]' (Gov.uk, 2014b). The new law also stipulates the different penalties applicable: 'on summary conviction' those found guilty would be liable 'to imprisonment for a term not exceeding 12 months or to a fine or both' and 'on conviction on indictment, to imprisonment for a term not exceeding 7 years' (Hansard, 2014: 86).

To mark the historic occasion of criminalising forced marriage, the Home Office together with the FMU, the Crown Prosecution Service (CPS), the Police and Freedom Charity released a video entitled #Freedom2Choose aimed at raising awareness of the landmark legislation (Freedom Charity, 2014). In the short film, the Home Secretary, Theresa May said:

> Forced marriage is a fundamental breach of human rights that robs people of the opportunity to choose their own future. It can lead to abuse, rape and even murder in the most tragic cases. That's why forced marriage is now a crime. Everyone should have the freedom to choose. (Freedom Charity, 2014)

Echoing her words, the Crime Prevention Minister, Norman Baker, in turn added:

> Forced marriage is an appalling form of abuse which crosses borders and cultural boundaries ... Legislation is the next key step in solving this problem and builds on the hard work already being done by the government and third sector organisations ... The message from the coalition government is clear – forced marriage is totally unacceptable and will not be tolerated. (Gov.uk, 2014b)

The official announcement regarding the new legislation was well-received across the board, particularly as many stakeholders had long campaigned to achieve this outcome. However, the deep-seated ideological divisions between those advocating criminalising forced marriage and those opposed to it were once more laid bare. Khanum reminds us of how 'forced marriage is universally condemned, even by the perpetrators. Few people openly support force in a marriage' (Khanum, 2008: 8). As a variant of domestic violence and human rights abuses, the use of coercion to compel someone to marry against their will is a practice indeed rejected by British society at large. Yet, given the complex nature of this 'honour' related offence, profound differences of opinion among interested parties remain as to how best frame forced marriage within the law and punish those – usually parents and close family members – who forcibly coerce their relations into marrying. A snapshot of stakeholders' reactions to the new law and accompanying arguments in favour and against making forced marriage a criminal offence is presented next.

The Case 'For' Criminalising Forced Marriage

Supporters of criminalising forced marriage in the UK have pointed to the case of Scotland where legislation outlawing the practice has already been in place since 2011. As the Scottish government states: 'It is everyone's human right to choose their own partner and if a family member or partner uses either emotional or physical pressure to force marriage upon you, then it is an abuse of your basic rights' (The Scottish Government, 2012). Consistent with the views expressed during the original public consultation on forced marriage in 2011, those advocating criminalisation 'felt that it would act as a deterrent and deliver a strong message', that such practice would not be tolerated and perpetrators would face prosecution; victims would in turn be empowered 'to come forward and report incidents of forced marriage' (Home Office, 2012: 5). Unsurprisingly grassroots women's groups which have long campaigned for the criminalisation of forced marriage were among the strongest advocates of the new legislation. Jasvinder Sanghera, founder of Karma Nirvana, for instance said:

> I sincerely welcome the Prime Minister's announcement that the Government is making forced marriage a criminal offence.
>
> Furthermore, I welcome the conviction in which David Cameron sends out the message; I hope other leaders will follow. I echo this conviction of how forced marriages are *'little short of slavery'* that it is necessary to make this a crime because it is an absolute abhorrent practice.
>
> I personally have campaigned for changes in the law for over 15 years. This for me will always be a historic day as the Government have listened to the many voices who call the Karma Nirvana Helpline which currently receives over 500 calls a month. (Sanghera cited in Karma Nirvana, 2013b)

In a similar way, Diana Nammi, Director of IKWRO, reiterated her backing of the legislation as a key measure in disincentivising prospective perpetrators:

> We have campaigned long and hard for the criminalisation of forced marriage, which equates to slavery, for a number of years because this is what the women that we represent tell us they want. Criminalisation makes it absolutely clear to everyone that forced marriage is not tolerated in the UK. The absence of a specific criminal offence thus far has undermined the movement to end forced marriage. Criminalisation is a crucial deterrent; many of our clients have told us that if forced marriage had been criminalised when they were facing it, their

families may not have gone ahead with it because they would have abided by the law. (Nammi cited in IKWRO, 2014a)

Besides long-established grassroots activists, newly formed organisations such as Freedom Charity also welcomed the new legislation. Anneta Prem, founder of Freedom Charity, which took part in the official *#Freedom2Choose* video launch, expressed her support for the new legislation as safeguarding individual human rights:

> I am delighted that the government has taken action to criminalise forced marriage. In the most tragic cases, people forced into marriage become domestic slaves by day and sexual slaves by night.
>
> Today's announcement sends out a powerful message that this indefensible abuse of human rights will be not be tolerated.
>
> Everyone should have the freedom to choose. (Prem cited in Gov.uk, 2014b)

Religious-based women's groupings like the Muslim Women's Network UK (MWNUK) similarly voiced their support for criminalising forced marriage. Faeeza Vaid, Executive Director of MWNUK, remarked:

> The impact of being forced into marriage can be devastating for its victims. In agreement with Universal Human Rights, I believe that Forced marriages are unacceptable and illegal in Islam. And so the introduction of these criminal laws is not about scapegoating parents, individuals or communities, they are about standing firm for justice ... we need to encourage victims not to suffer in silence. It is my personal hope that this law will act as a deterrent to those who think this abhorrent crime is acceptable. (Vaid cited in MWNUK, 2014)

Mainstream Third Sector organisations working in the domestic violence field likewise supported forced marriage becoming a crime. Sandra Horley CBE, Chief Executive of Refuge, the leading charity providing safe houses for women and children escaping domestic abuse, called for greater accountability for perpetrators together with preventive measures to avoid 'honour' crimes being committed; she said:

> Forcing someone to marry is a serious crime. Victims of this form of abuse are often threatened, intimidated, kidnapped, beaten, raped and even killed. I am pleased that, from today, perpetrators of this horrific behaviour will face the full weight of the criminal law ... Criminalising forced marriage sends a strong message to society. However, legislation alone will not end this form of abuse. Our law enforcement agencies must ensure that perpetrators are apprehended and prosecutions are rigorously pursued. Forced marriage must

also be prevented: this will require effective deterrent measures, expert training for professionals and far-reaching awareness-raising campaigns. And support for victims is also essential. (Horley cited in Refuge, 2014)

Backing for the new law was equally forthcoming from those working in the area of child protection, which saw the new legislation as a means to afford protection to vulnerable young people. Dr Ash Chand, Strategy Head for Minority Ethnic Children at the NSPCC, argued that:

The change in the law to make forced marriage a crime in England and Wales is a huge step forward which we hope will deter those plotting against their own children.

Many young people who call our ChildLine service about this issue are frightened, concerned and feel control of their lives is being wrenched from them. (Chand cited in Gov.uk, 2014b)

Professional bodies with legal expertise were also among those advocating the new legal framework. The Law Society, for instance, which represents 'more than 140,000 solicitors qualified in England and Wales' (The Law Society, 2012), stated its support of criminalisation in its response to the government's original public consultation on forced marriage:

The Law Society is in favour of making both forced marriage and the breach of Forced Marriage Protection Orders (FMPO) criminal offences. This would provide certainty to victims and would send a strong deterring signal to potential offenders. It would also ensure that victims who are emotionally coerced into a forced marriage have a means of legal redress and facilitate the prosecution of forced marriages.

The police recorded 2823 honour attacks in the UK in 2011. During the first two years and four months after the Forced Marriage (Civil Protection) Act 2007 came into force of the 293 FMPOs that were made, only one order was enforced with a jail sentence for breach. (The Law Society, 2012)

In addition, statutory bodies operating within the criminal justice system such as the CPS had argued for greater legal redress being afforded to victims of forced marriage:

Depending on the facts of the individual case, the CPS is currently able to prosecute FM related cases and the charge chosen will depend on the seriousness of the offending behaviour. If a new criminal offence was created for FM,

> depending on the facts and circumstances of the case, the CPS would still decide
> to charge other offences if that better reflected the gravity of the offending (e.g.
> rape, kidnapping etc.). (CPS cited in Home Office, 2012: 8)

Despite widespread support for criminalisation of forced marriage, the new legislation – as had its predecessor – came under close examination from a variety of stakeholders who voiced their concerns over the suitability of its new provisions. Some of their arguments are examined next.

The Case 'Against' Criminalising Forced Marriage

Opposition to making forced marriage a crime was presented both as a matter of principle as well as direct criticism of the new law, its perceived flaws and unintended consequences. Critics, for instance, pointed to existing UK legislation already dealing with associated offences committed when forcing someone to marry, such as human rights abuses, rape, abduction and so on. Rather than introducing additional legislation to deal specifically with forced marriage, current legislative measures should be instead fully implemented, they argued. Besides, the high burden of proof required under criminal law would make it more difficult to prosecute forced marriage cases. It was also claimed that new legislation would be counter-productive as victims would be discouraged from coming forward if their relatives faced a prison sentence as a result, thus driving the practice underground. Once again, these views were fully consistent with those previously expressed in the original public consultation on forced marriage in 2011 (Home Office, 2012: 5).

In contrast with Third Sector advocates of criminalising forced marriage, a number of their grassroots peers voiced their opposition to the new law. One of the strongest detractors of the legislation was SBS, the minority ethnic women's service provider, which, as already indicated, had been 'compelled to resign from the Working Group [on Forced Marriage] when the Group insisted on offering mediation and reconciliation as options to women [who] were at risk of forced marriage' (SBS, 2014b). With the new law now in place, its initial opposition to the criminalisation route remained. Whilst being 'sympathetic' to the principle of criminalising forced marriage, SBS argued that 'on balance, a new criminal offence would not serve the main objective of protecting women and girls from forced marriage', instead being 'very likely to drive the problem underground' (SBS, 2014b). SBS furthermore emphasised the impact that the legislation may have on victims coming forward:

> our experience showed us that the overwhelming majority of our service users,
> while wanting to escape a forced marriage, did not wish to criminalise their

parents and family members and would not come forward if they felt that this would be the end result of their complaint. We strongly felt that a more effective solution lay in providing properly resourced specialist services to meet emergency and long term support. (SBS, 2014b)

Imkaan, a 'national Black, Minority Ethnic and Refugee (BME) second-tier organisation dedicated to working on violence against women and girls (VAWG)' (Hansard, 2013b) expressed similar concerns regarding the criminalisation of forced marriage. In its written submission to the parliamentary *Anti-Social Behaviour, Crime and Policing Bill, Session 2013–2014*, it stated:

Imkaan welcomes the government's commitment to addressing forced marriage … However, we remain concerned about the proposal to create a specific criminal offence on forced marriage. As is the case with any area of work, prosecution cannot work on its own and is not enough. We remain concerned that criminalisation of forced marriage would further drive the practice underground, potentially resulting in more girls and boys being removed to other countries without warning. The new legislation would need to run in parallel with other sources of support if women and girls are to come forward for help and get timely and appropriate assistance and advice. (Hansard, 2013b)

The Henna Foundation, 'which has helped hundreds of victims of forced marriage over the last 15 years' (Barrett, 2014), also challenged the new law. Shereen Williams, speaking for the Foundation, said 'David Cameron was hell bent on making this a criminal offence but we're not sure how it will help'; she explained how 'Victims will be very reluctant to take action that could lead to the imprisonment of their parents or other family members' (Williams cited in Barrett, 2014). In its response to the government's initial consultation on forced marriage, the Henna Foundation had moreover alluded to the difficulties of prosecuting forced marriage cases:

Deep-rooted attitudes and indoctrination cannot be changed overnight or eradicated by the creation of a criminal offence. The CPS [Crown Prosecution Service] will need to satisfy the high criminal standard of proof, namely 'beyond reasonable doubt'. Considering the evidential difficulties of crimes the likelihood of a successful prosecution is very doubtful. It will be almost impossible to define a crime of forced marriage, as it would have to be drawn widely. The wider it is the more it lends itself to loopholes and defences being found to get round the charge(s). (Henna Foundation cited in Home Office, 2012: 10)

Another women's group which rejected the idea of criminalising forced marriage is Ashiana Network, a specialist refuge provided for women from

South Asian, Turkish and Iranian Diaspora communities in the UK. Ashiana Network objected to the new law mainly on the basis of existing legislation allowing for appropriate civil and criminal remedies being already in place:

> We do not support criminalisation of forced marriage. The current existing frameworks, combining criminal and civil legislation and the Forced Marriage Statutory Guidelines, provide adequate mechanisms to address forced marriage. Legislation in the UK does not operate in the same way as it does in other EU countries. It is designed with the specific aim to prosecute, not as a tool for changing attitudes or developing more responsive policies. Whilst we recognise the symbolic value of criminalising forced marriage, we are concerned that this will create an inadequate and inappropriate response to women fleeing forced marriage and therefore have limited impact. It may even deter women from seeking remedy through the civil courts. (Ashiana Network, 2012b: 10–11)

A further body that raised concerns about criminalising forced marriage was the Equality and Human Rights Commission (EHRC), whose parliamentary mandate is intended 'to challenge discrimination, and to protect and promote human rights' (EHRC, 2014). The EHRC welcomed the criminalisation of the breach of FMPOs, but it did not support turning forced marriage into a full-blown criminal offence on the basis that sufficient protection exists under current law:

> The Commission condemns forced marriages and considers that a forced marriage is a serious violation of human rights and one which may amount to domestic violence against women and children in some situations … The Commission supports the government's intention to make a breach of a forced marriage protection order a criminal offence. However, we are not sure that the case is yet made for the proposal that a forced marriage in itself be made a criminal offence. A new offence could have a deterrent effect and send a clear signal that the practice is unacceptable but we believe that the current law is adequate for the purposes of protection and prevention if properly enforced. (EHRC, 2012)

Given the complexity of the issues involved in making forced marriage a crime, it is not surprising that differences of opinions extended to various constituencies within religious groups, with the Muslim community providing a case in point. While the Muslim Women's Network UK (MWNUK), for example, welcomed the criminalisation of forced marriage, its peers from the Muslim Council of Britain (MCB) remained opposed to it. In line with the MCB's response to the original government consultation on forced marriage, its former Secretary General and Chairman of the East London Mosque Trust, Muhammad Abdul

Bari, reiterated his rejection of the new legislation. Echoing some of the now familiar arguments, he said: 'As criminal law already provides punishment for offences that may be committed when coercing someone into matrimony there is no necessity, in my opinion, to create a new law' (Bari, 2012). Victims of forced marriage too differed in their approach to the criminalisation question. On the one hand, there were those who recognised the vulnerability of their own position when being coerced into a marriage, as one female victim put it: 'Being in a situation where you have those you trust manipulating you to do something against your wishes is awful. You don't want to upset them, and they try lots of emotional ways to get you to agree' (victim cited in MWNUK, 2014). These individuals accordingly view the new law and the rights it confers them as empowering to women (IKWRO, 2012b). Other victims, however, find that very same law too exacting in its punishment of perpetrators, often their close family and relatives. In the words of another female victim: 'With regards to Forced Marriages being criminalized, I feel it is a bit too drastic … for example if someone's parents are involved then how can their child send them to jail or let them be punished' (Ashiana resident cited in Ashiana, 2012b: 10).

On the whole, notwithstanding the widespread support enjoyed by government policy on the legality of forced marriage, disagreements on the criminalisation question have remained throughout the 'reform' stage of this multilayered social problem and are likely to continue in the foreseeable future.

Conclusion

In tracing the evolution of forced marriage in contemporary British society, Fuller and Myers' (1941) 'Natural History' framework has provided a suitable empirical model that helps to explain the rise of this social problem from the margins of grassroots service provision to the centre of the government's political and legislative agenda. Consistent with the stages originally identified in their trailer campsites study in Detroit during the early twentieth century, forced marriage in modern Britain has largely progressed through the phases of 'awareness', 'policy determination' and 'reform'. From the outset, a peripheral issue relegated to the specialist area of domestic violence against minority ethnic women, knowledge and awareness of forced marriage and 'honour'-based violence remained largely limited to the local and regional community level for decades. In the late 1990s, a combination of political change, greater gender representation in parliament together with a number of high profile cases of 'honour' related offences reported in the press – including those of Rukhsana Naz, 'Jack' and 'Zena' Briggs and girl KR – heralded a period of 'awareness' in which the forced marriage problem moved from the fringes of British society to the mainstream. This process saw the 'honour' question acquiring an unprecedented degree of public prominence and was accompanied by a growing body of knowledge and evidence on the subject.

By 1999, the establishment of the government-led Working Group on Forced Marriage and the subsequent publication of *A Choice by Right* a year later signalled the transition of the forced marriage issue into its 'policy determination' phase. Here, the ground-breaking public policy consultation involving a wide range of stakeholders revealed a plethora of different and often opposing views on the subject of forced marriage, particularly regarding the contentious matter of making this practice a criminal offence. While the Working Group rejected the idea of criminalisation, underlying tensions remained well into the final 'reform' stage of this seemingly intractable social problem.

The publication of *A Choice by Right* in 2000 inaugurated an extended period of institutionalisation of the forced marriage question by successive governments. Over the past decade, a string of policy and legislative measures aimed at tackling forced marriage and 'honour' related offences have come to see the light: from the setting up of the Forced Marriage Unit (FMU) in 2005 to deal with the problem, to the publication of the *Forced Marriage (Civil Protection) Act 2007* introducing FMPOs as civil remedies and the eventual criminalisation of forced marriage in England, Wales and Northern Ireland – following the Scottish example – under provisions included in Part 10 of *the Anti-Social Behaviour, Crime and Policing Act 2014*. All of these new initiatives have served to illustrate the high status forced marriage has come to enjoy nowadays and the seriousness with which it is regarded by the British government and society at large. In line with Fuller and Myers' model, this final 'reform' stage in the 'Natural History' of the forced marriage problem remains an ongoing developmental process and thus continues to run its course at the present time.

Having mapped out the transformation of forced marriage from its humble grassroots origins to the epicentre of the British political establishment, the following chapter will focus attention on the collaborative nature of 'honour' related offences. Often perpetrated with the acquiescence of close relatives and members of the neighbouring community, forced marriages and 'honour' killings involve a collective effort habitually shrouded in a conspiracy of silence. Chapter 5 will thus examine the role played by family, kinship and community networks in the aiding and perpetuating of these crimes. Drawing from the book's feminist perspective, the chapter will moreover consider whether community and religious leaders may also play a part in either challenging or preserving the *status quo*.

Chapter 5
Community Leadership, Networks and the 'Politics from Back Home'

Patriarchal Diasporas: Gatekeepers of the *Status Quo?*

Questions have long been raised about the reactionary nature of community leadership in the UK and its apparent unwillingness to effectively address culturally challenging issues affecting their constituents (Home Office, 2001). The official publication in 2001 of *Community Cohesion: A Report of the Independent Review Team chaired by Ted Cantle* in response to urban disturbances in towns and cities across England laid bare some of the shortcomings of local stewardship at the time:

> The failure to communicate is compounded by the lack of an honest and robust debate, as people 'tiptoe around' the sensitive issues of race, religion and culture. This appears to be prevalent within the black and ethnic minority communities as well as between white and non-white communities. (Home Office, 2001: 18)

While recognising that 'Strong local leadership is an essential part of community cohesion' (Home Office, 2001: 46, para. 6.5), the *Cantle Report* acknowledged that 'the lack of leadership in some areas has undoubtedly led to the growth of racist and extremist groups' (Home Office, 2001: 21, para. 5.2.1).

Within the context of Britain's 'honour'-based cultures, dissatisfaction with institutional inertia and lack of direction from those supposedly representing the interests of their peers continues nowadays. Disappointment with community leadership has most strongly been voiced by victims of 'honour' offences and their families together with women's grassroots service providers and activists. Jagdeesh Singh, whose sister Surjit Athwal's 'honour' killing in 1998 was featured in Chapter 3, has for decades denounced the reluctance of Britain's Sikh community leaders and those of the wider 'honour'-based Diasporas to openly engage with the 'honour' question:

> There is this very distinctive and self-incriminating silence within communities that have a history of 'honour' killings ... The so-called community leaders, the influential religious groups and the local language newspapers remain deafeningly

silent when these killings happen. But that silence makes them just as guilty as the people who kill in the name of honour. (Singh cited in Taylor, 2009)

Some 'conservative and older elements' within Singh's Sikh community may regard him 'as a troublemaker who needlessly provokes controversy by shining an unwelcome spotlight on things that should not be aired in public' (Taylor, 2009). Singh however continues to argue that 'The communities that suffer from "honour" killings don't want to be drawn into a debate about a type of murder they would far rather ignore … But they need to start having that debate; because we're not going to win this fight without them' (Singh cited in Taylor, 2009).

Anne Cryer, MP for Keighley and veteran campaigner for women's rights, has also been the target of 'intense criticism from many male Muslim elders in her constituency' for her 'outspoken stance' on 'the problem of domestic violence and so-called "honour" killings of young Asian women in Britain by their families' (Drury, 2008). In 2010, Cryer described a conversation with a local community leader in which he justified the use of forced marriage among his constituents as a proxy for divorce. In her evidence of the *House of Commons Home Affairs Committee – Follow-up to the Committee's Report on Domestic Violence, Forced Marriage and Honour-Based Violence*, she recollects how:

> Less than a year ago one of the chief gatekeepers of my community actually said to me in great confidence, and I am sure he believed in what he was saying to me, 'You know, Ann, it's like this: these girls come to you and talk about forced marriages. They are not forced into marriage. It is just that there is a problem in our community about divorce and therefore they call divorce due to a forced marriage and it excuses it', and I said: 'Look: I just don't want to hear this'. It just was not the case. (Cryer cited in Hansard, 2010: Q33, Ev 6–7)

As revealed in Chapter 4, it has been mainly minority ethnic women's groups and in particular South Asian grassroots organisations which, unlike their male counterparts, have over the years led the way in service provision, lobbying and campaigning for victims of 'honour' offences. Their efforts to eradicate harmful practices such as forced marriage, FGM and 'honour' killings have frequently been at odds with the still largely paternalistic outlook of the population groups they work with. It is not surprising that female activists have come to view those in positions of authority among their own communities as being part of the problem, not the solution. In their written evidence to the *House of Commons, Home Affairs Committee, 'Forced Marriage', Eighth Report of Session 2010–2012*, the women's campaigning group Southall Black Sisters (SBS) provided an unequivocal assessment of their experience of Black and Minority Ethnic (BME) community leadership:

the leadership within BME communities is conservative and dominated by male community and religious leaders who will not proritiese [*sic*] or take action to tackle violence against BME women and girls. Indeed, some fundamentalist and orthodix [*sic*] sections will reinforce opporessive [*sic*] practices such as forced marriage and honour based violence. (SBS cited in Hansard, 2011a: Ev 22)

Diana Nammi, Director of the Iranian and Kurdish Women's Rights Organisation (IKWRO) and recipient of the Woman of the Year Award 2014,[1] furthermore illustrates the obstacles organisations such as IKWRO frequently encounter when highlighting the plight of their service users. Explaining her original decision to support making forced marriage a criminal offence, Nammi reveals how IKWRO had regularly faced attempts to silence them:

Some people have said that criminalising forced marriage will intensify negativity towards minority communities. IKWRO has repeatedly heard this argument made about all of our work raising awareness on all forms of 'honour' based violence. We have been told to be quiet about all negative issues within our communities. But we strongly disagree. We both represent and are largely made up of minority women and we must at the same time expose human rights abuses and fight racism; the two are not mutually exclusive. We believe that staying silent about human rights abuses faced by women and girls from minority communities is racist. By turning our back and allowing harmful practices such as forced marriage to continue unchallenged, we actually leave the community to face stigmatisation and discrimination. We must prioritise the safety of minority women and girls, we must protect their universal human rights and fight for equality. (Nammi quoted in IKWRO, 2014a)

Jasvinder Sanghera, founder of Karma Nirvana, has also faced hostility within the South Asian community she belongs to over her equally multi-award winning work and forthright views on the 'honour' question. In the past two decades, she has experienced intimidation, 'received countless death threats, had excrement smeared over her office windows and had people shout at her in public' as well as being the target of a hoax purporting to have placed a bomb underneath her car (Brooker, 2013). Sanghera has nevertheless been an ardent critic of cultural and religious traditions detrimental to women as well as the role that community leaders, particularly those within South Asian Diasporas, continue to play in sustaining such practices:

---

1   Diana Nammi received the Woman of the Year Award 2014 'for her work to protect the rights of Middle Eastern and North African women and to end "honour" based violence, forced marriage, female genital mutilation (FGM) and domestic violence' (IKWRO, 2014b).

I've yet to see community leaders, religious leaders, Asian councillors, politicians give real leadership on this ['honour'-related offences]. They don't because they know it makes them unpopular. They know this is happening. And to know that significant abuse in your communities is happening and not to demonstrate real leadership on this is extremely irresponsible. It's morally wrong and it's morally blind. (Shangera featured in BBC *Panorama*, 2012)

Even when male members of 'honour'-based communities speak out against 'honour' violence, they have often found themselves at the receiving end of hostility and threats from their own constituents. In 2010, Nazir Afzal, National Director for Community Liaison at the Crown Prosecution Service (CPS), described the difficulties facing minority ethnic 'male role models' who publicly denounce 'honour' related practices (Afzal cited in Hansard, 2010: Q24, Ev 5). At the time, Afzal was responding to a question put to him by David Davies MP during his evidence to the *House of Commons Home Affairs Committee – Follow-up to the Committee's Report on Domestic Violence, Forced Marriage and Honour-Based Violence*:

Q24 David Davies: Mr Afzal, we have heard from female members of minority communities like Jasvinder Sanghera but less so from male members. Within the communities where this is an issue, are there lots of male role models who are saying this is totally wrong and we have to change as a community?

Mr Afzal: 'Lots' might be an exaggeration but, yes, there are plenty of men who are speaking out now yet they themselves are being threatened. You can go on to the blogosphere and see people threatening me. Men have to be – and I am not speaking for myself – very bold and courageous to come out and they need to have safety in numbers, I guess, to speak out about this subject. I do think there are more and more. Very recently I was talking to the Islamic Cultural Centre here in London and they are working with 90 others around the country to send out some strong messages on this subject which would not have entered their radar a year or so ago. (Davies and Afzal cited in Hansard, 2010: Q24, Ev 5)

Despite the public awareness efforts described then, by 2000, the Home Office Working Group on Forced Marriage had already recognised the inadequate response to forced marriage among those in positions of influence within 'honour'-based Diasporas (Home Office, 2000). So-called 'opinion formers' identified by the Working Group included 'anyone who is able to influence values, attitudes and behaviours' such as 'Religious and community leaders', 'local and national politicians, leaders of community and women's groups' (Home Office, 2000: 20). Unhappiness with the performance of many of these individuals and organisations was the overriding assessment from the stakeholders' feedback gathered by the Working Group:

The Working Group has heard people talk of their disappointment with many of these opinion formers who have failed to speak out against forced marriage because it was seen as a 'taboo' subject. People who have spoken to the Working Group have an expectation that opinion formers will send a clear and consistent message about the unacceptability of forced marriage. It is hoped that following this report, opinion formers will be in a more robust position to lead and send a clear message about the unacceptability of forced marriage. (Home Office, 2000: 20)

It was precisely the prevalent views of 'opinion formers' consulted by the Working Group that led the latter to initially reject making forced marriage a criminal offence. It is worth remembering that during the subsequent public consultation that preceded the implementation of the *Anti-Social Behaviour, Crime and Policing Act 2014* (Hansard, 2014) and thus the *de facto* criminalisation of forced marriage, serious disagreements remained among those purporting to represent the interests of ethnic and religious minorities. While the Muslim Women's Network UK (MWNUK), for instance, advocated the making of forced marriage a criminal offence; their peers at the Muslim Council of Britain (MCB) strongly opposed such move.

Against the background of 'honour' related crimes, community leadership has furthermore come under criticism from those working within the criminal justice system. Cris McCurley, Partner at Ben Hoare Bell LLP, a 'senior family law practitioner in the north east of England … specialised in domestic violence work' and with over 22 years of experience dealing with BME communities, has stressed the patriarchal nature of her clients' community leadership (Hansard, 2011a: Ev 23). In her written evidence to the *House of Commons, Home Affairs Committee, 'Forced Marriage', Eighth Report of Session 2010–2012*, McCurley stated:

I am grateful to be able to evidence that the police in the North East of England have finally stopped referring matters of domestic violence, honour violence and forced marriage back to the [male] community leaders who are often self appointed in any event and, I know from my clients, uphold the very values and traditions that lead to the abuse of these women in many cases. (Hansard, 2011a: Ev 25–26)

Concerns have also been voiced regarding the high incidence of harmful 'honour'-based practices among certain minority groups and their apparent reluctance to address this seemingly intractable issue. Nazir Afzal from the CPS has highlighted the prevalence of 'honour' offences among the UK's Muslim community and how undue emphasis on cultural sensitivities may prevent meaningful steps being taken to tackle the problem:

It needs to be said that the vast majority [of 'honour'-related offences] that we see involve the Muslim community, of which I am member. My view is that there is no place for multicultural sensitivity in this situation. This is something that we cannot tolerate. The moment that I stop looking at a community because somebody tells me it's too sensitive, it's the moment I pack up my file and walk out of the door. (Afzal featured in BBC *Panorama*, 2012)

Afzal moreover argues that patriarchal attitudes to women among members of minority groups which abide by 'honour' codes may underline these communities' position regarding 'honour' crimes. He exemplifies the type of paternalistic mindsets spanning generations of those belonging to 'honour'-based cultures in contemporary British society by reference to the views of an ordinary Muslim young man he came in contact with:

I thought this was a generational thing; it was something that would die out with my generation. Unfortunately I've come across very young people who think the same way. One example: a young man, twenty years old, he says to me, 'Nazir, don't you understand?' he says … 'man is a piece of gold', he says 'woman is a piece of silk'. 'If you drop a piece of gold in mud, you can wipe it clean; but if you drop a piece of silk in mud [is] stained for ever!' That is his view of women. That's why he thinks that women must be controlled, that their behaviour cannot be allowed to just go unchecked. And so that's a twenty year old. (Afzal featured in BBC *Panorama*, 2012)

Such anecdotal evidence has long been echoed in the literature, with successive attitudinal surveys and scholarly research into UK minorities' perceptions of culturally based 'honour' traditions consistently pointing to a broad acceptance of the latter by Diasporas where such practices prevail (Samad and Eade, 2002; Brandon and Hafez, 2008; ComRes, 2014). Samad and Eade's (2002) study of *Community Perceptions of Forced Marriage* identified 'honour' based traditions as firmly rooted within Britain's South Asian communities, as did Brandon and Hafez's (2008) subsequent research into 'honour'-based offences. In 2006, an ICM poll conducted for the *Sunday Telegraph* revealed that 'Four out of 10 British Muslims want sharia law introduced into parts of the country' (Hennessy and Kite, 2006). At the time, 40 per cent of the British Muslims surveyed said they 'want to see Islamic sharia law in force in UK communities which are predominantly Muslim' (Hennessy, 2006). On the other hand, 41 per cent opposed such a move (Hennessy and Kite, 2006). Four in five of the respondents also said 'they still want to live in and accept Western society' and 'More than nine in 10 say they feel personally "loyal" to Britain' (Hennessy, 2006). Martin Boon, ICM polling expert, who had assessed British Muslims as 'still moderate in most senses' explained how 'We have run a number of these polls now over the past few years and it seems to me that as a group, British Muslims have now somewhat hardened their views' (Hennessy, 2006). Sadiq Khan, Labour Muslim MP, described the findings of the ICM polls as 'alarming', while Sir Iqbal Sacranie, then Secretary-General of the Muslim Council of Britain (MCB), argued that 'The results on the sharia law question reflect the degree of importance that many British Muslims attach to living by an Islamic code of ethics and morality' (Hennessy, 2006). A spokesperson for Charles Clarke, the then Home Secretary, in turn stated that 'It is critically important to ensure that Muslims, and all faiths, feel part of modern British society. Today's survey indicates we still have a long way to go … [but] we are committed to working with all faiths to ensure we achieve that end' (Hennessy and Kite, 2006).

In 2012, a further ComRes opinion poll was commissioned by the BBC's *Panorama* specifically to explore the attitudes of Asian groups living in Britain – including Indian, Pakistani, Bangladeshi, Mixed Asian and Other Asian – regarding 'honour'-based practices (ComRes, 2014). On this occasion, the research found that over two-thirds (69 per cent) of young UK-based Asians surveyed aged between 16 and 34 'agree that families should live according to the concept of "honour" or "*izzat*"' (ComRes, 2014). Young Asian men in particular were more likely than their female counterparts to agree that families should abide by 'honour' codes, with 75 per cent of men believing so compared with 63 per cent of women (ComRes, 2014). Similarly, younger people were more likely than older cohorts to wish to live in accordance with 'honour' traditions, with 73 per cent of 16–24-year-old Asians advocating 'honour'-based customs compared with 64 per cent of 25–34-year-olds (ComRes, 2014). Only 6 per cent of young Asians said that 'in certain circumstances it can be right to physically punish a female member of the family if she brings dishonour'; however when presented with a range of possible motives, 18 per cent of respondents chose at least one as a 'reasonable justification', with Asian women as likely as men to agree 'they should be punished' (ComRes, 2014). Reasons for punishing women included: 'disobeying a father' (8 per cent); 'marrying someone unacceptable' (7 per cent) or 'wanting to end a marriage' (7 per cent) (ComRes, 2014). On the other hand, when asked if 'there is ever a justification for so-called "honour" killings', the overwhelming majority (94 per cent) of young Asians did not think so under any circumstances, with only 3 per cent finding it acceptable (ComRes, 2014).

In order to fully understand the significance of these figures and the factors underlying gendered attitudes within Britain's 'honour'-based cultures, the UK's experience needs to be positioned within a wider international context. The next section therefore briefly considers the existence of a similar patriarchal outlook in the countries of origin of Britain's Diasporas where 'honour' offences prevail.

Home from Home

The migrant nature of Britain's 'honour'-based communities makes it perhaps not surprising that the paternalistic mindsets identified in the literature and the criticisms levelled against their leadership extend beyond the UK's borders into their own homelands, where the subordination of women has in some instances become institutionalised. This is particularly the case given that 'some 90% of honor killings in the contemporary world occur in Muslim countries' (Eisner and Ghuneim, 2013: 408). As already indicated, the ubiquitousness of 'honour' crimes and especially 'honour' killings in Muslim countries, including those in South Asia, the Middle East and North Africa (MENA), is well documented (UNFPA, 2000; UN Security Council, 2006; Kulczycki and Windle, 2011). In 2000, Asma Jahangir, UN Special Rapporteur on Extrajudicial, Summary or Arbitrary Executions, highlighted the role played by state institutions and those in positions of authority in such nations in perpetuating and even legitimising 'honour' violence against women:

> The Special Rapporteur notes that some countries [where 'honour' crimes prevail] retain legislation allowing for reduction of sentences and exemption from prosecution to those who kill in the name of honour. The authorities often maintain a deadly and deliberate silence over such killings, thereby encouraging perpetrators to adopt a self-righteous stance in regard to such inhuman crimes. The courts in many of these countries continue to justify such killings. Lesser punishment is often awarded on the grounds that the victim offered 'provocation' by disobeying or violating cultural norms. (Jahangir cited in UN Economic and Social Council, 2000: para. 81: 28)

Jahangir went on to criticise the detrimental attitudes to women among policy and law-makers alike as well as the unequal treatment of female victims of 'honour' offences before the law in comparison with that afforded to perpetrators:

> the Special Rapporteur was deeply troubled to read judgement upon judgement moralizing upon the conduct of the victims of 'honour killings', while justifying acts of murder by the very people who would be expected to feel love and closeness to the women they so heartlessly kill. The Special Rapporteur is also concerned at the policy adopted by some Governments to protect potential victims of 'honour killings'. While those threatening the lives of these women enjoy total freedom, the victims are placed in prisons or custodial and correctional homes, sometimes for years on end. They are not free to leave these institutions once confined to them. (Jahangir cited in UN Economic and Social Council, 2000: para. 83: 28)

The case of Pakistan was singled out as a Muslim state where the 'honour' violence problem is not only prevalent, but abetted by the nation's political elite and deeply embedded in the very fabric of civic society:

> The Special Rapporteur deplores the refusal of the Senate of Pakistan to discuss a resolution condemning 'honour killings'. The senators favouring such a resolution were physically intimated in the presence of the press and women activists attending the session. The Government of Pakistan has further refused to condemn honour killings despite public protests throughout the country against the decision of the Senate. The Special Rapporteur is deeply concerned at the Government's attitude of tolerance of such killings despite its statement to the contrary at the fifty-fifth session of the Commission on Human Rights. (Jahangir cited in UN Economic and Social Council, 2000: para. 81: 28)

In 2012, Rashida Manjoo, UN Special Rapporteur on Violence Against Women, its Causes and Consequences, similarly reported on persistent socially sanctioned paternalistic attitudes within the world's South Asian region, where individual countries continue to see increasing levels of 'honour' related violence against women (UN General Assembly, 2012). Majoo disclosed how 'despite progress in criminal law reform, the failure [in South Asia] to comprehensively address strong patriarchal values, the high premium on women's chastity and the subordination of women remains a key factor in the prevalence of gender-motivated killings of women in the region' (Manjoo cited in UN General Assembly, 2012: 5). She specifically referred to the cases of India and Nepal:

> despite the prohibition of dowry in the Penal Code of India, the reported number of dowry-related deaths of women had significantly increased from 4,836 (1990) to 8,383 (2009). The limited impact of criminalization in efforts to eradicate killings was also noted in the very low conviction rate (10 per cent). Suicides by women were reported to have become a 'pan-South Asian trend', with suicide due to domestic abuse, forced marriages, the casting out of widows and lack of inheritance rights emerging as the leading cause of death among Nepalese women in the prime reproductive age group (in 2008/2009). In the region, honour killings, acid burning attacks, witch-hunting, foeticide, gender-based violence during caste and communal conflict were also discussed in the context of a lack of acceptance of girls in society and the absence of adequate family support. (Manjoo cited in UN General Assembly, 2012: 5)

The extent to which state institutions, authorities and the courts are seen as perpetuating collective paternalistic mindsets by 'normalising' violence against women while fostering a climate of impunity for perpetrators of 'honour' related offences has also been documented (Al Ashqar, 2014; UN Human

Rights, 2010; UN, 2012b, North, 2013; Burke, 2012, 2013a and 2013b). In 2014, for example, Judge Ahmad Al Ashqar, reporting to the Office of the UN High Commissioner for Human Rights on the judicial implications of the *Murder of Women in Palestine under the pretext of Honour*, revealed that 'The Palestinian judiciary has tended, in the vast majority of its judicial decisions [78.6 per cent of the total number of judgements under review], to mitigate punishment for the perpetrators of the killing of women under the pretext of honour' (Al Ashqar, 2014: 12). This approach, Al Ashqar argued, 'has contributed to the collective consciousness that killing women under the pretext of honour will only be punished by a limited sentence' (Al Ashqar, 2014: 12). Four years earlier, Rabiha Diab, the Palestinian Minister of Women's Affairs, had denounced the persistent treatment of 'honour' killings as a taboo subject and publicly called upon 'the Palestinian Authority Institutions and religious leaders to prioritize its eradication from our society' (Diab cited in UN Human Rights, 2010).

In line with the UK experience, one of the social outcomes of such a collective mentality can be seen reflected in the attitudes of young people to 'honour' violence. Eisner and Ghuneim's (2013) study of *Honor Killing Attitudes Amongst Adolescents in Amman, Jordan* provides a case in point. As an 'extreme form of gendered violence', the authors explain, 'honour' killings ultimately occur 'in the context of societies with strong tribal traditions and a pronounced patriarchal social structure' (Eisner and Ghuneim, 2013: 406). In the case of Amman, Esner and Ghuneim found that 'a large proportion of the young generation in Jordan [about 40 per cent of boys and 20 per cent of girls] believes that killing a woman who has dishonored her family is morally right and justifiable' (Eisner and Ghuneim, 2013: 405 and 415). These common 'attitudes in support of honor killings', the authors contended, 'are anchored in a broader system of beliefs about patriarchal authority and dominance, and assumptions about female virginity and chastity' (Eisner and Ghuneim, 2013: 415). The results of their study suggested that:

> a considerable part of the respondents considered it acceptable to kill a sister, wife, or daughter who has dishonored the family. Boys were about twice as likely as girls to find honor killings acceptable. Within a country that is considered to be modern by Middle Eastern standards this represents a high proportion of young people who have at least some supportive attitudes to honor killing. (Eisner and Ghuneim, 2013: 413)

Elsewhere, socially constructed gendered value systems are seen as so central to understanding the wider phenomenon of 'honour'-based violence that they are now used as official criteria to measure the extent of the problem, particularly among Diaspora communities. In Sweden, for instance, law enforcement authorities assessing cases of 'patriarchal violence with honour as a motive' routinely refer to 'PATRIARCH', an 'evidence-based checklist' that features among 'risk factors': 'Attitudes that support honour violence'; 'Origin from an area with known sub-cultural values' and 'Lack of cultural integration' (Belfrage et al., 2012: 24). In 2011, Belfrage et al.'s six-year assessment of the implementation of PATRIARCH in Sweden revealed that the vast majority of 'honour' victims identified were women (84 per cent) and 'commonly from the Middle East', including countries such as Turkey (36 per cent), Iraq (16 per cent) and Iran (11 per cent) (Belfrage et al., 2012: 25–6).

Scholars and observers remain divided as to whether specific cultural traditions and religious norms may underline the widespread incidence of 'honour' violence in nations where such practices still endure (Kulczycki and Windle, 2011). As previously acknowledged, some authors contend that given the presence of 'honour' violence in many societies as well as at different periods in history, the practice cannot be associated with a specific culture or religion such as Islam (Begikhani et al., 2010; Faqir, 2001). Faqir (2001) has referred instead to the existence of a 'neopatriarchy' within 'honour' cultures and specifically Arab societies, 'where power relationships are not only influenced by gender, but also by class, clan and proximity to the regime. Such relations are based on the subordination of the disadvantaged and the disfranchised' (Fariq, 2001: 67). Within this context, Faqir expounds on the position of Islam:

> A parallel value system seems to exist which is in action not Islamic. Islam abolished the femicide or the burying of young girls in the *jahiliyya* [pre-Islamic] period. However, the protection of honour now takes priority over Islamic teachings. Societal and political structures conspire to form a parallel value system, which is stronger than the Islamic religion. (Fariq, 2001: 74)

In contrast, others view deep-seated paternalistic values, strict moral codes, restricted individual freedom and the oppression of women as intrinsic to Islamic tenets, thus fostering a climate where 'honour' violence against women proliferates (Ali, 2006a and 2007; Manji, 2005). Keith Porteous Wood, Executive Director of the UK's National Secular Society, has unequivocally categorised *Shari'a* Law as a 'non-democratically determined, non-human rights compliant and discriminatory code' under which women fare 'badly' (Wood cited in Bingham, 2014). Kulczycki and Windle's (2011) systematic review of the literature on 'honour' killings in the MENA region furthermore points to the overtly inequitable 'written laws' in Islamic states, which often feature non-democratic regimes, as 'comprising clear proof that honour crimes are sanctioned in many [MENA] countries' (Kulczycki and Windle, 2011: 1456). 'The state apparatus' in these nations, they explain, 'reproduces and effectively reinforces the entrenched patriarchal and other socio-cultural attitudes that give rise to these violent acts ... The view of women as being under the authority of their male kin is deeply culturally rooted, and Islamic tenants are often invoked to reinforce the subordination of women' (Kulczycki and Windle, 2011: 1455).

In 2014, countries in the MENA area registered 'the worst civil liberties scores of any region' in the world (Freedom House, 2014), with many of them lagging behind in human development (UNDP, 2014). Against this backdrop, Turkey provides a topical illustration of the prevailing gendered mindset among MENA nations. At the time of writing, Turkish President Recep Tayyip Erdoğan has publicly declared that equality between men and women is unnatural (Dearden, 2014a). Addressing the Women and Justice Summit in Istanbul in November 2014, President Erdoğan pronounced that 'You cannot make women and men equal; this is against nature'. He added: 'Equality is turning the victim into an oppressor by force or vice versa', before proposing that 'What women need is to be able to be equivalent, rather than equal' (Erdoğan cited in Dearden, 2014a). His remarks followed an earlier speech on 'moral corruption' by his Deputy Prime Minister, Bülent Arınç, in which he called for 'Turkish people to rediscover the Koran and stop moral regression' and suggested that women should protect their 'chasteness' and 'not laugh in public' (Arınç cited in Dearden, 2014b).

In the context of Britain's 'honour'-based Diasporas, it can be argued that the existence of a collective outlook among their members that condones 'patriarchal control, rigid sexual norms and harsh punishment for moral transgressions' (Eisner and Ghuneim, 2013: 408) is consistent with that displayed by their peers in their original homelands. Having thus explored the wider socio-cultural setting in which 'honour' violence takes place and the role played by those in positions of authority in perpetuating it, we shall turn our attention to the collaborative nature of 'honour' crimes. The following section will specifically focus on how Britain's 'honour'-based minorities may resort to the use of community networks and so-called 'bounty hunters' in order to preserve the *status quo*.

'Honour' Codes, Community Networks and 'Bounty Hunters'

'Honour' crimes are widely seen as collective endeavours typically involving several close family relatives of the victims and often members of the local community (Brandon and Hafez, 2008). The many 'honour' offences depicted in the book and particularly the 'honour' killings featured in Chapter 3 attest to the collaborative nature of such acts. From the overseas murder of Surjit Athwal in 1998, to the disappearance and subsequent discovery of Shafilea Ahmed's body in 2004, to the fatal multiple stabbing of Samaira Nazir in 2005, to the gang-rape and strangulation of Banaz Mahmod in 2006 and the ensuing concealing of her remains; all of these crimes entailed a significant degree of premeditated planning and coordination by the perpetrators. They also usually required the involvement of members of the victims' families' extended social networks, which were variously brought into the initial conspiracy to commit murder, the execution of the victims' killings and/or the disposal of the incriminating evidence, as was the case with the murders of Surjit and Banaz.

It is precisely the nature and influence of community networks that is broadly viewed in the literature as an integral part of the patriarchal socio-cultural setting in which 'honour'-based communities operate (Briggs and Briggs, 1997; Sanghera, 2009; BBC *Panorama*, 2012). With their wide ranging scope, community networks' reach may extend well beyond a victim's family's inner circle of relatives and friends. They may span a much broader web of contacts, including those in the resident neighbourhood, local community representatives and even state institutions such as education, health and welfare agencies. Reflecting on the nature of such extensive social networks, Sanghera explains how 'What we have are families living next to each other. They all become the eyes and the ears of the community and they will all be involved in the "honour" system' (Sanghera featured in BBC *Panorama*, 2012). In cases of forced marriages and 'honour' killings overseas, as the ones depicted in the book, community networks have been shown to cross over national boundaries.

Given the informal and secretive character of such socio-cultural networks, their existence remains largely under-researched and is generally only evidenced in personal accounts of survivors of 'honour' violence together with the authorities, practitioners and service providers' own reporting of their effects (Briggs and Briggs, 1997; Athwal, 2013; BBC *Panorama*, 2012; Hansard, 2008 and 2010). Nazir Afzal from the CPS has seen his organisation's efforts to prosecute perpetrators of 'honour' killings time and again thwarted by members of community networks protecting 'their own'. In 2010, during his evidence to the *House of Commons Home Affairs Committee – Follow-up to the Committee's Report on Domestic Violence, Forced Marriage and Honour-Based Violence*, Azfal recalled one such case:

> I prosecuted recently in the case of Tulay Goren, who was the 15-year-old girl who went missing 10 years ago. It took us 10 years to bring her father to justice because of the wall of silence that surrounded that family. We never found her body. I keep asking myself how many other unmarked graves are there around this country where people who are supposed to be protecting their child have not even reported the fact that their child is missing. (Afzal cited in Hansard, 2010: Ev 4)

Grassroots women's groups supporting victims of 'honour' violence have long been aware of the impact of community networks on their clients' lives and, in particular, an even more guarded manifestation of this phenomenon, namely: the hiring of bounty hunters. Philip Balmforth, a leading expert on forced marriages 'who has spent 15 years with West Yorkshire Police's race relations department' says that 'Bounty hunters are not an urban myth', on the contrary, 'Wherever you get an Asian community, someone sets up a business to bring runaway women back home' (Balmforth cited in Hill, 2004). Balmforth explains how:

> While it was once the case that bounty hunters were Asian men, it now includes men of all races, and increasingly women too. Women can get access to female refuges while white men can sometimes get information where Asian men cannot, because they are not suspected. (Balmforth cited in Hill, 2004)

Employed by families to track down missing relatives and runaways, bounty hunters will typically tap into their communities' far-reaching web of contacts to find women and young girls escaping forced marriages as well as those who have absconded against their family's wishes. Bounty hunters are known to 'pay taxi drivers and shop owners to carry photographs of the women and contact them with any information. They put pressure on employees in employment centres and benefit agencies to give out confidential information and infiltrate refuges and hostels' (Hill, 2004). Some families will indeed 'hire female bounty hunters to pose as domestic violence victims to enter refuges and find their target' (Badshah, 2010). Pursued by bounty hunters for over a decade, Jack Briggs, whose story and that of his former wife, Zena, is described in the following section, provides an insight into the inner workings of these shadowy figures:

> This bounty hunter is famous ... within the Asian community. The way it works is that he gets paid a sum in advance for finding a runaway girl, and he doesn't get settlement till he's found her. He uses his own network, the Asian network that stretches across Britain like a web, through restaurateurs, shopkeepers, minicab drivers and so on. He carries photographs and videos, and just goes from city to city, asking if people have seen the girls he's looking for. If they can't help immediately he'll ask them to ring him if they hear anything. And everybody he sees will be happy to co-operate, because no one wants these young women running away from their arranged marriages. It could be their daughter next. (Jack Briggs cited in Briggs and Briggs, 1997: 71)

Aided by such communal support system, a bounty hunter's ultimate 'mission' is to bring the runaways 'back to their families' (Badshah, 2010). Hannana Siddiqui from SBS reiterates the socio-cultural patriarchal basis behind the enduring presence of bounty hunters among 'honour' cultures:

Conservative sections of the community will go as far as hiring a bounty hunter as they have a shared value system which takes priority, along with patriarchal structures and religious value systems ... The family's future is down to marrying their daughter. Men can have friends, get an education and job, and can get married when they're older. But women are [seen as] the embodiment of honour, so their sexuality and moral behaviour is controlled. (Siddiqui cited in Badshah, 2010)

Zakir (assumed name), a 'veteran taxi driver' and former bounty hunter himself, would charge 'around £5,000' to trawl 'the streets of Bradford, Huddersfield, Leeds and Sheffield' searching for his charges (Badshah, 2010). Others can be rewarded with twice as much money (Badshah, 2010). Despite the hefty fees, bounty hunters are not likely to be primarily motivated by financial rewards, but rather by their shared belief in the 'honour' system. That was certainly the case with Zakir:

I did it as a favour to the families, as I knew most of them. It wasn't about the money. It was about *izzat* [honour]. I saw the effect it had on them when their daughter ran away. The worry and the shame from the community talking about them. I was part of the 'taxi driver network', so we shared information about who we picked up and where they got dropped off. (Zakir cited in Badshah, 2010)

Zakir eventually 'got tired of chasing people around' and ceased to be a bounty hunter; but he insists he 'didn't harm any of the girls' and only on 'a couple of occasions I had to speak forcefully to them because they wouldn't come home' (Zakir cited in Badshah, 2010). Increasingly, however, bounty hunters may not be as 'restrained' in the handling of their cargoes as Zakir was, particularly if confronted with Asian women and girls enjoying independent lifestyles. Kaveri Sharma, a legal adviser at the Newham Asian Women's Project in London, says: 'Because women are becoming harder to intimidate, this could mean bounty hunters using more force, or families telling them that, if the girl won't come home, they should not let her continue living' (Sharma cited in Hill, 2004).

One couple who experienced first-hand the lengths to which both bounty hunters as well as the families that hire them will go in order to achieve their objectives are Jack and Zena Briggs (assumed names) (Briggs and Briggs, 1997). Their high-profile case, which shone a rare light on this problem, is related next.

The Story of Jack and Zena Briggs

In 1997, the publication of *Jack & Zena: A True Story of Love and Danger* brought to public attention the remarkable experience of a married couple from Bradford who had spent years in hiding from bounty hunters (Briggs and Briggs, 1997). Dubbed a 'modern-day Romeo and Juliet', Jack and Zena Briggs had met and fell in love in the summer of 1992: she was a young woman from a 'high-caste Muslim family in Leeds'; he was an older local white Englishman from a working-class background (Briggs, 2009). Despite Zena's family's seemingly Westernised outlook, she was expected to marry Bilal, a cousin in Pakistan she hardly knew, by the time she came of age. Of Bilal, Zena says: 'I *knew* that a union between myself and Bilal would be a disaster. But that's not the way we do things in our community. We'd never even raise our eyebrows to our parents, let alone question them. What they said went' (Zena Briggs cited in Briggs and Briggs, 1997: 26). Despite her opposition to the union, Zena was well aware of the potential consequences of disobeying her parents:

> I knew that for my family it was completely out of the question for me to marry anybody but Bilal. Girls who resisted the system – who ran away, even with other Asian men – were ruthlessly hunted down and brought back. They and their families would be in disgrace. Sometimes it didn't stop there. There were stories you heard, or even occasionally read in the press, where women were crippled or murdered for their disobedience. (Zena Briggs cited in Briggs and Briggs, 1997: 38)

A year later, unable to conduct her relationship with Jack in public and faced with the prospect of being forced into a marriage, the couple decided to run away together. Zena's family responded swiftly by issuing death threats against them. On learning of their flight, Mohammed, Zena's father, said to her: 'You died for me the day you left'; he added 'You can't hide from us for ever, Zena. When we catch up with you you're both dead' (Zena Briggs cited in Briggs and Briggs, 1997: 120). Zena's brother, Kasim, went further in spelling out to Jack the punishment that awaited him and Zena should they be found:

> 'You're not going to get far, Jack', he [Kasim] said, and I was immediately shocked by the new cold, matter-of-fact tone in his voice. It was as if I was speaking to another person, not the charming, humorous Kasim I'd been mates with before. 'We've got a bounty hunter out looking for you', he went on. 'I'm selling my cars and I'm going to make it my life's mission to find you. And when we do find you I'm going to make sure you're killed. Slowly. You're both going to end up in binliners. Not one, but several. And when that happens we'll have stone-clad alibis. So you might as well just bring her [Zena] back and leave it at that'. (Jack Briggs, cited in Briggs and Briggs, 1997: 70)

'That was 1993', Zena recalls, 'I've lived my life on a witness protection scheme ever since. My name and address are closely guarded secrets because I fled an arranged marriage' (Briggs, 2009). Their elopement and subsequent marriage would indeed mark the beginning of years of living in hiding, surviving on benefits and frequently moving to different locations around the country; always in fear of their lives. In *Jack & Zena*'s autobiographical account, Zena describes what everyday life had become for the runaway couple:

> I only wish I could say that the whole horror is over, that we're reconciled with my family; or even just that my family have removed the death-threat, told us that they'll allow us to live together in peace ... But I can't. We're still in hiding, still living with the fear that one day they'll catch up with us. Jack still times my trips out to the shops. Even now we haven't unpacked our clothes. There are two big wardrobes in the flat we're in at the moment, but everything's still in bags at the side. That's just the mindset we've got into; we're always waiting, watching, scared inside. (Zenna Briggs cited in Briggs and Briggs, 1997: 218)

In 1999, Anne Cryer MP, who raised Jack and Zena's plight in a *House of Commons Debate on Human Rights (Women)* summed up their situation:

> On the fateful day six years ago when Jack and Zena decided to run away and marry, they knew that there would be problems but hoped that, eventually, her family would accept Jack, as his family accepted her. That was not to be. To this day, a death sentence hangs over the couple, and, over the years, the otherwise decent Bradford Asian family has employed private detectives, bounty hunters and hit men to seek out their once much-loved daughter for the purpose of killing her and her husband, even stooping to punishing them by terrifying Jack's elderly mother who was dying of cancer. (Cryer cited in Hansard, 1999)

By 2006, after 13 years living in hiding, the police informed Jack and Zena that 'their inquiries suggested there was no longer any "credible threat" to their safety' (Rawstorne, 2009). But their lengthy 'clandestine existence' had taken its toll on the couple's relationship and, in 2009, it was reported that Jack and Zena had separated (Rawstorne, 2009). Despite the time elapsed though, the threat to their lives, Jack says, 'is still there, and I don't think it will make a jot of difference when her family finds out that we have split up', 'In their eyes, the damage has been done'; he adds 'It goes back to the whole honour-based culture. We have put a mark – a stain – on their family and it will never go away' (Briggs cited in Rawstorne, 2009).

With the 'honour' question having blighted their lives for so long, Jack and Zena have subsequently been involved in campaigning and raising awareness of forced marriage and related issues (Rawstorne, 2009). Their predicament not only corroborated the existence of UK-based bounty hunters and their extensive community networks; but in line with the experience of other victims of 'honour' violence, it also highlighted significant gaps in available statutory support. Above all, Jack and Zena's story raises serious questions about the 'honour' cultures that turn individuals exercising their free will into fugitives, as well as the community leaders that continue to remain silent about such wrongdoings. While discussing Jack and Zena's case in parliament, Ann Cryer MP appealed to 'the leaders of the Asian Muslim community' to encourage their peers 'to put their daughters' happiness, welfare and human rights first'; she added 'Our Asian women constituents are perfectly entitled to expect the same human rights as are afforded to us and to our daughters. They are also entitled to expect us to help them to enjoy those human rights' (Cryer cited in Hansard, 1999). Back in 1997, Jack had similarly reflected on the wider implications of his and Zena's plight for British society at large:

> I feel so strongly that the problem we are the living embodiment of needs to be sorted out. People died in wars to keep this a free country. And, in the sense that I cannot live in peace and quiet with the woman I love, it is no longer a free country. (Jack Briggs cited in Briggs and Briggs, 1997: 114)

Given the complexity of the issues involved, any steps towards effectively addressing the 'honour' problem are likely to be challenging, if not unsurmountable. But as long as patriarchal attitudes and 'honour'-based collective mindsets prevail, those hired to hunt down other people's relatives will not be driven out of business. As former bounty hunter Zakir explains, 'Nothing'will stop the problem; 'Families will do anything in the name of honour' (Badshah, 2010).

Conclusion

In trying to understand the underlying social structures and values that sustain Britain's 'honour' cultures, the evidence here presented has revealed the existence of a deep-seated patriarchal mindset at the core of Diasporas that abide by 'honour' codes. With a mostly male-dominated reactionary outlook, community leaders have by and large proved unwilling to engage with culturally problematic issues. In particular, matters concerning widespread paternalistic attitudes to women and the inherently sanctioned gendered discrimination the latter are subjected to on cultural and religious grounds. It has therefore fallen to grassroots women's activists and service providers to spearhead the collective drive to deal with 'honour' violence among their constituents. Time and again, these experienced practitioners have not only criticised the conspicuous inaction of what Chris McCurley called 'self-appointed' ethnic minority leaders (Hansard, 2011a: Ev 25–26), but have seen them as part of the problem rather than the solution. In contrast, frontline specialists dealing with the 'honour' phenomenon and those speaking out against its harmful effects have found themselves at the receiving end of the very attitudes responsible for such transgressions. Whether Diana Nammi from IKWRO, Jasvinder Sanghera, from Karma Nirvana, the SBS or Anne Cryer MP; they have all been targeted and often intimidated for their views and efforts to eradicate 'honour'-based practices. Their male counterparts have not fared any better, as the cases of Nazil Afzal from the CPS and Jagdeesh Singh, brother of 'honour' killing victim Surjit Athwal, illustrate.

Scholarly research and attitudinal surveys both in the UK and abroad have corroborated the existence of a similarly paternalistic mindset in the countries of origin of Britain's Diasporas, where 'honour' offences still prevail. Successive UN reports monitoring the 'honour' situation in the world's MENA region have attested to the role played by state institutions, authorities and even legal systems in perpetuating and abating 'honour' violence against women. The literature has moreover confirmed that such gendered attitudes are passed on through generations, with young members of 'honour'-based cultures both at home and abroad embracing the views of their forebears. Within the context of Britain's 'honour'-based Diasporas, this intergenerational trend raises the issue of 'Lack of cultural integration' over time (Belfrage et al., 2012: 24). That is incidentally one of the 'risk factors' identified in Sweden's 'evidence-based list' PATRIARCH, which is regularly used to assess the extent of 'patriarchal violence with honour as a motive' among the Swedish nation's own Diasporas (Belfrage et al., 2012: 24).

Despite the documented prevalence of 'honour' crimes among certain communities and cultures, the literature remains divided regarding the influence that specific cultural and religious codes such as *Shari'a* Law may have in fostering gender discrimination and 'honour' violence against women. This particular debate is unsurprisingly expected to go on. There is however little doubt as to the collaborative nature of 'honour' offences. As Brandon and Hafez (2008) pointed out, 'honour' crimes typically involve a multiplicity of perpetrators colluding in the planning and execution of their offences. The many cases of forced marriages and 'honour' killings depicted in the book have further revealed how families of the victims will often tap into an extended web of connections beyond their inner circle of close relatives and friends, in order to ensure that their criminal acts come to fruition. By relating the story of Jack and Zena Briggs, this chapter has moreover shone a light on a particularly murky use of community networks, that is, the practice of hiring 'bounty hunters' to trace down transgressors of 'honour' codes. Jack and Zena's years in hiding not only illustrate the considerable influence of such community networks; but the lengths to which members of 'honour' cultures will go to protect the *status quo*. The couple's plight ultimately stands as a testament to the enduring power of 'honour'-based patriarchal belief systems, while raising questions as to their place in a wider liberal British society.

With these questions revisited again later in the book, the next chapter will focus instead on practical solutions to the 'honour' violence problem. Chapter 6 will therefore explore the experiences of practitioners and specialists in the front-line of service provision to victims of 'honour' violence, including grassroots women's organisations, government agencies and survivors themselves. Drawing from their experiences and expertise, the chapter will seek to identify key existing challenges and examples of good practice aimed at eradicating the seemingly intractable 'honour' problem.

Chapter 6

Front-Line Views: Challenges for Policy and Practice

Tackling 'Honour' Violence: A Multi-Agency Approach

Given the complex nature of 'honour'-based violence, strategies and interventions aimed at dealing with this phenomenon invariably require a multi-faceted approach involving a variety of stakeholders and agencies. Whether raising public awareness of the 'honour' issue, providing training to front-line professionals, support to victims, funding to grassroots service providers or enacting legislation to prosecute perpetrators; solutions to the 'honour' question seem as intricate and multi-dimensional as the very problem they seek to address. At the time of writing, the government's latest statutory guidance on forced marriage in England and Wales titled *Multi-Agency Practice Guidelines: Handling Cases of Forced Marriage* illustrates this point (HM Government, 2014a). The official publication states that 'As it is unlikely that any single agency will be able to meet all the needs of someone affected by forced marriage'; 'a multi-agency response' is needed that 'encourages agencies to cooperate and work together closely to protect victims' (HM Government, 2014a: 1). The document accordingly 'sets out the responsibilities of Chief Executives, Directors and Senior Managers within agencies involved with handling cases of forced marriage. It covers issues such as staff training, developing inter-agency policies and procedures, raising awareness and developing prevention programmes through outreach work' (HM Government, 2014a: 1). Bodies targeted include colleges and universities, children and adults' social care services, health professionals, local housing authorities, police officers and the Crown Prosecution Service (CPS) among others (HM Government, 2014a).

Four years earlier, the Coalition government had launched its overarching strategic vision to tackle gendered domestic abuse across the board, including 'honour' violence. On 25 November 2010, on the occasion of the International Day for the Elimination of Violence Against Women, a public policy document titled *Call to End Violence against Women and Girls* was published (HM Government, 2010). In her foreword, Theresa May, the Home Secretary, declared that 'No woman should have to live in fear of violence. No man should think it acceptable to perpetrate violence against women. No child should grow up in a home where violence is an everyday occurrence' (May cited in HM Government, 2010: 3). In keeping with the government's sanctioned 'multi-agency' approach, she laid out her Administration's plans to tackle violence against women and girls:

> The ambition of this government is to end violence against women and girls. This is not a short-term task, but a long-term goal, the achievement of which will not be easy ... This is not a task for central government alone. We will need to work with families and communities to change attitudes. Local authorities, Police and Crime Commissioners, voluntary and community organisations, Community Safety Partnerships, the NHS and developing public health service, and the devolved administrations will need to work together to meet the needs of their local communities ... Our work will not stop at the borders of the United Kingdom. For the first time our strategy will include the innovative work we are doing internationally to tackle this global problem. (May cited in HM Government, 2010: 3)

In trying to unravel the government's overarching 'honour' violence strategy, the following sections will highlight briefly some of the key issues identified in the literature and commonly raised by policymakers, practitioners and victims involved in the area of 'honour'-based violence. Given the limited space available here, this chapter can only provide a fleeting glimpse of some of the most salient priorities in an otherwise lengthy list of relevant concerns.

The Knowledge Gap

One of the main difficulties encountered by those involved in the 'honour'-based violence field is the lack of accurate evidence on the subject. Whether figures on forced marriages in the UK or those of British citizens forced to marry overseas, numbers of 'honour' killings on British soil or those of UK nationals perpetrated abroad, or data on school children either at risk of a forced marriage or those already removed from school rolls for that purpose; there are simply no accurate national statistics to speak of, but rather estimates of what is believed to be a much larger problem. As documented in this volume, the hidden nature of the 'honour' phenomenon makes it especially difficult for data to be collected; in addition, reluctance from victims to come forward only compounds the endemic under-reporting so characteristic of the 'honour' violence sector. By and large data collection remains generally fragmented and scattered across a range of sources such as government bodies like the flagship Forced Marriage Unit (FMU), criminal justice agencies such as the CPS, the Metropolitan Police Service and women's grassroots providers as well as scholarly research and the grey literature.

Despite increasing efforts to narrow the 'honour' knowledge gap, which this book seeks to contribute to, the persistent lack of a national standardised system of data collection and analysis continues to remain an obstacle in the mapping, monitoring and prevention of such practices. In 2008, Margaret Moran MP reflected on the effects of the prevalent uncertainty regarding the magnitude of the 'honour' violence problem:

> The true extent of forced marriage will never be known, because so few cases are reported to and recorded by statutory agencies, but local community organisations receive several hundred enquiries about forced marriage each year. Unfortunately, they do not have the counselling services and dedicated advice workers they need to offer support themselves rather than signposting them to other agencies. Consequently, many victims do not in practice have access to services they trust. Community groups involved with forced marriage therefore need core funding so that they can operate effectively. (Moran cited in Khanum, 2008: ii)

Brandon and Hafez (2008) have similarly drawn attention to some gaps in the existing 'honour' related official data when they pointed out how 'The government has not released any estimates on how many women holding British passports have been forcibly taken abroad by their relatives and not allowed to return' (Brandon and Hafez, 2008: 17). Many more examples of such deficiencies have been already revealed in this book, including the Freedom of Information (FOI) request made by the Iranian and Kurdish Women's Rights Organisation (IKWRO) in 2010. On this occasion, the group was seeking to learn about the incidence of 'honour'-based violence reported to the police across the UK during the course of a year (IKWRO, 2011), information which is not otherwise readily available. Most grassroots organisations such as Karma Nirvana and Southall Black Sisters (SBS) carry out their own research in continuing efforts to piece together the missing evidence from official records. Against this background, a more accurate picture of the actual extent of the 'honour' problem in Britain will remain elusive until a national standardised data-gathering and analysis system is put into place.

Limited Resources and No Recourse to Public Funds

In a perennially cash-strapped 'honour' violence sector, the chronic lack of adequate funding is often cited as a key concern by both those managing limited public resources and their counterparts involved in the actual provision of front-line services. The situation of SBS, which is indicative of a sector-wide problem, provides a case in point. In their written evidence submitted to the *House of Commons, Home Affairs Committee, 'Forced Marriage', Eighth Report of Session 2010–2012, Report* (Hansard, 2011a), SBS describe the serious impact of government cuts on the very survival of the organisation:

> Since the last select committee report, when Southall Black Sisters (SBS) faced closure as a result of funding cuts from London Borough of Ealing, a successful legal challange [*sic*] in July 2008 by our service users meant that Ealing Council could not withdraw our funding. Since then, we have been on interim funding, pending a review of local domestic violence services in Ealing. The Council is currently conducting research on domestic violence services in the borough, and will then make a decision on what cuts, if any, they will make to our services, which will come into effect either in October 2011 or April 2012. In the meantime, due to general public sector cuts in the borough, the level of future funding of our services remains uncertain ... Furthermore, increased competition for funding in the recession, has also made it more difficult to obtain funding from other sources such as donations and charitable trusts. We are therefore extremely uncertain about our survivial [*sic*] in the coming two to three years. (Hansard, 2011a: EV22)

In their *Call to End Violence against Women and Girls* strategy, the Coalition government recognises the reality of having to operate in 'an economic climate which requires us to spend less and work more efficiently' (HM Government, 2010: 15). Notwithstanding such environmental constrains, the Home Office has pledged its commitment to keeping 'Tackling violence against women and girls' as a 'key objective over the coming spending review period', while vowing to maintain 'a core of stable funding' to the sector (HM Government, 2010: 15). Such commitment involves a number of undertakings, including to:

- provide over £28m (in total) of stable Home Office funding for specialist services over the next four years ...
- maintain levels of funding support for specified national functions including making over £900,000 available per year over the next four years to support national helplines;
- continue to provide support to victims of forced marriage and frontline practitioners through the Forced Marriage Unit and its national helpline;
- identify an effective and sustainable solution to support women and their children who come to the United Kingdom on a spousal visa and who are forced to flee that relationship as a direct result of proven domestic violence. We will continue to fund support for victims in this situation until we have identified the most suitable way forward. (HM Government, 2010: 16–17)

Despite the government's assurances, grassroots women's groups experiencing similar financial difficulties to those described by SBS have repeatedly raised concerns about the impact that cuts in government funding may have on their ability to maintain an effective level of service provision, and in some cases, to ultimately continue operating.

Uncertainty surrounding SBS's future aside, the organisation has campaigned to draw attention to the plight of a particularly vulnerable client group, namely that of women of 'insecure immigration status' who have no recourse to public funds (Amnesty International UK and Southall Black Sisters, 2008). This cohort is made up of women experiencing multiple and complex needs, yet seemingly left outside of mainstream provision:

> Women with no recourse to public funds include those who entered the UK on valid visas as spouses, students, visitors or workers, women and girls whose visas have expired and who are therefore classified as over-stayers, and women and girls who have been trafficked into the UK. They also include women and girls from European Union access countries, who are also restricted in their ability to access public funds if they have been in the country less than a year, or if they are not registered under the workers registration scheme. (Amnesty International UK and Southall Black Sisters, 2008: 6)

SBS argue that 'no comprehensive UK-wide research' has been carried out 'into the numbers of women fleeing gender based violence who are affected by the no recourse to public funding requirement' (Amnesty International UK and Southall Black Sisters, 2008: 6). Their own estimates put the figure at 'about 600 domestic violence cases a year', but they claim that there may be 'up to 1,000 cases a year – with many going unreported because of the difficulties women face in seeking help' (Amnesty International UK and Southall Black Sisters, 2008: 6). They have consequently called upon the government to implement a number of remedial measures including:

- Guaranteeing the right of women with uncertain immigration status fleeing violence or its threat in the UK, access to crisis, temporary and permanent accommodation, specialist support services and essential financial support by: **exempting women fleeing violence from the no recourse to public funds requirement**.
- To put in place immediate emergency funding to help women across the UK.
- To guarantee adequate core funding of violence against women services and organisations, including specialist services for Black, Minority Ethnic and Refugee women across the UK. (Amnesty International UK and Southall Black Sisters, 2008: 30, original emphasis)

The government has in turn stated being aware of the plight of women with 'insecure immigration status' who 'may have experienced gender-specific violence and/or gender-specific persecution' (HM Government, 2010: 15), while reiterating its commitment to provide them with adequate support whenever feasible. As the *Call to End Violence against Women and Girls* policy document explains:

> Some women enter the United Kingdom on a spousal visa and are subsequently forced to flee that relationship as a direct result of domestic violence. Our intention is to ensure that such women and their children are supported while their case for indefinite leave to remain in the UK is developed and considered. We need to ensure that the solution is both financially viable and sustainable. (HM Government, 2010: 16)

In addition to SBS's calls to abolish the 'no recourse to public funds' requirement for women falling under the 'insecure immigration status' category, two further related issues have been highlighted by stakeholders and women's groups, namely, lack of adequate access to the law and police services. Both matters are examined next.

Accessing Legal and Police Services

Inadequate legal support has been identified by many practitioners and service providers as being detrimental to their constituents. This is particularly the case as vulnerable women escaping 'honour' violence will typically experience financial difficulties and may not be fully aware of their legal rights. Yet they are in great need of legal assistance. Diana Nammi, Director of IKWRO, has urged the government to implement a series of measures to ensure greater access to legal support and the criminal justice system for 'honour' violence victims as well as a better quality of service provision across the board (Nammi quoted in IKWRO, 2014a). She has argued for the delivery of 'Effective training for all professionals working with the public, including the police, judges, health professionals and social services'; raising awareness of 'changes in the law' among both potential victims and perpetrators; 'Provision within immigration law and procedures to permanently protect victims/survivors' and 'Access to justice through legal aid for victims/survivors' (Nammi quoted in IKWRO, 2014a).

Similarly, access to police services by victims of 'honour' violence has often proved problematic, with the many case-studies depicted in the book attesting both to considerable shortcomings as well as good practice. Perhaps the 'honour' killing of Banaz Mahamod in 2006 best exemplifies the two ends of the spectrum (Khan and Prindle, 2012; ITV *Exposure*, 2012). As documented in Chapter 3, having dismissed Banaz's repeated warnings with tragic consequences, the police went on to secure successful prosecutions of her killers in court following ground-breaking investigative and legal work (Khan and Prindle, 2012; ITV *Exposure*, 2012).

Police forces' varying standards of response to victims of 'honour' violence and in particular forced marriage was noted by the *House of Commons, Home Affairs Committee, 'Forced Marriage', Eighth Report of Session 2010–2012, Report* (Hansard, 2011a), which stated:

> The police have been leading the way in pursuing Forced Marriage Protection Orders for victims and potential victims of forced marriage. However, the response to victims varies greatly on a force-by-force basis. We were greatly disturbed by evidence from a victim of forced marriage that she was required to report her situation to a succession of police officers, none of whom treated it sufficiently seriously. We are pleased to note that the Government recognises the importance of training for frontline practitioners in its *Call to End Violence Against Women and Girls Action Plan* and we request information about the outcome of the review of the forced marriage e-learning tool. All appropriate police officers should receive training in recognising and responding to forced marriage and we recommend that the Government consider how best to ensure that this kind of learning is cascaded down to officers, as part of its current review of police training delivery. (Hansard, 2011a: para. 33: 14)

In the meanwhile, it is worth recalling the actual testimony of a forced marriage survivor who gave evidence to the House of Commons, Home Affairs Committee regarding her experience with the police:

> I went to the police. I wanted to take action, but I got told I had to have 15 pieces of evidence to go to court or else I can't go to court … the police officer would change every day. I would have to explain my story every day to someone, and it got really tedious because forced marriages, it is not a small matter, it is a big matter. (Forced marriage survivor cited in Hansard, 2011a: para. 31: 14)

When seeking to improve the experience of clients such as the above survivor in their dealings with the police, Sanghera, founder of Karma Nirvana, has pointed out that while 'the national guidance from the Association of Chief Police Officers had been helpful, effective action was currently dependent upon an officer driving it forward at force-level' (Sanghera cited in Hansard, 2011a: para. 31: 14).

Education and Awareness Raising

A key part of supporting 'honour' violence victims involves providing them with relevant information and advice as well as raising public awareness of their plight. As documented in Chapter 4, since the inception of the FMU in 2005, the Unit has led the government's efforts on the 'honour' violence education and awareness front (FMU, 2014). Besides the FMU's existing public helpline to support 'honour' violence victims and practitioners working with them, the Unit carries out a comprehensive outreach national programme as well as educational and media campaigns (FMU, 2014). The FMU Domestic Programme Fund (DPF) furthermore sponsors grassroots organisations and service providers delivering tailored-made 'honour'-related programmes to various communities and constituent groups (FMU, 2014).

As part of its remit, the FMU also works collaboratively with other government departments such as the Department for Children, Schools and Families (DCSF) to educate and increase awareness of 'honour'-based violence. In 2008, their joint efforts to disseminate information in schools were recognised by the *House of Commons, Home Affairs Committee, 'Domestic Violence, Forced Marriage and "Honour"-Based Violence, Sixth Report of Session 2007–08'* (Hansard, 2008). The report stated:

> We acknowledge that there are areas of good practice in education in schools
> on domestic violence and forced marriage, and we welcome the initiative by
> the Department for Children, Schools and Families (DCSF) to design 'school-
> friendly' materials in conjunction with the Forced Marriage Unit. We recommend
> that the DCSF and FMU work together proactively to distribute these materials
> to all schools, rather than waiting for materials to be requested. (Hansard, 2008:
> para. 93: 38)

Given the key role schools play in the lives of children, parents and communities, educational institutions are at the forefront of the government's strategy to tackle 'honour' violence. Not only schools are charged with instructing and raising awareness of 'honour'-based violence among pupils and their families, but they can identify vulnerable children at risk of forced marriage, providing them with support as well as alerting the authorities. Schools are moreover responsible for monitoring student attendance to ensure pupils who go missing from school rolls are accounted for. In line with the work of the FMU, there are many examples of good practice in the sector. Diana Nammi, from IKWRO, for instance, explains how her organisation is 'working in schools and colleges' to raise awareness of 'honour'-based violence by 'training all staff through inset says [*sic*], influencing students who may be potential victims, perpetrators or have influence to prevent forced marriage of others, and we are reaching parents through school coffee mornings' (Nammi quoted in IKWRO, 2014). Many other organisations such as the Freedom Charity reach out to school children and young people at risk of forced marriage through the use of helplines and social media (Freedom Charity, 2012). As shown in Chapter 4, the Freedom Charity jointly with the Home Office, the FMU and the CPS took part in the launch of the video *#Freedom2Choose*, which was released in June 2014 to mark the criminalisation of forced marriage and mostly aimed at school children and young people (Freedom Charity, 2014).

Nevertheless, the school sector has long come under criticism for its widespread unwillingness 'to engage with awareness-raising about force marriage' (Hansard, 2011a: para. 21: 10). The *House of Commons, Home Affairs Committee, 'Domestic Violence, Forced Marriage and "Honour"-Based Violence, Sixth Report of Session 2007–08'* believed that schools' reluctance stemmed 'from a fear of causing offence within communities where forced marriage is prevalent' (Hansard, 2011a: para. 21: 10). As the Report explains:

> we were alarmed by the evident resistance of some schools and local authorities to displaying information, particularly on forced marriage. Whilst schools should retain discretion about the most appropriate way to display materials, it is clear from survivors' accounts that schools can provide a lifeline to vulnerable pupils by providing information on support services. We strongly recommend that the Department for Children, Schools and Families take steps to ensure that all schools are promoting materials on forced marriage, whilst allowing them to retain discretion on the details. (Hansard, 2008: para. 94: 38)

Such concerns are echoed by Sanghera, from Karma Nirvana, who has worked extensively raising awareness of 'honour' violence within schools. She argues that 'despite some initial encouragement from Government, there is evidence that the statutory guidance is not being implemented on the ground' (Sanghera cited in Hansard, 2011a: para. 23: 11). Sanghera recalls her own experience of attempting to engage with schools' governing bodies for the purpose of disseminating information about 'honour' violence among their pupils:

> In March 2011 Karma Nirvana wrote to the Heads and Chair of Governors of schools across the country, seeking to highlight issues and concerns pertinent to school children with a view to offering free training to teachers and governors. At the very least we requested that the school put our forced marriage posters up. Since sending the letters to a hundred schools across the country, we have only received one response expressing a willingness to participate. (Sanghera cited in Hansard, 2011a: para. 22: 11)

Cris McCurley, an experienced 'practitioner and trainer in forced marriage and "honour"-based violence' (Hansard, 2011a: para. 20: 10), has similarly found widespread unawareness among the school population regarding the government's sponsored public campaigns on 'honour' violence:

> I work extensively with teenage girls from the Asian communities, none of whom have ever heard about forced marriage protection in schools. What we know from the schools in this region (and from what I know from colleagues across the UK about schools across the board) is that it is not on the curriculum, it is not on the agenda, and the posters are not on the walls. (McCurley cited in Hansard, 2011a: para. 22: 11)

Even Lynne Featherstone, Minister for Equalities, has expressed little confidence on the level of support schools afford to their pupils at risk of forced marriage (Hansard, 2011a: Q94, Ev 15). The following exchange with David Winnick MP, during her evidence to the *House of Commons, Home Affairs Committee, 'Forced Marriage', Eighth Report of Session 2010–2012, Report*, illustrates the Minister's views:

> **Q94 Mr Winnick:** Are you satisfied that if a pupil at a school – it would probably be a female but not necessarily – tells the teacher that she is under pressure to go to India or Pakistan and has the strongest suspicion that it is for the purpose of marriage, that school will alert the appropriate authorities and give protection, or not?

> **Lynne Featherstone:** Schools have an absolute duty to safeguard and if the front-line awareness is being raised enough, that should ring alarm bells, because it is a school's duty to then involve the local authority, which has the local duty of safeguarding children ... My feeling is, probably not. (Winnick and Featherstone cited in Hansard, 2011a: Q94, Ev 15)

Against such backdrop, Nammi, from IKWRO, has led calls for making 'honour' violence education compulsory teaching in schools as well as ensuring that robust monitoring systems are in place (IKWRO, 2014). However, the Minister for Equalities has conceded that 'It is very unlikely' for the subject of domestic violence 'to be made compulsory' learning as part of the curriculum (Featherstone cited in Hansard, 2011a: Q90–93, Ev 15).

Changing Attitudes

The final, but perhaps most important factor to consider in efforts to eradicate 'honour' violence is the need to challenge the gendered attitudes that give rise to domestic abuse in the first place. As Nichola Sharp, Policy Manager at Refuge in Central London, has put it: 'Violence is a choice that people make' (Sharp cited in Brandon and Hafez, 2008: 35). Although the final chapter of the book will revisit this issue, it is worth considering here the paternalistic attitudes prevalent among 'honour'-based communities by reference to the government's own views as well as those of grassroots services provides and survivors. *A Call to End Violence against Women and Girls: Action Plan 2014* makes it clear that the government deems culturally based patriarchal attitudes as playing a central part in promoting violence against women:

> We also need to recognise that attitudes which are entrenched in some segments of society need to be tackled to make a real sustainable change – attitudes which foster ongoing gender inequality, that provide cultural excuses or exemptions for illegal activity and attitudes of ambivalence and it being someone else's problem or responsibility. (HM Government, 2014b: 13)

The many personal accounts of women and young girls brought up in Britain within 'honour'-based cultures have time and again revealed their gendered existence as diametrically opposed to that of their male counterparts. Sarbjit Athwal, the sister-in-law of honour killing victim, Surjit Athwal, whose story featured in Chapter 3, recalls, for instance, a conversation with her father regarding his plans to prepare her for womanhood:

> 'I'm taking you to India to learn the ways of our country', he [dad] said emphatically. 'Your grandmother and your aunts will teach you to be a woman. They will teach you how to look after a family, how to run a house, how to clean and how to cook the Indian way'. (Athwal, 2013: 28)

Athwal's narrative has been replicated numerous times in the course of this volume, and continues to do so many more times over in the everyday lives of local school girls and women across Britain's 'honour' communities. Within this context, the government has set out its vision on how to tackle such paternalistic outlook:

> This latest Action Plan frames Government activity against the need for this fundamental shift in attitudes, focusing on what we can do to ensure the accountability of professionals, how we can develop and build on our campaigns on teenage relationships and body confidence, and how we can

support initiatives such as bystander programmes, which support people to intervene safely if they witness violence and empower the public to challenge unacceptable attitudes and behaviour. It also clearly sets out how we will build on the growing momentum to end practices like female genital mutilation and forced marriage by engaging directly with communities and faith leaders. (HM Government, 2014b: 13)

As the final chapter of the book will show, the scholarly literature has identified the prevalence of culturally sanctioned patriarchal mindsets as key to fostering 'honour' violence (Eisner and Ghuneim, 2013: 415). Eradicating such value systems across whole communities would require a long-term commitment and a multi-dimensional approach not dissimilar to the government's original 'Multi-agency' model. As Essner and Ghuneim (2013) explain:

> Any meaningful attempt to reduce attitudes in support of honor killings therefore probably requires a broader societal commitment to changing the underlying cultural support for patriarchal dominance, including the moral justification of private violence against transgressors. Addressing such issues probably would require measures at several levels, including decisive action by the criminal justice system against honor-related and patriarchal violence against women, coherent messages about the wrongfulness of honor-related violence by the political, religious and economic elites, and curricula in the education system that actively promote gender equality. (Eisner and Ghuneim, 2013: 415)

Brandon and Hafez (2008) have similarly pointed out how deep-seated attitudes which have been handed down from generation to generation can prove exceedingly difficult to shift. Even 'members of the most prosperous and long-established immigrant groups in the UK', the authors argue, 'can preserve their traditional "honour"-based value systems for centuries despite being exposed to a range of competing ideas and value-systems' (Brandon and Hafez, 2008: 31).

Next Steps

In *A Call to End Violence against Women and Girls: Action Plan 2014*, the government pledged to continue 'to support under-represented groups, for example girls at risk from gang violence or from honour based violence such as female genital mutilation or forced marriage, with a concerted programme of events, including an FGM awareness raising campaign and an EU wide event to share best practice' (HM Government, 2014b: 16–17). In addition, the government has vowed to 'Increase DFID's [Department for International Development] programming on early and forced marriage and work across donor countries to ensure a coordinated, strategic effort to galvanise action to bring an end to forced marriage' (HM Government, 2014b: 36).

In his Ministerial Foreword to *A Call to End Violence against Women and Girls: Action Plan 2014*, Noman Baker, Minister for Crime Prevention, outlined the Coalition government's efforts thus far to tackle 'honour' violence:

> The Coalition Government has made good progress on this agenda, including taking forward legislation to criminalise forced marriage in England and Wales, and extending the domestic violence definition to include those aged 16–17 and to cover coercive control. We will continue to work with the College of Policing and other key partners to support the development of expertise across the police and other first responders to tackle issues such as stalking and abusive crimes taking place online.

> The National Group on Sexual Violence Against Women and Vulnerable People, which I lead, is delivering a number of significant improvements to the Government's response to sexual violence and, importantly, will drive a significant cultural shift so that the focus of the criminal justice system is on the credibility of the allegation rather than the credibility of the individual. (HM Government, 2014b: 5)

In a clear recognition of the need to address the underlying causes behind the 'honour' violence problem, the government's long-term emphasis seems firmly focused on the stated goal of effecting a cultural shift among 'honour' cultures in Britain. By 2015, the Coalition government's 'ambition is to have increased awareness of violence against women and girls that begins at birth and continues for life' (HM Government, 2010: 9). The Administration's key message is that 'there are attitudes and behaviours that are wrong because they impact on the lives of women and girls and cause fear' (HM Government, 2010: 9). Individuals 'who think those attitudes and behaviours are right' will be challenged and measures put in place 'to prevent this violence from happening' (HM Government, 2010: 9).

Conclusion

By drawing from the wide-ranging expertise of policymakers and professionals working in the 'honour' violence sector as well as the experiences of their constituents, this chapter has identified a number of key relevant issues for policy and practice. From the outset, the complexity of the 'honour' violence problem has seen the government adopting a 'multi-agency' approach involving an array of stakeholders as well as different areas of intervention. The lack of available standardised national data on the 'honour' violence phenomenon has only compounded an already challenging problem. Despite the efforts of the FMU to provide some semblance of a national picture, data-gathering continues to remain scattered around a range of government departments, criminal justice bureaux, grassroots service providers as well as independent academic institutions. As a result, the unavailability of an overarching knowledge-based coordinated system has made it difficult to ascertain the actual scale of the 'honour' violence problem, which continues to rely on underestimates. It has also proved an obstacle to devising appropriate solutions. This was particularly evident when dealing with women of 'insecure immigration status' whose vulnerable situation and complex needs are not helped by uncertainty about their true numbers. Incidentally, uncertainty of a financial kind has affected the very charities working with these client groups, as they have become victims themselves of a challenging financial environment that, in some instances, threatens their own survival.

In line with other public services, 'honour' victims and practitioners have reported dissatisfaction in their dealings with the legal profession and the police. The former has been difficult to access and the latter has shown varying standards of response to the public. Similarly, despite government and grassroots groups' efforts to engage with the education sector, schools by and large have proved reluctant to raise awareness of 'honour' violence or be drawn into suspected cases of pupils at risk of forced marriages. Even the Minister for Equalities expressed lack of confidence on the level of support afforded to would-be 'honour' victims by the school system.

Despite the many shortcomings here exposed, the chapter has also illustrated many instances of good practice and collaborative work both at national and local level: from the extensive outreach, awareness-raising and ongoing funding initiatives under the FMU, to the individual educational, support and campaigning efforts of grassroots organisations such as Karma Nirvana, SBS, the Freedom Charity and IKWRO, among others.

Underlying these examples of best practice though, there remains the most difficult and intractable challenge of all; that is, changing the deep-seated paternalistic attitudes of Britain's 'honour'-based cultures. With pervasive gendered value systems widely acknowledged to be at the root of the 'honour' violence problem, the government has pledged to renew its efforts to challenge them. It is precisely this patriarchal mindset and its impact on the wider British civic society that are the focus of the book's concluding chapter.

PART III
Conclusion

Chapter 7
Making 'Honour' Violence History? British Multiculturalism Revisited

Another Day, Another 'Honour' Victim

On 4 June 2014, Ahmed Al-Khatib, a 35-year-old 'Syrian-born Muslim, who fled the Middle East for Britain' (Webb, 2014) was convicted of having murdered his wife Rania Alayed, 25, in an 'honour' killing and sentenced to 20 years' imprisonment (Brown, 2014; Narain, 2014; Webb, 2014). Manchester Crown Court heard how, in January 2013, after years of domestic abuse, the mother of three had left the family home in Longsight, Manchester, with her children and moved to a refuge. In an effort to rebuild her life, she had enrolled in a local college, made new friends and forgone wearing traditional garments. A few months after leaving home, Rania, who had married Ahmed aged 15, filed for divorce (Narain, 2014; Brown, 2014). Her husband's family 'were very angry she had had the audacity to go to the law … They believed she was establishing an independent life … Therefore it was decided she should either be coerced to comply or be killed' (Narain, 2014). For that reason, Rania was lured into a meeting at a flat in Salford, Greater Manchester, where Ahmed 'murdered her, stripped her of her clothes and concealed her body in a suitcase. It is believed the children were in the next room when the attack happened' (Brown, 2014). With the help of Ahmed's two brothers, Rania's body was then moved to 'the back of a motorhome' and driven '87 miles to Thirsk, North Yorkshire' where it is understood 'to have been buried next to a layby' (Narain, 2014). Despite repeated efforts by the police to locate Rania's body, her remains have never been found. Describing Rania's murder Detective Chief Inspector Phil Reade, of Greater Manchester Police's Major Incident Team, said:

> make no mistake, this was an honour killing … Al-Khatib's murderous actions were motivated by his outrage and jealousy that Rania would attempt to take control of her own life and live a more Westernised life, after suffering years of abuse at his hands … His male 'pride' clearly couldn't take a strong woman trying to determine her own fate, so he carried out one final act that would ensure she could never defy him again … The irony is that this horrific act of self-pity has brought nothing but shame on him and his family. (Webb, 2014)

At the time of writing, Rania has become the latest reported casualty in a lengthy list of young girls and women falling victims to 'honour' violence in Britain now spanning decades. The newest figures from the FMU indicate that from January to December 2013, the FMU 'gave advice or support related to a possible forced marriage in 1302 cases' alone, with 82 per cent of cases involving female victims and 18 per cent male victims (FMU, 2013). In line with FMU's data from previous years, the majority of the 74 countries involved hailed from South Asia as well as the Middle East and North Africa (MENA) region, with under half of the total (42.7 per cent) concerning Pakistan, followed by India (10.9 per cent) and Bangladesh (9.8 per cent) (FMU, 2013).

The continuing existence of 'honour'-based violence in the UK and its prevalence among certain minority groups is seen by some observers as the result of tensions between the country's egalitarian liberal discourse and the prevailing patriarchal outlook of such 'honour'-based communities (Brandon and Hafez, 2008: 37). Brandon and Hafez (2008) argue that 'honour' violence against women is 'often used by families and spouses to ensure that women conform to their community's traditions and cultural norms. Such violence is also used to punish women for actions or behaviour which the community may consider "unacceptable"' (Brandon and Hafez, 2008: 28). Torn between 'how women are told to act by their families and the personal freedoms which they see enjoyed by the wider society can create complex psychological problems' (Brandon and Hafez, 2008: 24). Many women, who are bound themselves by 'honour' codes, continue to be unable to resolve these conflicts with serious consequences, often remaining trapped in unwanted and violent marriages. Others, like Rania, who manage to break free from domestic abuse and the 'honour' cultures that engender it, are nevertheless murdered in an attempt to silence them for ever. As the 'honour' killings depicted in Chapter 3 illustrate, these women's violent deaths ultimately serve as a warning to would-be transgressors. The ritualised murder of Banaz Mahmod, in particular, clearly exemplifies this trend. 'Honour' killings, Brandon and Hafez (2008) conclude, 'are the most extreme example of instances where community values and interests are imposed on individuals at the expense of the most basic human right: the right to life' (Brandon and Hafez, 2008: 37). Nazir Afzal, the Crown Prosecution Service's lead on 'honour'-based violence, likewise sees victims of 'honour' violence as caught up in between two seemingly incompatible worlds that pull them in different directions. On the one hand, the patriarchal family traditions at home and, on the other hand, the liberal values of the wider British society in which they live. Members of 'honour'-based communities will penalise those who embrace the latter. Afzal says:

> A factor that links integration and honour-crimes is that obviously women are more likely to be exposed to foreign ideas than they would be in South Asia.

This leads to tensions within the community and within the family that leads to honour-based violence. The women who are trying to integrate are more likely to become victims of honour-based violence. (Nazir Afzal cited in Brandon and Hafez, 2008: 39)

The many accounts of 'honour' victims featured in this volume attest to the inner conflicts they have experienced between the traditional values upheld at home and those of the wider British society; between the gendered restrictions imposed on them by the paternalistic cultures they were brought up in and the freedoms afforded to their 'white' peers in the outside world. Whether survivors of 'honour' violence such as Kiranjit Ahluwalia, Jasvinder Sanghera, Sarbjit Athwal and Gina Satvir Singh, or casualties such as Surjit Athwal, Heshu Yones, Shafilea Ahmed, Samaira Nazir and Banaz Mahmod, they all invariably faced persecution and in some cases death at the hands of their own families over their 'Westernised' ways. The case of Jack and Zena Briggs furthermore exemplifies the extent to which community networks will acquiesce in hunting down those who transgress 'honour' codes. As Afzal pointed out, it is individuals who seek to exercise their agency and fully participate in mainstream civic society that are seen to contravene 'honour' cultures and therefore deemed in need of punishment and reform. Given that the vast majority of 'honour' victims are women and the perpetrators men, the feminist literature has justifiably focused on the underlying gendered value systems that produce and sustain such power imbalances.

'Honour' Violence and the Intersectionality Paradigm: Feminist Perspectives

The patriarchal nature of 'honour'-based communities and cultures, particularly within multicultural settings, has by and large been recognised in the feminist literature (Okin, 1999; Phillips and Dustin, 2004; Siddiqui, 2005). Viewing the experiences of 'honour' victims through an intersectionality theoretical lens has moreover afforded scholars, practitioners and activists alike an insight into the complex intersections of gender, ethnicity, class and culture present in the everyday lives of female members of 'honour'-based communities (Thiara and Gill, 2010). Still, deep ideological discrepancies persist concerning the role that specific cultural or religious traditions may play in perpetuating 'honour' violence against women and in particular the construction of 'honour' violence as a 'South Asian' or 'Muslim' issue (Hester et al., 2007; Gangoli et al., 2006; Sen, 2005; Philips and Dustin, 2004; Begikhani et al., 2010; Ali, 2006a and 2007). Some in the literature have challenged what they perceive to be 'simplistic notions of culture' (Kelly, 2010: 12; Volpp, 2001) together with so-called 'cultural essentialism' and 'the tendency to represent individuals from minority or non-Western groups as driven by their culture and compelled by cultural dictates to behave in particular ways', ultimately denying them any 'human agency' (Phillips, 2007: 8–9). At the same time, there has been recognition of the need to explore the prevalence of 'honour' violence within certain ethnic minority and religious cultures. Kelly (2010) has, for instance, argued that we must 'dare to ask whether VAW [violence against women], and each of its forms, is more common for some groups of women, or in specific contexts, and if so, why?' (Kelly, 2010: 12–13). Phillips (2007) has similarly pointed out that:

> even though there is inequality and oppression in all societies, it would be rather a coincidence if societies were all equally sexist, racist, and homophobic … Moreover, while there is much to be said for sorting out one's own backyard before embarking on a mission to sort out everyone else's, there is also merit in a political activism that looks beyond one's immediate neighbourhood or reference group. (Phillips, 2007: 29)

Against this background, the many autobiographical narratives and personal experiences of 'honour' victims depicted in this book contribute to the current debate by attesting to the influence that ubiquitous patriarchal traditions inherent in Britain's 'honour'-based Diasporas have on the lives of ordinary young girls and women. Sanghera's account of the gendered values she was brought up to believe in under the auspices of her family's Sikh religion provides a case in point:

> I was conditioned to learn that from a very young age it is dishonourable to make eye contact with men, sit with men and the rules shift and change as you get older. You are not allowed to have boyfriends, be seen talking to the opposite sex, cut your hair, wear makeup. You are taught these are all dishonourable acts of behaviour; and what you understand as a young person is if you engage in this behaviour, you will put yourself at risk. They can be triggers for significant harm, a forced marriage or even murder. (Sanghera featured in BBC *Panorama*, 2012)

Sanghera's description of her upbringing is mirrored in another young woman's family life, namely, Sarbjit Athwal. A fellow member of Britain's Sikh community and the sister-in-law of 'honour' killing victim, Surjit Athwal, Sarbjit's own story of a forced marriage was featured in Chapter 3. Recalling her formative years, Sarbjit reflects on the gendered values that had been instilled in her from a very young age, while contrasting her acquiescence with Surjit's independence and inquiring mind:

rightly or wrongly I'd been raised to believe we had our roles in life. Whatever my instincts, it had been hammered into me long before my finishing school in India that we needed to concentrate on being good daughters, mothers and wives … That's how deep the indoctrination of my culture ran inside me. I suppose we [Sarbjit and her sister-in-law Surjit] were two sides of the same coin. Except, where Surjit questioned everything, I just plodded along the path that had been chosen for me. I regret it now and I would certainly never wish my old docility on my daughters today. (Athwal, 2013: 120)

Sarbjit's internalising of the very traditions that curtailed her individual freedom is in turn echoed in the experience of Zena Briggs, whose story and that of her husband Jack's years in hiding from bounty hunters was depicted in Chapter 5. Zena describes the expectations placed on women by her Asian community:

It's all too easy for Asian girls to get branded as 'dirty property'; then they may be rejected by their fiancé's parents and bring shame on their family. A daughter, basically, has to make sure that there is never even the faintest reason for slander against her; she has to be totally pure. (Zena Briggs cited in Briggs and Briggs, 1997: 37)

Even after Zena had left home and 'disowned' her family by eloping with Jack, she nevertheless felt bound by the religious traditions she acknowledged discriminated against her own kind, specifically notions of female purity and virginity:

Just because I'd run away from my family didn't mean I'd abandoned my religion, or the principles I'd learnt from that religion. It was very important to me that I was a virgin when I married. (Zena Briggs cited in Briggs and Briggs, 1997: 123)

The literature on Britain's South Asian and Muslim Diasporas is filled with similar accounts of gendered cultural and religious traditions detrimental to women's rights, especially as Chapter 2 showed, from those at the receiving end of such practices (Ahluwalia and Gupta, 2008; Sanghera, 2007 and 2009; Athwal, 2013; Younis, 2013; Shah, 2010; Muhsen and Crofts, 2004). Even studies that challenge perceived stereotypical depictions of South Asian and Muslim women as devoid of any agency, acknowledge the gendered outlook of their constituents' cultures. Herbert and Rodger's (2008) narrative analysis of South Asian Muslim women in Leicester, for instance, warns of the dangers of viewing these minority women as 'passive victims whereby a series of unfortunate events simply happened to them or reproducing particular stereotypes such as the Muslim home as an oppressive arena or South Asian marriages as forced marriages' (Herbert and Rodger, 2008: 58). On the other hand, their study reveals how the same women had 'contended with their parents gendered expectations which attempted to define appropriate behaviour and monitor their conduct' (Herbert and Rodger, 2008: 57). One of the respondents, Munisa, for example, 'conveyed the sense of burden and frustration she felt by stressing how her life was constrained by gender roles, and by contrasting her obligations within the household with the freedom permitted to her brothers' (Herbert and Rodger, 2008: 57). In Munisa's own words:

> I felt because I was the only girl I felt my brothers were spoilt. My mum and dad thoroughly spoilt them ... I mean I did everything for them; they used to come from school, throw their things, their satchel and their shoes around you know you were forever picking things up ... my mum would make tea for them and all that and literally everything was in a mess you know and they could just leave it and go out to play, we would you know my mum and I would cook for them and all that. And so I was, in spite of all that, helping in the shop and helping my mum ... my dad would not let me go out anywhere. (Munisa cited in Herbert and Rodger, 2008: 57)

Herbert and Rodger (2008) reported how Munisa's experience was shared by many of the South Asian women in their study who felt highly pressurised to acquiesce with their parents' wishes in the knowledge that their actions were answerable not only to their close family members, but the whole community in which they live. It is precisely this gulf between the family home and the outside world, between 'honour' cultures' patriarchal mindset and mainstream society's liberal outlook that has raised questions about the desirability of Britain's multiculturalism.

From Multiculturalism to Post-Multiculturalism

In line with the UK experience, rejection of the core civic values of the societies in which 'honour'-based communities live has been seized in the literature as a symptom of the failings of state-sponsored multicultural policies (Vertovec, 2010; Vertovec and Wessendorf, 2010; Gozdecka et al., 2014). Reflecting on the continuing demand for 'recognition' of group identity and rights by minority ethnic cultures, Taylor contends that 'there are substantial numbers of people who are citizens and also belong to the culture that calls into question our [mainstream liberal] philosophical boundaries. The challenge is to deal with their sense of marginalisation without compromising our basic political principles' (Taylor, 1992: 63). In trying to resolve this ideological conflict, he postulated that 'liberalism can't and shouldn't claim complete neutrality', for 'Liberalism is also a fighting creed' (Taylor, 1992: 62). For over three decades now, a number of nations, including Britain, under the common banner of 'multiculturalism' have accordingly sought to accommodate minority cultures while preserving their country's national identities and values. They have done so by enacting social programmes whose overall goal is 'the promotion of tolerance and respect for group identities, particularly of immigrants and ethnic minorities' (Vertovec, 2010: 83). However, the many problematic aspects of multiculturalism, such as gendered 'honour'-based violence, perceived threats to social cohesion and socio-cultural and linguistic fragmentation among others (Julios, 2008), have seen the multicultural project largely regarded as having either failed or become redundant. Vertovec explains how:

> From the political Right many critics now see multiculturalism as a foremost contributor to social breakdown, ethnic tension and the growth of extremism and terrorism. From the Left, where numerous commentators were long dubious of a seeming complicity with Empire and willing blindness to class-based inequalities, even previous supporters of multiculturalism came to question the model as contributing to a demise of the welfare state and the failure of public services. (Vertovec, 2010: 83)

In a post-9/11 environment, the literature has responded to widespread calls to 'rethink' multiculturalism by challenging its very own *raison d'être* and perceived detrimental impact while taking into account wider geopolitical factors such as changing demographics, transnationalism and globalisation (Julios, 2008; Parekh, 2006; Joppke, 2004; Hewitt, 2005; Kivisto, 2005). With multiculturalism now being considered by many as legitimising 'a retreat into culturally and physically separate minority communities' (Vertovec, 2010: 90), the transition towards so-called 'post-multiculturalism' has been characterised by a focus on remedial policies aimed at fostering integration and social cohesion. In Britain, this well-documented public policy trend has seen, over the past decade, the implementation of an array of education, citizenship and migration policies aimed at promoting British nationality, while fostering shared common values including the English language and the rule of law (Julios, 2008). The publication of the *Cantle Report* in 2001 (Home Office, 2001), the *Nationality Immigration and Asylum Act 2002* (Hansard, 2002b), *Life in the United Kingdom – A Journey to Citizenship* in 2004 (Home Office, 2004) and *Our Shared Future* in 2007 (Commission on Integration and Cohesion, 2007) are but a few examples of the integrationist strategy pursued by successive UK governments (Julios, 2008). The findings of the *Cantle Report* perhaps best illustrates some of the underlying reasons behind such an approach:

> Whilst the physical segregation of housing estates and inner city areas came as no surprise, the team was particularly struck by the depth of polarisation of our

FORCED MARRIAGE AND 'HONOUR' KILLINGS IN BRITAIN

towns and cities. The extent to which these physical divisions were compounded by so many other aspects of our daily lives, was very evident. Separate educational arrangements, community and voluntary bodies, employment, places of worship, language, social and cultural networks, means that many communities operate on the basis of a series of parallel lives. These lives often do not seem to touch at any point, let alone overlap and promote any meaningful interchanges. (Home Office, 2001: 9, para. 2.1)

At the time, the Community Cohesion Review Team (CCRT) recommended the establishing and 'championing' of a relevant notion of British 'citizenship' which acknowledges 'the contribution of all cultures to this Nation's development throughout its history, but establishes a clear primary loyalty to this Nation' (Home Office, 2001: 20, para. 5.1.15). Within the context of 'honour'-based violence in Britain, the many policy initiatives and legislative changes that have hitherto been enacted to protect 'honour' victims' rights against the wishes of their families corroborate the continuation, if not acceleration, of the officially sanctioned integrationist drive. From the setting up of the FMU in 2005, to the implementation of the *Forced Marriage (Civil Protection Act) 2007* (Hansard, 2007) and the subsequent criminalisation of forced marriage under provisions contained in the *Anti-Social Behaviour, Crime and Policing Act 2014* (Hansard, 2014), all of these measures can be seen as an integral part of Britain's 'post-multiculturalist' realm. One in which the state actively seeks to prevent female members of 'honour' cultures from facing the same upbringing as that of Sarbjit Athwal (Athwal, 2013), who as a teenage in 1980, started secondary education at Brentford School for Girls having never spoken before 'to anyone of a different religion or race' outside of school (Athwal, 2013: 28). Her experience is symptomatic of the wider concerns identified in the literature regarding the pitfalls of multiculturalism and the unwillingness of 'honour'-based cultures to embrace mainstream British society and its liberal 'Western' values. Of her subsequent decision to go ahead with an unwanted arranged marriage, Sarbjit says:

I'm sure many readers of this book [*Shamed*] will not be able to understand why I would go through with something [arranged marriage] that was so much against my will. The truth is, if you were raised in my [Indian Sikh] family, you would do the same. Yes, perhaps if I had the choice I might have been out enjoying myself like other teenagers. But you have to remember that I had never been out, never socialised, never seen a glimpse of that side of life. I'd never even been on an underground train! You can't miss something you don't know exists. (Athwal, 2013: 79)

Against this background, John McCarthy, a former hostage who wrote the introduction to *Jack & Zena: A True Story of Love and Danger* (Briggs and Briggs, 1997), ponders the implications of such an outlook, which was largely shared by Zena's family, for the future of the British nation:

> It is very hard to believe that this is happening in Britain today. But it is, and the story [of Jack and Zena] raises important questions about how we move on as a multiracial society. How can a family be free to plan to kill a daughter and the man she loves while the establishment appears unable or unwilling to work for a resolution? It is too simple to say that her family must just be made to drop their threats. Their actions come out of a cultural tradition that needs to be understood before it can be reformed. Reformed it must be for the sake of many other youngsters who wish to take up the personal opportunities of living in a multicultural society. It is vital for us to learn from this story to be better equipped to fight against racism. It is a tragic irony that it is Jack and Zena, the victims of this awful culture clash, who are the shining light of race relations in this situation. (McCarthy cited in Briggs and Briggs, 1997: 9)

His words are in turn echoed by Khanum, whose earlier research on forced marriage and community cohesion in Luton considered similar challenges (Khanum, 2008). Khanum maintains that 'a fundamental feature of the British way of life must continue to be based on a commitment to universal human rights and that no groups or individuals can opt out of this commitment on cultural, traditional or any other spurious grounds' (Khanum, 2008: 4).

Conclusion

In tracing the development of the UK's forced marriage and 'honour' killings phenomenon, this book has revealed the extent and complexity of the problem as well as the considerable challenges faced when attempting to tackle it. A multi-faceted socio-cultural phenomenon deeply embedded in paternalistic mindsets, forced marriages and 'honour' killings continue to prevail among Britain's South Asian and MENA Diasporas, particularly those bound by religious traditions. While scholars and practitioners remain divided as to the appropriate framing of the 'honour' question, its scope, underlying causes and the best way to address it, there is little doubt about the undiminished pace of 'honour' violence over time. Once thought to be the preserve of first-generation immigrants, 'honour' crimes have long become an indigenous, self-perpetuating practice handed down to successive generations of UK-born citizens. Despite the government's best efforts, ground-breaking legislation and grassroots interventions, abidance by 'honour' codes continues to see ordinary parents turn to filicide and siblings fratricide in the name of 'honour'. In line with international indicators, attitudinal surveys furthermore largely point to general support of gendered attitudes among younger members of Britain's 'honour'-based cultures.

It is above all this unabated intergenerational trend that has cast serious doubts on the expediency of Britain's prevailing multicultural discourse. Unresolved questions remain regarding the safeguarding of minority group rights that are in conflict with the rights of the majority British population and the rule of law, as well as the preservation of cultural and religious traditions that overtly curtail women's individual freedoms and human rights. With a myriad of conflicting perspectives on the disputed subject of multiculturalism and gender, the feminist literature has afforded contrasting views on the matter rather than definitive answers or an overarching cohesive perspective. The intersectionality paradigm has nevertheless served to shed some light on the multiplicity of factors and intersections between gender, ethnicity and socio-cultural background shaping the experiences of 'honour' victims. By taking a holistic approach, the intersectionality model has allowed for the unequal power structures that continue to disadvantage minority ethnic women in Britain's 'honour'-based cultures to be put into a wider context. In doing so, it has helped to place the 'honour' violence debate within the wider field of human rights. By interrogating the notion of 'consent' and the circumstances in which it may be obtain through an intersectionality lens, the hitherto uncontested official rhetoric that defines an 'arranged' marriage as unproblematic has moreover come to be challenged. It is within this context that the array of narratives and personal accounts of forced marriage survivors and 'honour' killings victims depicted in this book have contributed to further this analysis.

As for a way forward in tackling 'honour' violence in Britain, it is worth considering what has been achieved so far. Given the sheer complexity of the problem, it is to our credit as a nation that significant steps have already been taken to eradicate this practice. As already indicated, from the setting up of the FMU in 2005, to the enactment of the ground-breaking *Forced Marriage (Civil Protection Act) 2007*, to the subsequent criminalisation of forced marriage and successful prosecutions of perpetrators both at home and abroad; successive UK governments and their enforcement agencies together with women's grassroots organisations have led the way in effectively responding to this seemingly intractable problem. In addition, the growing body of scholarly and grey literature on 'honour' violence together with the autobiographical accounts of survivors, parliamentary debates and media coverage have raised the profile of the 'honour' issue while fostering much needed public debate.

Notwithstanding the progress made, serious challenges remain. As illustrated in this book, the growing body of literature on Britain's 'honour' cultures is overwhelmingly focused on the South Asian and Muslim communities where is it most prevalent; but little is known, by comparison, about this phenomenon in other Diasporas including white minorities. Similarly the experiences of male victims of 'honour' crimes are overshadowed by those of their female counterparts and the accounts of perpetrators eclipsed by those of their victims. Despite the evidence regularly collected by government and law enforcement agencies together with front-line service providers, coordinated standardised data collection across the board still remains elusive. A synchronised national response particularly comprising education, welfare and law enforcement agencies has also been found wanting, as have the standards of service provision. Limited available resources, including lack of recourse to public funds for those of 'insecure immigration status', furthermore exacerbate already stretched grassroots support to victims of 'honour'-based domestic violence.

In the final analysis though, no amount of intervention can succeed without a fundamental paradigm shift among members of 'honour'-based cultures. It is after all the patriarchal values they espouse that largely engender, perpetuate and justify violence against women across generations. To date, it has been mostly 'honour' victims, practitioners and activists who, often at great personal risk, have dared to challenge the *status quo*. In contrast, community and religious leaders, still mainly seen as an integral part of the problem, have remained conspicuously silent. Unless they too become part of the solution, forced marriage and 'honour' killings will carry on claiming new victims in Britain for the foreseeable future. As Zakir, the former bounty hunter, knows only too well, demand for his services is unlikely to fall as long as families are willing to do 'anything' in the name of 'honour'.

Bibliography

Abbott, P., Tyler, M. and Wallance, C. (2005) *An Introduction to Sociology: Feminist Perspectives*, 3rd edn. London: Routledge.

Abrams, F. (1996) 'The Mystery of the Missing Muslim Girls', *Independent*, 15 February 1996 [online] at http://www.independent.co.uk/news/education/education-news/the-mystery-of-the-missing-muslim-girls-1319082.html (accessed 30 September 2012).

Ahluwalia, K. and Gupta, R. (2008) *Provoked: The Story of Kiranjit Ahluwalia*. New Delhi: HarperCollins Publishers India.

Ahmed (R on the application of) v. *Her Majesty's South and East Cumbria* [2009] EWHC 1653 (Admin).

Al Ashqar, A., Judge (2014) Office of the UN High Commissioner for Human Rights – Occupied Palestinian Territory, *Women Human Rights and Justice: Murder of Women in Palestine under the pretext of Honour – Legislation and Jurisprudence Analytical Sudy [sic]: Executive Summary* [online] at http://www.ohchr.org/Documents/Issues/Women/WRGS/Executive_summary_study_called_honour_killings_Palestine.pdf (accessed 19 November 2014).

Ali, A.H. (2006a) *The Caged Virgin: A Muslim Woman's Cry for Reason*. London: The Free Press.

Ali, A.H. (2006b) 'Muslim Women and the Key to Change', *Sunday Times*, 29 October 2006 [online] at http://www.timesonline.co.uk/article/0,2092–2426413,00.html (accessed 1 March 2007).

Ali, A.H. (2007) *Infidel – My Life*. London: The Free Press.

Allison, R. (2003) 'Where is the Honour in this?', *Guardian*, 3 October 2003 [online] at http://www.theguardian.com/world/2003/oct/03/gender.uk (accessed 18 May 2014).

Amnesty International (2007) 'Israel: Conflict, Occupation and Patriarchy: Women Carry the Burden', Amnesty International [online] at http://web.amnesty.org/library/pdf/MDE15016200ENGLISH/$File/MDE1501605.Toameth (accessed 11 May 2008).

Amnesty International UK and Southall Black Sisters (SBS) (2008) *'No Recourse' – No Safety: The Government's Failure to Protect Women from Violence*. London: Amnesty International UK and SBS.

Amos, Baroness (2002) 'Research into Community Perceptions of Forced Marriage', Speech by Baroness Amos, Parliamentary Under-Secretary of State at the Foreign and Commonwealth Office (FCO), at the launch of the FCO-sponsored report 'Community Perceptions of Forced Marriage', 12 November 2002, FCO [online] at http://www.fco.gov.uk/en/newsroom/latest-news/?view=Speech&id=2037065 (accessed 8 April 2008).

Anitha, S. and Gill, A. (2009) 'Coercion, Consent and the Forced Marriage Debate in the UK', *Feminist Legal Studies*, 17: 165–84.

Association of Chief Police Officers of England, Wales & Northern Ireland (ACPO) (2008) 'Honour Based Violence Strategy' [online] at http://www.acpo.police.uk/documents/crime/2008/200810CRIHBV01.pdf (accessed 4 June 2013).

Association of Chief Police Officers of England, Wales & Northern Ireland (ACPO) (2013) 'Honour Based Violence and Forced Marriage – The Definition of Honour-Based Violence and Forced Marriage Offences' [online] at http://www.cps.gov.uk/legal/h_to_k/honour_based_violence_and_forced_marriage/#a01 (accessed 5 June 2013).

Ashiana Network (2012a) 'Ashiana – Safe Heaven' [online] at http://www.ashiana.org.uk (accessed 9 August 2014).

Ashiana Network (2012b) 'Forced Marriage Consultation – March 2012' [online] at http://www.ashiana.org.uk/attachments/article/5/Ashiana%20Network%20Response%20to%20Forced%20Marriage%20Consultation%202012.pdf (accessed 19 September 2014).

Athwal, S.K. (2013) *Shamed: The Honour Killing that Shocked Britain – by the Sister who Fought for Justice*. Croydon: Virgin Books.

Badshah, N. (2010) 'The Bounty Hunter: Nadeem Badshah Talks to the Taxi Driver who also had another Job – Finding and Returning Young Women who had Fled Forced Marriages', *Guardian*, G2, 30 August 2010 [online] at http://www.lexisnexis.com.ezproxy.lib.bbk.ac.uk/uk/nexis/search/newssubmitForm.do (accessed 30 November 2014).

Baig, A. (2012) 'I Wed Aged FIVE ... in the UK: Shocking Story from a British Town', *Sun*, 8 April 2012 [online] at http://www.thesun.co.uk/sol/homepage/news/4244979/I-married-at-the-age-of-FIVE-in-the-UK.html (accessed 27 April 2012).

Bari, M.A. (2012) 'Forced Marriage is Criminal, but Criminalising it is not the Best Solution', Aljazeera – Opinion [online] at http://www.aljazeera.com/indepth/opinion/2012/06/2012622112715670229.html (accessed 19 September 2014).

Barrett, D. (2014) 'Outlawing Forced Marriage will not Work, Say Campaigners', *Telegraph*, 16 June 2014 [online] at http://www.telegraph.co.uk/news/uknews/law-and-order/10901216/Outlawing-forced-marriage-will-not-work-say-campaigners.html (accessed 19 September 2014).

Barton, F. (2007) 'Murder Girl's Five Cries for Help that were Ignored', *Daily Mail*, 12 June 2007 [online] at http://www.dailymail.co.uk/pages/live/

articles/news/news.html?in_article_id=461280&in_page_id=1770&in_a_ source (accessed 2 May 2008).

Bauman, G. (1999) *The Multicultural Riddle*. London: Routledge.

BBC (2002) 'Father Jailed over Daughter's Murder', BBC News [online] at http://news.bbc.co.uk./1/hi/england/1827623.stm (accessed 21 April 2008).

BBC (2003) 'Life for "Honour Killing"', BBC News [online] at http://news.bbc.co.uk/1/hi/england/london/3172202.stm (accessed 21 April 2008).

BBC (2005) 'Police Urge Forced Marriage Law', BBC News [online] at http://news.bbc.co.uk/1/hi/uk/4367087.stm (accessed 28 March 2008).

BBC (2007) 'Life for Murder Plot Grandmother', BBC News [online] at http://www.bbc.co.uk/1/hi/england/london/7002404.stm (accessed 20 April 2008).

BBC (2008) 'Lost Girls in "Forced Marriages"', BBC News [online] at http://news.bbc.co.uk/1/hi/uk/7280970.stm (accessed 30 September 2012).

BBC (2011) 'New Forced Marriage Law comes into Effect in Scotland' [online] at http://www.bbc.co.uk/news/uk-scotland-15909237 (accessed 10 June 2013).

BBC News (2011) '"Real Honour Crime Figures Far Darker" says Campaigner' [online] at http://www.bbc.co.uk/news/uk-16017110 (accessed 4 June 2013).

BBC *Panorama* (2012) 'Britain's Crimes of Honour' film [online] at http://www.youtube.com/watch?v=eDnVjfbvsyQ (accessed 25 May 2013).

Becker, H. (ed.) (1966) *Social Problems: A Modern Approach*. New York: John Wiley.

Begikhani, N., Gill, A., Hague, G. and Ibraheem, K. (2010) 'Final Report – Honour-based Violence (HBV) and Honour-based Killings in Iraqi Kurdistan and in the Kurdish Diaspora in the UK'. Centre for Gender and Violence Research, University of Bristol, UK, and Roehampton University, UK, in partnership with Kurdish Women's Rights Watch [online] at http://www.bristol.ac.uk/sps/research/projects/reports/2010/rw9038reportenglish.pdf (accessed 1 June 2013).

Belfast Telegraph (2010) 'Court Stops Girls "Being Sent Abroad for Marriage"', 20 April 2010, News, 12 [online] at http://www.lexisnexis.com.ezproxy.lib.bbk.ac.uk/uk/nexis/results/docview/docview.do?docLinkInd=true&risb=21_T15798969343&format=GNBFI&sort=BOOLEAN&startDocNo=1&resultsUrlKey=29_T1 (accessed 17 October 2012).

Belfrage, H., Strand, S., Ekman, L. and Hasselborg, A.K. (2012) 'Assessing Risk of Patriarchal Violence with Honour as a Motive: Six Years Experience using the PATRIARCH Checklist', *International Journal of Police Science & Management*, 14(1): 20–29 [online] at http://web.b.ebscohost.com.ezproxy.lib.bbk.ac.uk/ehost/pdfviewer/pdfviewer?vid=4&sid=0b4598e4-ee36–464d-931c-bce6d737c908%40sessionmgr110&hid=109 (accessed 20 November 2014).

Bennetto, J. and Judd, T. (2004) 'Police Launch Review of Suspected Honour Killings', *Independent*, 23 June 2004, News, 20.

Best, J. (2002) 'Review Essay – Constructing the Sociology of Social Problems: Spector and Kitsuse Twenty-Five Years Later', *Sociological Forum*, 17(4): 699–706.

Bhopal, K. (1999) 'South Asian Women and Arranged Marriages in East London'. In Barot, R., Bradley, H. and Fenton, S. (eds) *Ethnicity, Gender and Social Change*. Basingstoke: Macmillan Press Ltd., 117–34.

Bingham, J. (2008) 'Forced Marriage Doctor cannot be Abducted from UK, Court Rules', *Telegraph*, 19 December 2008 [online] at http://www.telegraph.co.uk/news/uknews/law-and-order/3850790/Forced-marriage-doctor-cannot-be-abucted-from-UK-court-rule.html (accessed 14 December 2014).

Bingham, J. (2012) 'Five-Year-Old Girl a Victim of Forced Marriage', *Telegraph*, 31 March 2012 [online] at http://www.telegraph.co.uk/news/religion/9176207/Five-year-old-girl-a-victim-of-forced-marriage.html (accessed 27 April 2012).

Bingham, J. (2014) 'Sharia Law Guidelines Abandoned as Law Society Apologises', *Telegraph*, 24 November 2014 [online] at http://www.telegraph.co.uk/news/religion/11250643/Sharia-law-guidelines-abandoned-as-Law-Society-apologises.html (accessed 24 November 2014).

Bird, S. (2007) 'Having Fled Iraq, She Died at the Hands of Her Father', *The Times*, 12 June 2007 [online] at http://www.timesonline.co.uk/tol/news/uk/crime/arices1918019.ece (accessed 11 May 2008).

Boseley, S. (2013) 'Marriage between First Cousins Doubles Risk of Birth Defects, say Researchers', *Guardian*, 4 July 2013 [online] at http://www.theguardian.com/science/2013/jul/04/marriage-first-cousins-birth-defects (accessed 16 January 2014).

Bowcott, O. (2003) 'Killer's Helper Found Guilty of Bride's Murder', *Guardian*, 16 October 2003 [online] at http://www.guardian.co.uk/uk/2003/oct/16/ukcrime.owenbowcott (accessed 10 June 2013).

Bradby, H. (1999) 'Negotiating Marriage: Young Punjabi Women's Assessment of Their Individual and Family Interests'. In Barot, R., Bradley, H. and Fenton, S. (eds) *Ethnicity, Gender and Social Change*. Basingstoke: Macmillan Press Ltd., 152–66.

Brady, B. (2008) 'Special Investigation: Britain's Hidden Scandal – A Question of Honour', *Independent on Sunday*, 10 February 2008, 8–9.

Brandon, J. and Hafez, S. (2008) *Crimes of the Community: Honour-based Violence in the UK*. London: Centre for Social Cohesion.

Briggs, J. and Briggs, Z. (1997) *Jack & Zena: A True Story of Love and Danger*. London: Victor Gollancz.

Briggs, Z. (2009) 'My Dangerous Love, Trampled on the Run', *The Sunday Times*, 30 August 2009 [online] at http://www.lexisnexis.com.ezproxy.lib.bbk.ac.uk/uk/nexis/results/docview/docview.do?start=5&sort=BOOLEAN&format=GNBFI&risb=21_T21053755547 (accessed 1 December 2014).

Brooke, C. (2008) 'Dozens of Missing School Children Feared Forced into Arranged Marriages', *Mail Online*, 5 March 2008 [online] at http://www.dailymail.co.uk/news/article-526233/Dozens-missing-schoolchildren-feared-forced-arranged-marriages.html (accessed 30 September 2012).

Brooker, N. (2013) 'Jasvinder Sanghera on Her Campaign against Forced Marriage', *Financial Times*, 23 August 2013 [online] at http://www.ft.com/cms/s/2/af84f04a-058d-11e3-8ed5-00144feab7de.html#axzz3GOWgRtdm (accessed 17 October 2014).

Brown, J. (2012) 'Parents of Teenager Shafilea Ahmed are Jailed for Life for Her Murder', *i*, 4 August 2012, 9.

Brown, J. (2014) 'Jealous Husband Jailed for 20 Years for Honour Killing of His Wife', *Independent*, 4 June 2014 [online] at https://www.nexis.com/results/docview/docview.do?start=2&sort=BOOLEAN&format=GNBFI&risb=21_T21101923178 (accessed 8 December 2014).

Brown, M. (2007) 'Lover Tells of Torment as 3 get Life for Honour Killing', *Express*, 21 July 2007 [online] at http://www.express.co.uk/news/uk/14246/Lover-tells-of-torment-as-3-get-life-for-honour-killing (accessed 30 May 2014).

Buncombe, A. (2013) 'Uproar as Guru Claims Delhi Rape Victim was Partly to Blame', *Independent*, 8 January 2013 [online] at http://www.independent.co.uk/news/world/asia/uproar-as-guru-claims-delhi-rape-victim-was-partly-to-blame-8443327.html (accessed 9 January 2013).

Burke, J. (2012) 'Delhi Bus Gang Rape: "What is Going Wrong with Our Society?"' *Guardian*, 19 December 2012 [online] at http://www.theguardian.com/world/2012/dec/19/delhi-bus-gang-rape (accessed 20 November 2014).

Burke, J. (2013a) 'Rape Protests Spread beyond India', *Guardian*, 4 January 2013 [online] at http://www.guardian.co.uk/world/2013/jan/04/rape-protests-spread-beyond-india?intcmp=239 (accessed 5 January 2013).

Burke, J. (2013b) 'Indian Gang-Rape Accused Appear in Delhi Court', *Guardian*, 7 January 2013 [online] at http://www.guardian.co.uk/world/2013/jan/07/indian-gang-rape-accused-delhi (accessed 9 January 2013).

Butt, R. (2006) '"You're not my mother any more", Shouted Samaira. Then Her Family Killed Her', *Guardian*, 15 July 2006 [online] at http://www.theguardian.com/uk/2006/jul/15/ukcrime.mainsection (accessed 28 May 2014).

Commission on Integration and Cohesion (2007) *Our Shared Future*. West Yorkshire: Commission on Integration and Cohesion.

ComRes (2014) 'Poll Digest – Social – BBC Panorama Honour Crime Survey' [online] at http://www.comres.co.uk/poll/631/bbc-panorama-honour-crime-survey.htm (accessed 23 October 2014).

Co-ordinated Action Against Domestic Abuse (CAADA) (2012) *Financial Statements, Co-ordinated Action Against Domestic Abuse (Company Limited by Guarantee) – For the Year Ended 30 June 2012* [online] at http://www.caada.org.

uk/aboutus/Caada_accounts_2011_12_FINAL_document.pdf (accessed 3 July 2014).

Cameron, D. (2011) 'Prime Minister's Speech on Immigration' – A Transcript of Prime Minister David Cameron's Speech on Immigration, given on 10 October 2011, *Number 10*, The Official Site of the British Prime Minister's Office [online] http://www.number10.gov.uk/news/prime-ministers-speech-on-immigration (accessed 10 October 2011).

Carter, H. (2012) 'Shafilea Ahmed's Parents Jailed for Her Murder', *Guardian*, 3 August 2012 [online] at http://www.theguardian.com/uk/2012/aug/03/shafilea-ahmed-parents-guilty-murder (accessed 2 September 2013).

CNN Today's News (2007) 'Unbelievable Kurdish Violence – Woman gets Stoned to Death', YouTube [online] at http://www.youtube.com/watch?v=jF9uB8fBBTw&feature=related (accessed 27 April 2008).

Coleman, J. (2011) '"Honour" Crimes: Six Cases', *Guardian*, 3 December 2011 [online] at http://www.guardian.co.uk/uk/2011/dec/03/honour-crimes-cases (accessed 15 May 2013).

Concise Oxford English Dictionary (2006), edited by C. Soanes and A. Stevenson, eleventh edition. Oxford: Oxford University Press.

Cooper, C. (2012) 'Support for "Honour" Violence in Poll', *Independent*, 20 March 2012 [online] at http://www.independent.co.uk/news/uk/crime/support-for-honour-violence-in-poll-7578177.html?origin=internalSearch (accessed 10 October 2013).

Corbin, J. (2013) 'Inside Britain's Sharia Courts', *Telegraph*, 7 April 2013 [online] at http://www.telegraph.co.uk/news/uknews/law-and-order/9975937/Inside-Britains-Sharia-courts.html (accessed 9 May 2013).

Crenshaw, K. (1991) 'Mapping the Margins: Intersectionality, Identity Politics and Violence against Women of Colour', *Stanford Law Review*, 43(6): 1241–99.

Crompton, R. (1997) *Women and Work in Modern Britain*. Oxford: Oxford University Press.

Crompton, R. (2006) *Employment and the Family: The Reconfiguration of Work and Family Life in Contemporary Societies*. Cambridge: Cambridge University Press.

Crown Prosecution Service (CPS) (2006) 'CPS Statement: Murder of Samaira Nazir', CPS [online] at http://www.cps.gov.uk/news/latest_news/145_06/index.html (accessed 22 May 2014).

Crown Prosecution Service (CPS) (2007a) 'Family Members Found Guilty in "Honour Killing" Case', CPS [online] at http://www.cps.gov.uk/news/latest_news/150_07/index.html (accessed 22 May 2014).

Crown Prosecution Service (CPS) (2007b) 'Men Found Guilty of Murder in Honour Killing', CPS [online] at http://www.cps.gov.uk/news/latest_news/133_07/index.html (accessed 30 May 2014).

Crown Prosecution Service (CPS) (2008) *CPS Pilot on Forced Marriage and So-called 'Honour' Crime – Findings*, December 2008. London: CPS.

Crown Prosecution Service (CPS) (2009) 'Extradition of Mohammed Saleh Ali from Iraq', CPS [online] at http://www.cps.gov.uk/news/latest_news/extradition_of_mohammed_saleh_ali_from_iraq/index.html (accessed 30 May 2014).

Crown Prosecution Service (CPS) (2012) 'Parents Convicted for Murder of Shafilea Ahmed', CPS [online] at http://www.cps.gov.uk/news/latest_news/cps_statement_on_shafilea_ahmed/index.html (accessed 22 May 2014).

Crown Prosecution Service (CPS) (2013) 'Honour Based Violence and Forced Marriage – The Definition of Honour-Based Violence and Forced Marriage Offences', CPS [online] at http://www.cps.gov.uk/legal/h_to_k/honour_based_violence_and_forced_marriage/#a01 (accessed 5 June 2013).

Daily Mail (2007) 'Grandmother Jailed for Life over Honour Killing of "Cheating" Daughter-in-Law', 19 September 2007 [online] at http://www.dailymail.co.uk/pages/live/articles/news/news.html?in_article_id=482669&in_page_id=1770 (accessed 20 April 2008).

Das, L. (2003) 'Honour Killings, and Why My Muslim Father Wants Me Dead …', *Daily Mail*, 2 October 2003 [online] at http://www.lexisnexis.com.ezproxy.lib.bbk.ac.uk/uk/nexis/search/newssubmitForm.do (accessed 1 December 2014).

Dearden, L. (2014a) 'Turkish President: "Equality between Men and Women is against Nature"', *Independent*, 24 November 2014 [online] at http://www.independent.co.uk/news/world/europe/turkish-president-equality-between-men-and-women-is-against-nature-9879993.html (accessed 24 November 2014).

Dearden, L. (2014b) '"Women should not laugh in public", says Turkey's Deputy Prime Minister in Morality Speech', *Independent*, 29 July 2014 [online] at http://www.independent.co.uk/news/world/europe/women-should-not-laugh-in-public-says-turkeys-deputy-prime-minister-in-morality-speech-9635526.html?origin=internalSearch (accessed 24 November 2014).

Dhaliwal, N. (2006) 'Shame of the Honour Killings in Suburbia', *London Evening Standard*, 18 July 2006, A Merge, 12.

Dodd, V. (2003) 'Kurd who Slit Daughter's Throat in "Honour Killing" is Jailed for Life', *Guardian*, 30 September 2003 [online] at http://www.theguardian.com/uk/2003/sep/30/religion.world (accessed 2 September 2013).

Doughty, S. (2012) 'Girl of Five is Youngest UK Victim of Forced Marriage as Home Office Looks at Prosecuting Families', *Mail Online*, 30 March 2012 [online] at http://www.dailymail.co.uk/news/article-2122736/Forced-marriage-British-girl-5-UKs-youngest-victim.html (accessed 12 September 2012).

Drury, I. (2008) 'Veteran Campaigning Labour MP Anne Cryer to Step Down at Next General Election "Due to Decreasing Energy Levels"', *Mail Online*, 21 August 2008 [online] at http://www.dailymail.co.uk/news/article-1047729/Veteran-campaigning-Labour-MP-Anne-Cryer-step-general-election-decreasing-energy-levels.html (accessed 6 November 2014).

Eisner, M. and Ghuneim, L. (2013) 'Honor Killing Attitudes Amongst Adolescents in Amman, Jordan', *Aggressive Behaviour*, 39: 405–17 [online] at http://web.b.ebscohost.com.ezproxy.lib.bbk.ac.uk/ehost/pdfviewer/pdfviewer?sid=5a832076–87a3–4427–8ea6-fb782ffcc87d%40sessionmgr115&vid=4&hid=101 (accessed 22 November 2014).

Equality and Human Rights Commission (EHRC) (2012) 'Response to Consultation on Forced Marriage: Issued by the Home Office, December 2011' [online] at http://www.equalityhumanrights.com/legal-and-policy/our-legal-work/consultation-responses/response-to-consultation-on-forced-marriage (accessed 15 September 2014).

Equality and Human Rights Commission (EHRC) (2014) 'Our Vision and Mission' [online] at http://www.equalityhumanrights.com/about-us/about-the-commission/our-vision-and-mission (accessed on 19 September 2014).

Erdem, S. (2012) 'Murder most Foul; Thousands of Asian Teenagers are Forced into Arranged Marriages, and Some Face Death for Rebelling. The Government is Taking Notice but is it Too Little, Too Late?', *The Times*, 11 June 2012, 36–7 [online] at http://www.lexisnexis.com.ezproxy.lib.bbk.ac.uk/uk/nexis/results/docview/docview.do?docLinkInd=true&risb=21_T15813852962&format=GNBFI&sort=BOOLEAN&startDocNo=1&result (accessed 18 October 2012).

European Commission (EC) (2005) *Report on Inequality between Women and Men 2004*. Luxembourg: Office for Official Publications of the European Communities.

Evans, M. (2012) 'Shafilea Ahmed's Sister Alesha avoids Jail over Robbery in "Case of Mercy"', *Telegraph*, 16 November 2012 [online] at http://www.telegraph.co.uk/news/uknews/crime/9683180/Shafilea-Ahmeds-sister-Alesha-avoids-jail-over-robbery-in-case-of-mercy.html (accessed 22 May 2014).

Eysenck, M. (2013) *Simply Psychology*, 3rd edn. Hove: Psychology Press.

Faqir, F. (2001) 'Intrafamily Femicide in Defence of Honour: The Case of Jordan', *Third World Quarterly*, 22(1): 65–82 [online] at http://web.b.ebscohost.com.ezproxy.lib.bbk.ac.uk/ehost/pdfviewer/pdfviewer?vid=4&sid=ac719cc1-b67a-47ee-a843–4737e5bac630%40sessionmgr115&hid=128 (accessed 2 December 2014).

Finn, M. (2002) 'Nadia's Choice', *Guardian*, 1 April 2002 [online] at http://www.theguardian.com/world/2002/apr/01/gender.uk (accessed 16 January 2014).

Forced Marriage Unit (FMU) (2012) 'Statistics January to December 2012', Gov.uk [online] at https://www.gov.uk/government/uploads/system/uploads/attachment_data/file/141823/Stats_2012.pdf (accessed 27 April 2013).

Forced Marriage Unit (FMU) (2013) 'Statistics January to December 2013', Gov.uk [online] at https://www.gov.uk/government/uploads/system/

uploads/attachment_data/file/291855/FMU_2013_statistics.pdf (accessed 4 December 2014).

Forced Marriage Unit (FMU) (2014) 'Guidance: Forced Marriage – Forced Marriage Unit' [online] at https://www.gov.uk/forced-marriage#our-publications-and-other-resources (accessed 19 June 2014).

Foreign and Commonwealth Office (FCO) (2004) *Young People & Vulnerable Adults Facing Forced Marriage: Practice Guidance for Social Workers*. London: FCO.

Foreign and Commonwealth Office (FCO) (2005) *Dealing with Cases of Forced Marriage: Guidance for Education Professionals*, 1st edn. London: FCO.

Foreign and Commonwealth Office (FCO) (2007) *Dealing with Cases of Forced Marriage: Practice Guidance for Health Professionals*, 1st edn. London: FCO.

Foreign and Commonwealth Office (FCO) (2012a) 'News – Forced Marriage Warning as Summer Holidays Approach', FCO [online] at http://www.fco.gov.uk/en/news/latest-news/?id=787139282&view=News (accessed 26 September 2012).

Foreign and Commonwealth Office (FCO) (2012b) 'Travel and Living Abroad – Forced Marriage: Forced Marriage Unit', FMU [online] at http://www.fco.gov.uk/en/travel-and-living-abroad/when-things-go-wrong/forced-marriage (accessed on 13 June 2012).

Frean, A. (2000) 'Tricked into "Holiday" in Yemen', *The Times*, 4 March 2000 [online] at http://www.lexisnexis.com.ezproxy.lib.bbk.ac.uk/uk/nexis/results/docview/docview.do?docLinkInd=true&risb=21_T19008209918&format=GNBFI&sort=BOOLEAN&startDocNo=1&resultsUrlKey (accessed 16 January 2014).

Freedom Charity (2012) 'What We Do' [online] at http://www.freedomcharity.org.uk/what-we-do (accessed 20 August 2014).

Freedom Charity (2014) '#Freedom2Choose Film With Home Secretary' [online] at https://www.youtube.com/watch?v=wd0PtkhP10s (accessed 5 September 2014).

Freedom House (2014) *Freedom in the World 2014* [online] at https://freedomhouse.org/report/freedom-world/freedom-world-2014#.VHb8bDGsW_l (accessed 27 November 2014).

Fuller, R.C. and Myers, R.R. (1941) 'The Natural History of a Social Problem', *American Sociological Review*, 6(3): 320–329.

Gangoli, G., Razak, A. and McCarry, M. (2006) 'Forced Marriage and Domestic Violence among South Asian Communities in North East England', School for Policy Studies, University of Bristol and Northern Rock Foundation [online] at http://www.bris.ac.uk/sps/research/projects/completed/2006/rj4334/rj4334finalreport.pdf (accessed 2 June 2013).

Gilbert, S. (2013) 'Pressure Mounts on Government to Help Bring Killers of Coventry Mom to Justice', *Coventry Telegraph*, 17 July 2013 [online] at http://

www.coventrytelegraph.net/news/coventry-news/family-coventry-honour-killing-victim-5117272 (accessed 9 May 2014).

Gill, A. (2006) 'Patriarchal Violence in the Name of "Honour"', *International Journal of Criminal Justice Sciences*, 1(1) [online] at http://www.sascv.org/ijcjs/aisha.html (accessed 19 May 2014).

Gill, A.K. and Anitha, S. (eds) (2011) *Forced Marriage: Introducing A Social Justice and Human Rights Perspective*. London: Zed Books.

Gov.uk (Prime Minister's Office, 10 Downing Street) (2012) 'News Story: "Forced Marriage to Become Criminal Offence"', 8 June 2012 [online] at https://www.gov.uk/government/news/forced-marriage-to-become-criminal-offence (accessed 7 June 2013).

Gov.uk (2014a) 'Guidance: Domestic Programme Fund: Bidding Process – Successful Projects 2013 to 2014' [online] at https://www.gov.uk/domestic-programme-fund-bidding-process#successful-projects-2013-to-2014 (accessed 25 August 2014).

Gov.uk (2014b) 'News Story: Forced Marriage Now a Crime' [online] at https://www.gov.uk/government/news/forced-marriage-now-a-crime (accessed 6 September 2014).

Gozdecka, D.A., Ercan, S.A. and Kmak, M. (2014) 'From Multiculturalism to Post-Multiculturalism: Trends and Paradoxes', *Journal of Sociology*, 50(1): 51–64 [online] at http://jos.sagepub.com.libezproxy.open.ac.uk/content/50/1/51.full.pdf+html (accessed 4 December 2014).

Greater Manchester Police (GMP) (2008) 'Domestic Abuse – Forced Marriage', GMP [online] at http://www.gmp.police.uk/mainsite/pages/forcedmarriage.htm (accessed 27 March 2008).

Guardian (2012) 'Shafilea Ahmed: A Girl Betrayed', 4 August 2012, Guardian Leader, 42.

Hall, S. (1999) 'Life for "Honour" Killing of Pregnant Teenager by Mother and Brother', *Guardian*, 26 May 1999 [online] at http://www.theguardian.com/uk/1999/may/26/sarahhall (accessed 9 August 2014).

Hansard (1999) *House of Commons Debates, Human Rights (Women)*, 10 February 1999 [online] at http://www.publications.parliament.uk/pa/cm199899/cmhansrd/vo990210/debtext/90210–07.htm#90210–07_head0 (accessed 1 December 2014).

Hansard (2002a) *House of Commons, Select Committee on Foreign Affairs, Minutes of Evidence, 16 July 2002, Supplementary Memorandum from the Foreign and Commonwealth Office, 'FCO Annual Report Evidence Session – How the FCO's forced marriage assistance figures relate to the estimated overall figure of those affected, and details of relevant research'*, paras. 11–15, Parliament UK [online] at http://www.publications.parliament.uk/pa/cm200102/cmselect/cmfaff/826/2072619.htm (accessed 28 September 2012).

Hansard (2002b) *Nationality, Immigration and Asylum Act 2002 (c.41)*. Norwich: TSO.

Hansard (2007) *Forced Marriage (Civil Protection Act) 2007*. Norwich: TSO.

Hansard (2008) *House of Commons, Home Affairs Committee, 'Domestic Violence, Forced Marriage and "Honour"-Based Violence', Sixth Report of Session 2007–08*, volumes I and II, HC 263–I–II, Oral and Written Evidence. London: TSO.

Hansard (2009) *House of Commons, Written Answers – 'Forced Marriage: Prosecutions'*, 11 November 2009, Column 476W [online] at http://www.publications. parliament.uk/pa/cm200809/cmhansrd/cm091111/text/91111w0026. htm#09111186001763 (accessed 6 June 2014).

Hansard (2010) *House of Commons Home Affairs Committee – Follow-up to the Committee's Report on Domestic Violence, Forced Marriage and Honour-Based Violence, Oral and Written Evidence*, 9 March 2010, HC 429-i. London: TSO [online] at http://www.publications.parliament.uk/pa/cm200910/cmselect/ cmhaff/429/429i.pdf (accessed 6 November 2014).

Hansard (2011a) *House of Commons, Home Affairs Committee, 'Forced Marriage', Eighth Report of Session 2010–2012, Report, together with formal minutes, oral and written evidence*, HC 880. London: TSO.

Hansard (2011b) *Forced Marriage etc. (Protection and Jurisdiction) (Scotland) Act 2011* [online] at http://www.legislation.gov.uk/asp/2011/15/pdfs/ asp_20110015_en.pdf (accessed 2 September 2013).

Hansard (2011c) *House of Commons, Written Answers – 'Crimes of Violence: Women'*, 7 March 2011, Column 867W [online] at http://www.publications. parliament.uk/pa/cm201011/cmhansrd/cm110307/text/110307w0005. htm#11030812000015 (accessed 6 June 2014).

Hansard (2013a) *Marriage (Same Sex Couples) Act 2013*. Norwich. TSO [online] at http://www.legislation.gov.uk/ukpga/2013/30/pdfs/ukpga_20130030_ en.pdf (accessed 5 October 2013).

Hansard (2013b) *Anti-Social Behaviour, Crime and Policing Bill, Session 2013–2014, Written Evidence from Imkaan (ASB 30)* [online] at http://www.publications. parliament.uk/pa/cm201314/cmpublic/antisocialbehaviour/memo/asb30. htm (accessed 19 September 2014).

Hansard (2014) *Anti-Social Behaviour, Crime and Policing Act 2014 (c. 12)*. Norwich: TSO [online] at http://www.legislation.gov.uk/ukpga/2014/12/contents (accessed 16 June 2014).

Heaton QC, C., McCallum, L. and Jogi, R. (2009) *Forced Marriage: A Special Bulletin*. Bristol: Family Law.

Hennessy, P. (2006) 'Survey's Finding of Growing Anger in the Islamic Community are Described as "Alarming" by Leading Muslim Labour MP', *Telegraph*, 19 February 2006 [online] at http://www.telegraph.co.uk/ news/uknews/1510865/Surveys-finding-of-growing-anger-in-the-Islamic-community-are-described-as-alarming-by-leading-Muslim-Labour-MP.html (accessed 25 October 2014).

Hennessy, P. and Kite, M. (2006) 'Poll Reveals 40pc of Muslims want Sharia Law in UK', *Telegraph*, 19 February 2006 [online] at http://www.telegraph. co.uk/news/uknews/1510866/Poll-reveals-40pc-of-Muslims-want-sharia-law-in-UK.html (accessed 24 October 2014).

Herbert, J. and Rodger, R. (2008) 'Narratives of South Asian Muslim Women in Leicester 1964–2004', *Oral History*, 36(2) 54–63 [online] at http://www. jstor.org.ezproxy.lib.bbk.ac.uk/stable/10.2307/40179992?Search=yes&resul tItemClick=true&searchText=Narratives&searchText=of&searchText=Sou th&searchText=Asian&searchText=Muslim&searchText=Women&searchT ext=in&searchText=Leicester&searchText=1964–2004&searchUri=%2Fac tion%2FdoBasicSearch%3FQuery%3DNarratives%2Bof%2BSouth%2BAs ian%2BMuslim%2BWomen%2Bin%2BLeicester%2B1964–2004%26amp% 3Bacc%3Don%26amp%3Bwc%3Don%26amp%3Bfc%3Doff (accessed 30 October 2014).

Hester, M., Chantler, K., Gangoli, G., Devgon, J., Sharma, S. and Singleton, A. (2007) 'Forced Marriage: The Risk Factors and the Effect of Raising the Minimum Age for a Sponsor, and of Leave to Enter the UK as a Spouse or Fiancé(e)', Centre for Gender and Violence Research, University of Bristol [online] at http://www.bris.ac.uk/sps/research/projects/completed/2007/ rk6612/rk6612finalreport.pdf (accessed 1 June 2013).

Hewitt, R. (2005) *White Backlash and the Politics of Multiculturalism.* Cambridge: Cambridge University Press.

Hill, A. (2004) 'Runaways Stalked by Bounty Thugs', *Observer*, 18 April 2004 [online] at http://www.lexisnexis.com.ezproxy.lib.bbk.ac.uk/uk/nexis/ search/newssubmitForm.do (accessed 1 December 2014).

Hindustan Times (2013) 'Most Outrageous Remarks on Rape', 7 January 2013 [online] at http://www.hindustantimes.com/India-news/NewDelhi/Most-outrageous-remarks-on-rape/Article1–986108.aspx (accessed 9 January 2013).

HM Government (2010) *Call to End Violence against Women and Girls* [online] at https://www.gov.uk/government/uploads/system/uploads/attachment_ data/file/118150/vawg-paper.pdf (accessed 14 December 2014).

HM Government (2011) *Call to End Violence against Women and Girls: Action Plan.* London: Cabinet Office [online] at https://www.gov.uk/government/ uploads/system/uploads/attachment_data/file/97903/vawg-action-plan. pdf (accessed 14 December 2014).

HM Government (2014a) *Multi-Agency Practice Guidelines: Handling Cases of Forced Marriage.* London: Cabinet Office.

HM Government (2014b) *A Call to End Violence against Women and Girls: Action Plan 2014* [online] at https://www.gov.uk/government/uploads/system/ uploads/attachment_data/file/287758/VAWG_Action_Plan.pdf (accessed 14 December 2014).

Hofstede, G. (1980) *Culture's Consequences: International Differences in Work-Related Values*. Beverly Hills: Sage.

Home Office (2000) *A Choice by Right: The Report of the Working Group on Forced Marriage* [online] at http://www.nordaf.co.uk/public/Editor/assets/Library/Forced%20Marriage%20A%20Choice%20By%20Right.pdf (accessed 7 June 2013).

Home Office (2001) *Community Cohesion: A Report of the Independent Review Team Chaired by Ted Cantle*. London: Home Office.

Home Office (2004) *Life in the United Kingdom – A Journey to Citizenship*, published on behalf of the Life in the United Kingdom Advisory Group. Norwich: TSO.

Home Office (2012) *Forced Marriage – A Consultation: Summary of Responses* [online] at https://www.gov.uk/government/uploads/system/uploads/attachment_data/file/157829/forced-marriage-response.pdf (accessed 5 June 2013).

Hope, J. (2013) 'Warning Over Cousin Marriages: Unions between Blood Relatives in Pakistani Community Account for Third of Birth Defects in their Children', *Mail Online*, 4 July 2013 [online] at http://www.dailymail.co.uk/news/article-2355277/Warning-cousin-marriages-Unions-blood-relatives-Pakistani-community-account-birth-defects-children.html (accessed 4 July 2013).

H.O.P.E. (Helping Other People Everyday) Training & Consultancy (2009) *An Insight into Forced Marriages & Honour Based Violence*, film. Leicester: Holyk Films.

Husseini, R. (2009) *Murder in the Name of Honour: The True Story of One Woman's Heroic Fight against an Unbelievable Crime*. Oxford: Oneworld.

Idriss, M.M. and Abbas, T. (eds) (2011) *Honour, Violence, Women and Islam*. Abingdon: Routledge.

Independent (2012) 'British Asians back Family "Honour"', 19 March 2012 [online] at http://www.independent.co.uk/news/uk/home-news/british-asians-back-family-honour-7577031.html?origin=internalSearch (accessed 10 October 2013).

Indian Express (2013) 'Delhi Gangrape Protest is India's Arab Spring: Fareed Zakaria', 8 January 2013 [online] at http://www.indianexpress.com/news/delhi-gangrape-protest-is-indias-arab-spring--fareed-zakaria/1056197/1 (accessed 9 January 2013).

Iranian and Kurdish Women's Rights Organisation (IKWRO) (2011) 'Nearly 3000 Cases of "Honour" Violence Every Year in the UK' [online] at http://ikwro.org.uk/2011/12/03/nearly-3000-cases-of-honour-violence-every-year-in-the-uk (accessed 4 June 2013).

Iranian and Kurdish Women's Rights Organisation (IKWRO) (2012a) 'Criminalisation of Forced Marriage by Diana Nammi, Director of IKWRO',

15 June 2012 [online] at http://ikwro.org.uk/2012/06/15/criminalisation-of-forced-marriage (accessed 7 June 2013).

Iranian and Kurdish Women's Rights Organisation (IKWRO) (2012b) 'Criminalisation of Forced Marriage – IKWRO Statement of Support' [online] at http://ikwro.org.uk/2012/03/criminalisation-of-forced-marriage-%E2%80%93-ikwro-statement-of-support (accessed 19 September 2014).

Iranian and Kurdish Women's Rights Organisation (IKWRO) (2014a) 'Leading Women's Rights Charity Welcomes New Law Making Forced Marriage a Criminal Offence' [online] at http://ikwro.org.uk/2014/06/welcomes-marriage-criminal (accessed 4 September 2014).

Iranian and Kurdish Women's Rights Organisation (IKWRO) (2014b) 'Diana Nammi, Women's Rights Activist, named Woman of the Year' [online] at http://ikwro.org.uk/2014/10/womens-rights-activist (accessed 17 October 2014).

ITV *Exposure* (2012) 'Banaz: An Honour Killing' film, broadcast on ITV on 31 October 2012 at 22:35hrs [excerpt online] at http://www.itv.com/news/2012–10–31/video-of-honour-killing-victims-prediction-of-own-fate-to-be-shown (accessed 31 May 2013).

John, C. (2003) 'The Long Search for Surjit', *BBC News*, 6 November 2003 [online] at http://news.bbc.co.uk/1/hi/england/3241503.stm (accessed 16 May 2014).

Johnston, P. (2001) 'My Escape from a Forced Marriage: Student Tells of Six-Month Captivity as Britain Offers to Help other Muslim Girls', *Daily Telegraph*, 7 November 2001, 15 [online] at http://www.lexisnexis.com.ezproxy.lib.bbk.ac.uk/uk/nexis/search/newssubmitForm.do (accessed 17 October 2012).

Johnstone, H. (1999) '"Shame" Murder Mother Gets Life', *The Times*, 26 May 1999 [online] at http://www.lexisnexis.com.ezproxy.lib.bbk.ac.uk/uk/nexis/results/docview/docview.do?docLinkInd=true&risb=21_T20360217118&format=GNBFI&sort=BOOLEAN&startDocNo=1&resultsUrlKey=29_T20360217122&cisb=22_T20 (accessed 9 August 2014).

Jones, S. (2006) 'Bullying Mother-in-Law must Pay £35,000', *Guardian*, 25 July 2006 [online] at http://www.theguardian.com/uk/2006/jul/25/law.topstories3 (accessed 22 November 2013).

Joppke, C. (2004) 'The Retreat of Multiculturalism in the Liberal State: Theory and Policy', *The British Journal of Sociology*, 55(2): 237–57.

Joppke, C. (2009) 'Limits of Integration Policy: Britain and Her Muslims', *Journal of Ethnic and Migration Studies*, 35(3): 453–72.

Judd, T. (2006) 'Stabbed to Death as Her Family Watched ... for Honour', *Independent*, 15 July 2006 [online] at http://www.independent.co.uk/news/uk/crime/stabbed-to-death-as-her-family-watched-for-honour-407984.html (accessed 27 May 2014).

Julios, C. (2008) *Contemporary British Identity: English Language, Migrants and Public Discourse*. Aldershot: Ashgate.

Karma Nirvana (2012) 'History', Karma Nirvana [online] at http://www.karmanirvana.org.uk/the-story-of-karma-nirvana.html (accessed 13 June 2012).

Karma Nirvana (2013a) 'Karma Nirvana – About' [online] at http://www.karmanirvana.org.uk/about (accessed 9 August 2014).

Karma Nirvana (2013b) 'Jasvinder Statement' [online] at http://www.karmanirvana.org.uk/jasvinder-statement (accessed 5 September 2013).

Kazimirski, A., Keogh, P., Kumari, V., Smith, R., Gowland, S., Purdon, S. and Khanum, N. (2009) *Forced Marriage: Prevalence and Service Response*, National Centre for Social Research, Research Report No DCSF-RR128. Published by the Department for Children Schools and Family (DCSF) [online] at http://www.natcen.ac.uk/media/659806/c0f6680f-c723–4955-bf08-e64073fad61b.pdf (accessed 14 July 2013).

Kelly, L. (2010) 'Foreword'. In Thiara, R.K. and Gill, A.K. (eds) *Violence Against Women in South Asian Communities: Issues for Policy and Practice*. London: Jessica Kingsley Publishers, 9–13.

Khan, D. and Prindle, D. (directors) (2012) *Banaz: A Love Story*, film. Oslo: Fuuse Films [online] at http://fuuse.net/banaz-a-love-story (accessed 6 June 2014).

Khan, T.S. (2006) *Beyond Honour: A Historical Materialistic Explanation of Honour Related Violence*. Oxford: Oxford University Press.

Khanum, N. (2008) *Forced Marriage, Family Cohesion and Community Engagement: National Learning through a Case Study of Luton*. Watford: Equality in Diversity.

Kivisto, P. (2005) *Incorporating Diversity – Rethinking Assimilation in a Multicultural Age*. Colorado: Paradigm Publishers.

The Koran (2003) translated by N.J. Dawood. London: Penguin Books.

Kulczycki, A. and Windle, S. (2011) 'Honor Killings in the Middle East and North Africa: A Systematic Review of the Literature', *Violence Against Women*, 17: 1442–64 [online] at http://vaw.sagepub.com.libezproxy.open.ac.uk/content/17/11/1442.full.pdf+html (accessed 24 November 2014).

Kymlicka, W. (1995) *Multicultural Citizenship: A Liberal Theory Of Minority Rights*. Oxford: Clarendon.

Kymlicka, W. (1999) 'Liberal Complacencies'. In Okin, S.M. (ed.) *Is Multiculturalism Bad for Women?* Princeton: Princeton University Press, 31–4.

Lakhani, N. (2009) 'Forced Marriage: "I can't forgive or forget what they did to me"', *Independent*, 5 July 2009 [online] at http://www.independent.co.uk/news/uk/home-news/forced-marriage-i-cant-forgive-or-forget-what-they-did-to-me-1732170.html (accessed 14 December 2014).

Lakhani, N. (2012) 'Society's Shame: The Five-Year-Old Girl Forced into Marriage', *Independent*, 31 March 2012 [online] at http://www.independent.

co.uk/news/uk/home-news/societys-shame-the-fiveyearold-girl-forced-into-marriage-7604140.html (accessed 7 September 2012).

The Law Society (2012) 'Forced Marriage Consultation Response – Law Society of England and Wales', March 2012 [online] at https://www.lawsociety.org.uk/representation/policy-discussion/documents/consultation-on-forced-marriage--law-society-response-(pdf-232kkb) (accessed 6 September 2014).

Lemert, E.M. (1951) 'Is There a Natural History of Social Problems?', *American Sociological Review*, 16(2): 217–23.

Lightfoot-Klein, H. (1989) 'The Sexual Experience and Marital Adjustment of Genitally Circumcised and Infibulated Females in The Sudan', *Journal of Sex Research*, 26(3): 375–92 [online] at http://www.fgmnetwork.org/authors/Lightfoot-klein/sexualexperience.htm (accessed 22 July 2008).

Lord Lester of Herne Hill (2007) 'Uncivil Ceremonies', Policy Focus: Legal Reform, *The House Magazine*, 22 January 2007, 25.

Mahr, K. (2013) 'India's Gang-Rape Case: As Accused Go to Court, Unease Settles over Delhi', *Time*, 7 January 2013 [online] at http://world.time.com/2013/01/07/indias-gang-rape-case-as-accused-go-to-court-unease-settles-over-delhi (accessed 9 January 2013).

Mail Online (2012) 'Shafilea Ahmed Father "Had Briefcase Full of Gold Bars so He Could Flee Justice at any Moment"', 7 August 2012 [online] at http://www.dailymail.co.uk/news/article-2184750/Shafilea-Ahmeds-father-briefcase-gold-bars-flee-justice-moment.html (accessed 21 May 2014).

Manji, I. (2005) *The Trouble with Islam Today: A Wake-up Call for Honesty and Change*. Toronto: Vintage Canada.

Marsden, S. (2012) 'Numerous Opportunities Missed to Protect "First" White Honour Killing Victim', *Telegraph*, 29 May 2012 [online] at http://www.telegraph.co.uk/news/uknews/crime/9297748/Numerous-opportunities-missed-to-protect-first-white-honour-killing-victim.html (accessed 25 April 2014).

McDowell, L. (1997) *Capital Culture: Gender at Work in the City*. Oxford: Blackwell.

McGirk, J. (2003) 'Court Frees Briton Imprisoned and Tricked into Marriage', *Independent*, 7 May 2003 [online] at http://www.lexisnexis.com.ezproxy.lib.bbk.ac.uk/uk/nexis/results/docview/docview.do?docLinkInd=true&risb=21_T19008209918&format=GNBFI&sort=BOOLEAN&startDocNo=1&resultsUrlKey=29_T19008209922&cisb=22_T19008209921&treeMax=true&treeWidth=0&selRCNodeID=2&nodeStateId=101en_GB,1&docsInCategory=1&csi=8200&docNo=1 (accessed 16 January 2014).

McVeigh, K. (2007a) '"Honour" Killer Boasted of Stamping on Woman's Neck', *Guardian*, 20 July 2007 [online] at http://www.guardian.co.uk/uk/2007/jul/20/ukcrime.uknews4 (accessed 5 June 2013).

McVeigh, K. (2007b) '"Honour" Killing: Pressure Grows on UK to Extradite Suspect from Iraq', *Guardian*, 22 November 2007 [online] at http://www.guardian.co.uk/Iraq/Story/0,ww15030,00.html (accessed 2 May 2008).

McVeigh, K. (2007c) 'Woman Arranged "Honour" Killing of Daughter-in-Law during Trip to India', *Guardian*, 27 July 2007 [online] at http://www.theguardian.com/uk/2007/jul/27/ukcrime.uknews4 (accessed 16 May 2014).

McVeigh, T. (2009) 'Ending the Silence on "Honour Killing"', *Guardian*, 25 October 2009 [online] at http://www.theguardian.com/society/2009/oct/25/honour-killings-victims-domestic-violence (accessed 2 September 2013).

McVeigh, T. (2013) 'Her Film about an "Honour" Killing Won an Emmy. Now it's Being Used to Train Police', *Observer*, 13 October 2013 [online] at http://www.theguardian.com/society/2013/oct/13/emmy-honour-killing (accessed 30 May 2013).

Milton Keynes Citizen (2010) 'Girls Aged 12 Forced to Wed', 8 April 2010 [online] at http://www.lexisnexis.com.ezproxy.lib.bbk.ac.uk/uk/nexis/search/newssubmitForm.do (accessed 18 October 2012).

Mirror (2012) '"I fled in just the clothes I was wearing": How One Muslim Woman Escaped Arranged Marriage', 17 September 2012 [online] at http://www.mirror.co.uk/news/real-life-stories/shafilea-ahmed-murder-how-i-escaped-1327180 (accessed 9 June 2013).

Modood, T. (2005) *Multicultural Politics: Racism, Ethnicity and Muslims in Britain.* Edinburgh: Edinburgh University Press.

Mogra, S.I. (2012) 'Unacceptable and Un-Islamic: Imam's Fury at Wedding of Girl 5', *Sun*, 9 April 2012, News, 18 [online] at http://www.lexisnexis.com.ezproxy.lib.bbk.ac.uk/uk/nexis/search/newssubmitForm.do (accessed 14 October 2012).

Moore, S. (2012) 'Delhi Gang-Rape: In India, Anger is Overtaking Fear', *Guardian*, 31 December 2012 [online] at http://www.guardian.co.uk/commentisfree/2012/dec/31/delhi-rape-india-damini (accessed 5 January 2013).

Muhsen, Z. with Crofts, A. (2004) *Sold: A Story of Modern-Day Slavery.* London: Time Warner Paperbacks.

Muslim Council of Britain (MCB) (2005) 'The Muslim Council of Britain (MCB) Response to Consultation Paper: "FORCED MARRIAGE" – A Wrong not a Right' [online] at http://mcb.org.uk/uploads/wrongnotright.pdf (accessed 7 June 2013).

Muslim Women's Network UK (MWNUK) (2014) 'Muslim Women's Network UK Welcomes Criminalising Forced Marriage' [online] at http://www.mwnuk.co.uk/Muslim_Womens_Network_UK_Welcomes_Criminalising_Forced_Marriage_236_noticeDetail.php (accessed 13 September 2014).

Narain, J. (2014) 'Husband Killed His Wife for Being Too Westernised', *Daily Mail*, 5 June 2014 [online] at https://www.nexis.com/results/docview/docview.

do?docLinkInd=true&risb=21_T21102148797&format=GNBFI&sort=B OOLEAN&startDocNo=1&resultsUrlKey=29_T21102158601&cisb=22_ T21102158600&treeMax=true&treeWidth=0&selRCNodeID=8&nodeStat eId=411en_US,1,5&docsInCategory=1&csi=138794&docNo=1 (accessed 8 December 2014).

National Society for the Prevention of Cruelty to Children (NSPCC) (2014) 'Forced Marriage Feared by Schoolchildren', Press Releases, 16 June 2014 [online] at http://www.nspcc.org.uk/news-and-views/media-centre/press-releases/2014/forced-marriage-childline/forced-marriage-animation_wdn103034.html (accessed 18 June 2014).

North, A. (2013) 'Is Delhi Gang Rape India's "Rosa Parks Moment"?' BBC News India [online] at http://www.bbc.co.uk/news/world-asia-india-21228923 (accessed 20 November 2014).

Office for National Statistics (ONS) (2011) 'Population Estimates by Ethnic Group 2002–2009', Statistical Bulletin. Newport: ONS.

Okin, S.M. (1999) *Is Multiculturalism Bad for Women?* Princeton: Princeton University Press.

Okin, S.M. (2013) *Women in Western Political Thought.* Princeton: Princeton University Press.

Onal, A. (2008) *Honour Killing: Stories of Men Who Killed.* London: Saqi Books.

Organisation for Economic Cooperation and Development (OECD) (2012) *Closing the Gender Gap: Act Now.* OECD Publishing [online] at http://www.oecd-ilibrary.org/social-issues-migration-health/close-the-gender-gap-now_9789264179370-en (accessed 17 December 2013).

Parekh, B. (2000) *Rethinking Multiculturalism: Cultural Diversity and Political Theory.* London: Palgrave.

Parekh, B. (2006) *Rethinking Multiculturalism: Cultural Diversity and Political Theory,* 2nd edn. Basingstoke: Palgrave Macmillan.

Peachey, P. (2012) '"Still now they follow me". Footage of Banaz Mahmod Warning Police Before Her "Honour" Killing to be Shown for the First Time', *Independent,* 24 September 2012 [online] at http://www.independent.co.uk/news/uk/crime/still-now-they-follow-me-footage-of-banaz-mahmod-warning-police-before-her-honour-killing-to-be-shown-for-the-first-time-8168099.html (accessed 30 May 2014).

Penn, R. (2011) 'Arranged Marriages in Western Europe: Media Representations and Social Mobility', *Journal of Comparative Family Studies,* 42(5): 637–50.

Penn, R. and Lambert, P. (2009) *Children of International Migrants in Europe.* London: Palgrave.

Phillips, A. (2007) *Multiculturalism without Culture.* Princeton: Princeton University Press.

Phillips, A. and Dustin, M. (2004) 'UK Initiatives on Forced Marriage: Regulation, Dialogue and Exit', *Political Studies,* 52: 531–51.

Pope, N. (2012) *Honour Killings in the Twenty-First Century*. New York: Palgrave Macmillan.

R v. *Athwal and ors* [2009] EWCA Crim 789.

R v. *Mahmod (Mahmod Babakir)* [2009] EWCA Crim 775.

R v. *Nazir* [2009] EWCA Crim 213.

R v. *Yones* [2007] EWHC 1306 (QB).

Rawstorne, T. (2006) 'Out of the Shadow of Death', *Daily Mail*, 26 May 2006 [online] at http://www.lexisnexis.com.ezproxy.lib.bbk.ac.uk/uk/nexis/results/docview/docview.do?docLinkInd=true&risb=21_T20360252840&format=GNBFI&sort=BOOLEAN&startDocNo=1&resultsUrlKey=29_T20360252844&cisb=22_T20360252843&treeMax=true&treeWidth=0&csi=138794&docNo=3 (accessed 9 August 2014).

Rawstorne, T. (2009) 'Across the Cultural Divide: The Muslim Woman and Older British Man whose Love Survived Death Threats but was Doomed to Fail', *Mail Online*, 2 September 2009 [online] http://www.dailymail.co.uk/femail/article-1199279/Across-cultural-divide-The-Muslim-woman-older-Brit-love-survived-death-threats-doomed-fail.html (accessed 1 December 2014).

Refuge (2006) 'Refuge Response to the Forced Marriage Consultation – a Wrong not a Right', January 2006 [online] at https://refuge.org.uk/cms_content_refuge/attachments/25–0601-Forced%20Marriage%20Consultation-A%20Wrong%20not%20a%20Right.pdf (accessed 7 June 2013).

Refuge (2013) *Annual Report and Financial Statements 31 March 2013* [online] at http://refuge.org.uk/files/Refuge-Annual-report-to-31-March-2013.pdf (accessed 3 July 2014).

Refuge (2014) 'Refuge Welcomes Criminalisation of Forced Marriage' [online] at http://www.refuge.org.uk/2014/06/16/refuge-welcomes-criminalisation-of-forced-marriage (accessed 6 September 2014).

Rehman, Y., Kelly, L. and Siddiqui, H. (eds) (2013) *Moving in the Shadows: Violence in the Lives of Minority Women and Children*. Surrey: Ashgate Publishing.

Respect (2014) 'Perpetrators of Domestic Violence' [online] at http://respect.uk.net/work/work-perpetrators-domestic-violence (accessed 5 July 2014).

Roald, A.S. (2001) *Women in Islam: The Western Experience*. London: Routledge.

Rosley, J. (2006) 'Mother-in-Law Harassment: Singh v Bhakar', *Family Law*, 36 (November): 967–69.

The Runnymede Trust (2000) *The Future of Multi-Ethnic Britain – The Parekh Report*, Report of the Commission on the Future of Multi-Ethnic Britain. London: Profile Books.

Said, E.W. (2003) *Orientalism*. London: Penguin.

Samad, Y. and Eade, J. (2002) *Community Perceptions of Forced Marriage*. London: Community Liaison Unit, Foreign and Commonwealth Office (FCO).

Saner, E. (2007) 'Dishonourable Acts', *Guardian*, 13 June 2007 [online] at http://www.theguardian.com/uk/2007/jun/13/ukcrime.prisonsandprobation (accessed 30 May 2014).

Sanghera, J. (2007) *Shame*. London: Hodder & Stoughton Ltd.

Sanghera, J. (2009) *Daughters of Shame*. London: Hodder & Stoughton Ltd.

Sanghera, J. (2012) 'Girls' Lives Must be Theirs to Live', *Sun*, 8 April 2012 [online] at http://www.thesun.co.uk/sol/homepage/news/4244979/I-married-at-the-age-of-FIVE-in-the-UK.html (accessed 27 April 2012).

Sardar, Z. (2008a) 'Family – First Person: Arranged Marriages Fascinate People in the UK "Like Watching Horror Films". Don't Scoff, says Ziauddin Sardar, British Society Could Learn a Lot from the Asian Experience', *Guardian*, 13 September 2008, 3.

Sardar, Z. (2008b) *Balti Britain: A Journey through the British Asian Experience*. London: Granta Books.

The Scottish Government (2012) 'Forced Marriage in Scotland' [online] at http://www.scotland.gov.uk/Topics/Justice/crimes/forced-marriage (accessed 14 September 2012).

Sears, N. (2006) 'Woman Wins £35,000 Damages from Bullying Mother-in-Law', *Mail Online*, 25 July 2006 [online] at http://www.dailymail.co.uk/news/article-397446/Woman-wins-35–000-damages-bullying-mother-law.html (accessed 22 November 2013).

Sen, P. (2005) '"Crimes of Honour", Value and Meaning'. In Welchman, L. and Hossain, S. (eds) *'Honour': Crimes, Paradigms, and Violence Against Women*. London: Zed Books, 42–63.

Sewell, B. (1999) 'Rukhsana, Martyr to a Cruel and Barbaric Tradition', *The Evening Standard*, 1 June 1999 [online] at http://www.lexisnexis.com.ezproxy.lib.bbk.ac.uk/uk/nexis/results/docview/docview.do?docLinkInd=true&risb=21_T20360217118&format=GNBFI&sort=BOOLEAN&startDocNo=1&resultsUrlKey=29_T20360217122&cisb=22_T20360217121&treeMax=true&treeWidth=0&selRCNodeID=5&nodeStateId=411en_GB,1,2 (accessed 9 August 2014).

Shackles, S. (2012) '"Honour Killings" are just Murder – it's as Simple as that', *New Statesman*, 7 August 2012 [online] at http://www.newstatesman.com/blogs/lifestyle/2012/08/honour-killings-are-just-murder-its-simple (accessed 9 June 2013).

Shah, H. (2010) *The Imam's Daughter*. London: Rider Books.

Sheridan, E., Wright, J., Small, N., Corry, P.C., Oddie, S., Whibley, C., Petherick, E.S., Malik, T., Pawson, N., McKinney, P.A. and Parslow, R.C. (2013) 'Risk Factors for Congenital Anomaly in a Multi-Ethnic Birth Cohort: An Analysis of the Born in Bradford Study', *The Lancet*, 19 October 2013, 382(9901): 1350–1359.

Siddiqui, H. (2005) "'There is no 'Honour' in Domestic Violence, Only Shame!" Women's Struggle against "Honour" Crimes in the UK'. In Welchman, L. and Hossain, S. (eds) *'Honour': Crimes, Paradigms, and Violence Against Women.* London: Zed Books, 263–81.

Siddique, H. (2007) 'Mother and Son Jailed over "Honour" Killing', *Guardian*, 19 September 2007 [online] at http://www.theguardian.com/uk/2007/sep/19/ukcrime.haroonsiddique (accessed 2 September 2013).

Sieghart, M.A. (2006) 'What Right Have Muslims to Claim Moral Superiority?', *The Times*, 20 July 2006, Features, Times 2, 7.

Singh v. *Bhakar* [2007] 1 F.L.R. 880 (CC (Nottingham)).

Smith, J.D. (2007) 'Death in the Name of Pride', *Sunday Times Magazine*, 11 November 2007, 64–77.

Smith, J.D. (2012) 'A Plate of Tuna Pasta – and then Murder', *The Sunday Times*, 5 August 2012, News Review, Features, 7.

Smith-Squire, A. (2008) 'I was Forced to Marry My Cousin – it's Normal in My Culture, but SO WRONG', *Daily Mail*, 11 February 2008 [online] at http://www.dailymail.co.uk/pages/live/femail/article.html?in_article_id=513757&in_page_id=1879 (accessed 12 February 2008).

Southall Black Sisters (SBS) (2013) 'Kiranjit Ahluwalia' [online] at http://www.southallblacksisters.org.uk/campaigns/kiranjit-ahluwalia (accessed 5 June 2013).

Southall Black Sisters (SBS) (2014a) 'Southall Black Sisters – About Us' [online] at http://www.southallblacksisters.org.uk/about-us (accessed 9 August 2014).

Southall Black Sisters (SBS) (2014b) 'The Forced Marriage Campaign' [online] at http://www.southallblacksisters.org.uk/campaigns/forced-marriage-campaign (accessed 19 September 2014).

Spector, M. and Kitsuse, J.I. (1977) *Constructing Social Problems.* California: Benjamin-Cummings Publishing Company.

The Star (2006) 'Killings a "Distortion of Honour" – Judge', 22 July 2006 [online] at http://www.thestar.co.uk/what-s-on/out-about/killings-a-distortion-of-honour-judge-1–271183 (accessed 25 May 2014).

Steele, J. (2006) 'Woman Stabbed to Death by Family for Loving Wrong Man', *Telegraph*, 15 July 2006 [online] at http://www.telegraph.co.uk/news/uknews/1523949/Woman-stabbed-to-death-by-family-for-loving-wrong-man.html (accessed 23 May 2014).

Taneja, P. (2012) 'Forced Marriage: Girl Aged Five among 400 Minors Helped', BBC, 30 March 2012 [online] at http://www.bbc.co.uk/news/uk-17534262 (accessed 13 September 2012).

Taylor, C. (1992) *Multiculturalism and 'The Politics of Recognition': An Essay by Charles Taylor.* Princeton: Princeton University Press.

Taylor, J. (2009) 'My People Refuse to Talk about Honour Killings', *Independent*, 19 December 2009 [online] at http://www.independent.co.uk/news/

uk/crime/my-people-refuse-to-talk-about-honour-killings-1845103.html (accessed 6 November 2014).

Taylor, J. and Hughes, M. (2008) 'Mystery of Bradford's Missing Children: Were They Forced into Marriages Abroad?', *Independent*, 4 February 2008 [online] at http://www.independent.co.uk/news/uk/home-news/mystery-of-bradfords-missing-children-were-they-forced-into-marriages-abroad-777684.html (accessed 2 October 2012).

Telegraph (2004) 'Affairs of the Heart that Ended in Tragedy', 7 December 2004 [online] at http://www.telegraph.co.uk/news/uknews/1478400/Affairs-of-the-heart-that-ended-in-tragedy.html (accessed 17 May 2013).

Telegraph (2012) 'Sonia Gandhi Pays Tribute to Gang-Rape Victim and Pledges Justice', 29 December 2012 [online] at http://www.telegraph.co.uk/news/worldnews/asia/india/9770697/Sonia-Gandhi-pays-tribute-to-gang-rape-victim-and-pledges-justice.html (accessed 5 January 2013).

Thiara, R.K. and Gill, A.K. (eds) (2010) *Violence Against Women in South Asian Communities: Issues for Policy and Practice*. London: Jessica Kingsley Publishers.

Thomas, C. (2009) 'Forced and Early Marriage: A Focus on Central and Eastern Europe and Former Soviet Union Countries with Selected Laws from Other Countries', EGM/GPLHP/2009/EP.08. Expert paper prepared by: Cheryl Thomas, Director, Women's Human Rights Program, The Advocates for Human Rights, Minnesota, USA. United Nations Division for the Advancement of Women, and United Nations Economic Commission for Africa, Expert Group Meeting on good practices in legislation to address harmful practices against women. United Nations Conference Centre, Addis Ababa, Ethiopia, 25 to 28 May 2009 [online] at http://www.un.org/womenwatch/daw/egm/vaw_legislation_2009/Expert%20Paper%20EGMGPLHP%20_Cheryl%20Thomas%20revised_.pdf (accessed 15 January 2014).

Tickle, L. (2012) 'Forced Marriage: The Pupils Who Vanish in the Holidays', *Guardian*, 9 April 2012 [online] at http://www.guardian.co.uk/education/2012/apr/09/forced-marriage-british-pupils (accessed 27 September 2012).

Triandis, H.C., McCusker, C., Betancourt, H., Iwao, S., Leung, K., Salazar, J.M., Setiadi, B., Sinha, J.B.P., Touzard, H. and Zaleski, Z. (1993) 'An Etic-Emic Analysis of Individualism and Collectivism', *Journal of Cross Cultural Psychology*, 24: 366–84.

United Nations (UN) (1962) Office of the High Commissioner for Human Rights, *Convention on Consent to Marriage, Minimum Age for Marriage and Registration of Marriages 1962* [online] at http://www.ohchr.org/EN/ProfessionalInterest/Pages/MinimumAgeForMarriage.aspx (accessed 15 January 2014).

United Nations (UN) (1979) UN Women, *Convention on the Elimination of All Forms of Discrimination against Women (CEDAW) 1979* [online] at http://

www.un.org/womenwatch/daw/cedaw/text/econvention.htm (accessed 15 January 2014).

United Nations (UN) (2005) Office on Drugs and Crime – Division for the Advancement of Women, 'Violence against Women: Good Practices in Combating and Eliminating Violence against Women', UN [online] at http://www.un.org/womenwatch/daw/egm/vaw-gp-2005/docs/experts/khafagy. honourcrimes.pdf (accessed 11 May 2008).

United Nations (UN) (2012a) Secretary General Ban Ki-moon, Latest Statements, 'New York, 29 December 2012 – Statement attributable to the Spokesperson for the Secretary-General on death of Delhi student' [online] at http://www.un.org/sg/statements/?nid=6533 (accessed 20 February 2013).

United Nations (UN) (2012b) UN News Centre, 'UN Human Rights Chief Calls for Profound Change in India in Wake of Gang-Rape Tragedy' [online] at http://www.un.org/apps/news/story.asp?NewsID=43862#.USSOXx1hiyg (accessed 20 February 2013).

UN Assistance Mission for Iraq (UNAMI) (2007) *Human Rights Report 1 April – 30 June 2007* [online] at http://www.uniraq.org/FileLib/misc/HR%20 Report%20Apr%20Jun%202007%20EN.pdf (accessed 26 April 2008).

UN Children's Fund (UNICEF) (2000) 'Unicef Fact Sheet no. 241: Female Genital Mutilation' [online] at http://www.who.int/mediacentre/factsheets/ fs241/en (accessed 11 May 2008).

UN Children's Fund (UNICEF) (2006) 'Unicef Child Protection Information Sheet: Female Genital Mutilation/Cutting', Unicef [online] at http://wwww. unicef.org./protection/files/FGM.pdf (accessed 11 May 2008).

UN Economic and Social Council (ECOSOC) (2000) Commission on Human Rights, Fifty-sixth session, Item 11 (b) of the provisional agenda, 'Civil and Political Rights, Including Questions of: Disappearances and Summary Executions', Extrajudicial, Summary or Arbitrary Executions, Report of the Special Rapporteur, Ms Asma Jahangir, submitted pursuant to Commission on Human Rights resolution 1999/35, E/CN.4/2000/3, 25 January 2000. New York: UN.

UN General Assembly (2012) Human Rights Council, Twentieth session, Agenda item 3: Promotion and protection of all human rights, civil, political, economic, social and cultural rights, including the right to development, *Report of the Special Rapporteur on violence against women, its causes and consequences, Rashida Manjoo – Addendum: Summary report on the expert group meeting on gender-motivated killings of women,* A/HRC/20/16/Add.4 [online] at http://www. ohchr.org/Documents/HRBodies/HRCouncil/RegularSession/Session20/ A-HRC-20–16-Add4_en.pdf (accessed 20 November 2014).

UN Human Development Programme (UNDP) (2014) *Human Development Report 2014 – Sustaining Human Progress: Reducing Vulnerabilities and Building*

Resilience. New York: UNDP [online] at http://hdr.undp.org/sites/default/files/hdr14-report-en-1.pdf (accessed 27 November 2014).

UN Human Rights (2010) Office of the High Commissioner for Human Rights, 'Murder in the Name of Family Honour' [online] at http://www.ohchr.org/EN/NewsEvents/Pages/MurderInTheNameOfFamilyHonour.aspx (accessed 20 November 2014).

UN Population Fund (UNFPA) (2000) *State of World Population 2000: Lives Together, Worlds Apart – Men and Women in a Time of Change*. New York: UNFPA [online] at http://www.unfpa.org/swp/2000/english/ch03.html#3 (accessed 30 May 2013).

UN Population Fund (UNFPA) (2012) *Marrying Too Young – End Child Marriage*. New York: UNFPA.

UN Population Fund (UNFPA) (2013) *State of World Population 2013: Motherhood in Childhood – Facing the Challenge of Adolescent Pregnancy*. New York: UNFPA.

UN Security Council (2006) 'Report of the Secretary-General pursuant to paragraph 30 of Resolution 1546 (2004)', UNAMI [online] at http://www.uniraq.org/FileLib/misc/SG_Report_S_2006_360_EN.pdf (accessed 26 April 2008).

UNFPA-UNICEF (2012) *Joint Programme on Female Genital Mutilation/Cutting: Accelerating Change – Annual Report 2012*. New York: UNFPA-UNICEF.

Vertovec, S. (2010) 'Towards Post-Multiculturalism? Changing Communities, Conditions and Contexts of Diversity', *International Social Science Journal*, 61(199): 83–95.

Vertovec, S. and Wessendorf, S. (eds) (2010) *The Multiculturalism Backlash: European Discourses, Policies and Practices*. London: Routledge.

Volpp, L. (2001) 'Feminism versus Multiculturalism', *Columbia Law Review*, 101(5): 1181–218 [online] at http://www.jstor.org.ezproxy.lib.bbk.ac.uk/stable/pdfplus/10.2307/1123774.pdf?acceptTC=true (accessed 19 November 2014).

Walby, S. (1993) *Theorizing Patriarchy*. Oxford: Blackwell Publishers.

Ward, D. (2007) 'Sikh Wife's "Disgrace" Sparked Killing, Court Told', *Guardian*, 3 May 2007 [online] at http://www.guardian.co.uk/crime/article/0,2071126,00.html (accessed 20 April 2008).

Watson-Smyth, K. (1999) 'Mother Murdered Pregnant Daughter', *Independent*, 26 May 1999 [online] at http://www.independent.co.uk/news/mother-murdered-pregnant-daughter-1095933.html (accessed 10 June 2013).

Weathers, H. (2007) '"Honour Killing" Sister Breaks Her Silence', *Daily Mail*, 17 June 2007 [online] at http://www.dailymail.co.uk/pages/live/femail/article.html?in_article_id=462342&in_page_id=1879 (accessed 27 April 2008).

Webb, S. (2014) 'Husband Who Lured His "Westernised" Wife to Her Death in "Honour Killing" then Dressed up in Her Clothes to Convince Family and Friends She was Still Alive is Jailed', *Mail Online*, 5 June 2014 [online] at https://www.nexis.com/results/docview/docview.do?docLinkInd=true&risb=21_

T21102148797&format=GNBFI&sort=BOOLEAN&startDocNo=1&res
ultsUrlKey=29_T21102158601&cisb=22_T21102158600&treeMax=true&t
reeWidth=0&selRCNodeID=12&nodeStateId=411en_US,1,5&docsInCate
gory=14&csi=397135&docNo=1 (accessed 8 December 2014).

Welchman, L. and Hossain, S. (eds) (2005) *'Honour': Crimes, Paradigms, and
Violence Against Women*. London: Zed Books.

White, M. (2007) 'Westminster Divided over Curbs on Forced Marriages',
Guardian, 26 January 2007 [online] at http://www.guardian.co.uk/
commentisfree/2007/jan/26/politics.uk (accessed 7 June 2013).

Women's Aid (2014) *Women's Aid Annual Review: A Tour of 2013–2014* [online]
at http://www.womensaid.org.uk/landing_page.asp?section=000100010019
&sectionTitle=About+us (accessed 3 July 2014).

World Economic Forum (WEF) (2013) *The Global Gender Gap Report 2013*.
Geneva: WEF.

Younis, S. (2013) *Shackled to My Family*. Oxford: Oxford eBooks.

Zoepf, K. (2007) 'A Dishonourable Affair', *New York Times*, 23 September
2007 [online] at http://www.nytimes.com/2007/09/23/magazine/23wwln-
syria-t.html?pagewanted=1&_r=1&adznnlz=1197896704-zsV9V%20
zicZUq/Bi0hjl90w (accessed 11 May 2007).

Index